STUART MULLI

*A defining moment in the
history of child abduction*

UNMASKING THE KILLER OF THE MISSING BEAUMONT CHILDREN

*An unsolved crime so
heart-breaking, so shocking,
it shook Australia to its core
and changed the country forever*

Unmasking the Killer of the Missing Beaumont Children
© Stuart Mullins and Bill Hayes 2022

ISBN: 978-1-922757-10-4 (paperback)
         978-1-922757-11-1 (eBook)

 A catalogue record for this
book is available from the
National Library of Australia

Printed in Australia by Ocean Reeve Publishing
www.oceanreevepublishing.com
Published by Stuart Mullins, Bill Hayes and Ocean Reeve Publishing

Ocean
REEVE
PUBLISHING

Contents

About the Authors

Bill Hayes was born in Northern Ireland and later spent a part of his childhood in London's famous East End. He left school and joined the Merchant Navy at age fifteen, going on to enlist in the UK Armed Forces where amongst other qualifications he earned the famous British Airborne Paratroop wings, Bill served in the jungles of East Asia, Hong Kong, and the New Territories, the deserts of Libya, Australia, the South Arabian Peninsula, and Northern Ireland. Migrating to Australia, he had also joined the Australian Army Reserve, where he was commissioned as an officer. In his civilian career, he joined the Australian Federal Police and was posted to Woomera, the home of the top-secret rocket range in the far north of South Australia. After a couple of years, he joined the South Australia Police (SAPOL), serving for some years as a uniform patrol officer and then in the Criminal Investigation Branch (CIB) as a detective. He was also trained as an advanced hostage negotiator. During his CIB service, he served at the Elizabeth Branch of the CIB with a number of secondments to the Major Crime Squad before joining the Special Crime Squad based in Adelaide. Later, Bill joined the Major Crime Squad, which at that time consisted of two sections, Armed Robbery and Homicide. During his time in the Major Crime Squad in the 1980s, he was tasked with reading part of the many boxes of statements pertaining to the case of the missing Beaumont children, which he reviewed. In Bill's words, 'It is fair to say that in the short time that I had, I only really scratched the surface.'

It was an eye-opening read and gave Bill a much greater appreciation of the size of the task that the police had faced in 1966, as well as a solid understanding of the case. One thing that became obvious to him at that time was that the children appeared to have gone willingly with their abductor. If they had been taken kicking and screaming, there was no doubt that, given the crowd at Glenelg that day, it would have been easily seen and a different outcome achieved.

After a successful time as a detective, Bill resigned after a total of fifteen years' service and went into the private sector and set up his own successful private investigation company, where he remains.

Bill was approached by Stuart Mullins in June 2008 to assist in uncovering the dark and deviant side of Harry Phipps and his possible link to the Beaumont children's abduction. Bill's impressive investigative skills and his unique knowledge of the Beaumont disappearance were utilised extensively when getting eyewitness evidence that exposed Harry Phipps as being the lead person of interest in this crime, as was later outlined in the publication *The Satin Man: Uncovering the Mystery of the Missing Beaumont Children*.

Bill is happily married with three children and four grand-children and now lives on the south coast of South Australia.

Bill has several undergraduate and postgraduate qualifica-tions. He is a qualified lead auditor, has a Master of Business Administration (MBA) degree, and holds fellowships in both the Australian Institute of Company Directors and the Australian Institute of Private Investigators.

Bill holds a senior black belt in Tang Soo Do Karate and is a Kodanja of the Asia Pacific Tang Soo Do Federation. He is a gold medal winner in the World Tang Soo Do Karate World Championship held in the USA. He is also a former Australian representative in powerlifting, where he won the gold medal in the International Law Enforcement Olympics.

***

Stuart Mullins was born in Glenelg, South Australia, in the late 1950s. He grew up in Seacombe Gardens, a mere five kilometres from Somerton Park, where the Beaumont family resided. In 1966, Stuart was the same age as Arnna Beaumont. He attended Darlington Primary School, which was in the same school sport competitive set as Paringa Park Primary School, which Jane and Arnna attended. Also, his grandmother at the time lived in Somerton, not too far from where the Beaumont family resided. He is also the cousin of Mostyn Matters, the first detective to meet a distressed Jim and Nancy Beaumont that fateful day in 1966 and the last of the detectives still standing.

By 1971, Stuart's family had moved interstate to Richmond, New South Wales. After leaving school, he attended Nepean College of Advanced Education, Penrith, now the University of Western Sydney, where he obtained his teaching qualifications. He taught for only a short time in Australia before travelling overseas. Stuart became an outward-bound instructor working with former SAS personnel for the Scottish Adventure School on the island of Raasay in north-west Scotland, working with unemployed teenagers from Glasgow, Dundee, and Stirling. He followed this by securing a role for two years as a Physical Education teacher in Durban, South Africa, where Stuart also played first-grade cricket for several seasons. Durban was the location of his first marathon and certainly has not been his last. He later spent time with Club Mediterranean South Pacific as recreation manager, then at the five-star Hayman Island Resort North Queensland. Following on from this, he spent two years in Japan working in an executive search company, finally returning to Australia to start his own hospitality recruitment company, which he still runs today.

Stuart assisted Alan Whiticker in his research for Alan's book *Searching for the Beaumont Children*, published in 2006. He then teamed up with Alan as co-author of the bestselling *The Satin Man: Uncovering the Mystery of the Missing Beaumont Children*. Stuart was also the writer for *Joe Bugner: My Story* about the only heavyweight boxer to go the distance twice with the greatest, Muhammad Ali. Stuart lives in a seaside suburb of south Queensland with his lovely wife and has two grown children and two grandchildren.

Introduction

People who say it cannot be done should not interrupt those who are doing it.[1]

—George Bernard Shaw

The disappearance of the Beaumont children was an event that worked itself into the story and psyche of Australia and haunted a family for more than fifty years. Still today, the images of nine-year-old Jane, seven-year-old Arnna, and four-year-old Grant represent the moment life changed forever in Australia on Australia Day, 26 January, in 1966. The children waved goodbye to their mother Nancy at the front gate of their home in a quiet seaside suburb of Somerton Park, twelve kilometres south-west of Adelaide, for a day out at nearby Glenelg beach. She never saw them again. Nancy went to her grave broken-hearted, not knowing what had happened to her children.

This inconceivable disappearance was a defining moment in the history of child abduction—an unsolved, heart-breaking crime so shocking that it shook Australia to its core, changed the country forever, and reverberated worldwide. Hidden among the crowd at Glenelg beach on Wednesday, 26 January 1966 was a predator on the hunt for his prey. The prey? Jane, Arnna, and Grant Beaumont. The case quickly turned from a disappearance into an abduction and led to one of the largest manhunts in Australian criminal history. What followed were fake leads, false trails, bizarre encounters with controversial clairvoyants, and numerous conspiracy theories—but nothing that led to the missing children. Over the decades, several suspects were put forward and investigated, with all coming to a dead end. Thus, fifty years later, the case remains unsolved—until now. Enter Harry Phipps.

In the 2013 bestselling book *The Satin Man: Uncovering the Mystery of the Missing Beaumont Children,* we, along with co-author Alan Whiticker, uncovered incriminating information regarding Phipps alluding to his alleged involvement in some way in the disappearance of the Beaumont children.[2] Now, in *Unmasking the Killer of the Missing Beaumont Children,* we offer further extensive, damning, and alarming information based on a thorough, painstaking investigation over fourteen years, which now exposes Harry Phipps as the prime suspect in the abduction, disappearance, and likely murder of the Beaumont children. We set out why Harry Phipps was a preferential child molester and that there is no doubt that he committed child molestation offences before and since the Beaumont children. As Dr Xanthé Mallett, arguably Australia's leading criminologist, states:

> I have to say that in my opinion, Harry Phipps is the best suspect that has ever been put forward in the Beaumont abduction and disappearance. I consider him my number one suspect in this case.[3]

Over years of thorough investigation and research, we have identified Phipps, whom we believe is likely to have abducted and murdered the Beaumont children—a man who stood head and shoulders above all others and against whom the circumstantial evidence is compelling and overwhelming.

Harry Phipps was a pillar of old Adelaide society—a man of wealth, power, influence, and standing in the community. He was a well-respected businessman, a family patriarch, charming, persuasive, generous, and charismatic. On the surface, he was a gentleman, but in reality, he was a vicious, manipulative, and cunning predator. Unbeknown to the public, behind the walls of his Glenelg mansion in 1966 and decades onwards resided a violent, serial sexual predator—a man with a penchant for child sex. Harry Phipps was a wolf dressed in sheep's clothing hidden under a cloak of respectability.

Armed with further disturbing information, we detail the lie lived by Harry Phipps, a serial sexual predator whose crimes went undetected for over four decades. He lived a mere 190 metres from Colley Reserve, where the Beaumont children were last seen playing with an individual who appeared to uncannily fit the physical description of Phipps. How was he able to avoid detection for so long, indeed going to his grave in 2004 with a clean record?

During this era, when hunting paedophiles and child-killers, police did not look for a respected, well-groomed man like Harry Phipps, no more than they looked at the clergy, the businessman, the entertainer, the parent, or the kind uncle or aunt, teacher, or swim coach. Police looked for an individual who fitted the 1960s view of a paedophile: a dirty old man. Now, in the twenty-first century, police know better.

But could this abduction and disappearance be that simple? Could the perpetrator in one of the most baffling missing-persons cases in Australian criminal history have lived in plain sight all along? Could the Beaumont children have died so close to the spot they had vanished from that same day? We detail why this may be the case and methodically expose Harry Phipps as the likely killer of the missing Beaumont children.

Chapter 1:
The Beaumont Generation

Be home before the street lights come on.

—Parents of the 1960s

It was love at first sight when thirty-one year old Jim Beaumont set eyes on twenty-eight year old Nancy Ellis at the Victoria Hotel in Adelaide in 1955. Jim knew that Nancy was 'the one' and vice versa. He was struck by her natural beauty, captivating brown eyes, and coy smile. Nancy was outgoing, friendly, and a natural conversationalist who loved to laugh. Jim was so enamoured by her charm that he took the next nervous step to ask her out. A yes followed, capping off a memorable day that saw him win handsomely at the Balaklava races ninety kilometres north of Adelaide. The couple's first date was at the Gepps Cross Drive-In, and six weeks later, Jim proposed. Though initially hesitant, Nancy accepted, and they married in December 1955.

As a teenager, Jim joined the army, serving in the 2/24th Battalion in Borneo in 1945. Even though he was christened Grant, he was known to his army buddies as Jim, and the name stuck. In the final year of World War 2, he received a shrapnel wound in the battle of Tarakan and was flown to Moroka Island Eastern Philippines for treatment, and this is where he saw out the rest of the war.[4]

After the end of hostilities, Jim decided not to go home, as his father had passed away while he was overseas. So, he volunteered in 1945 for the occupation units in Japan for two years, as he believed this to be an exciting opportunity to explore a different country. Upon return, Jim was discharged. He bought several taxis and began work for Adelaide's largest taxi company. Nancy, on the other hand, was a typist at the City Meat Company in North Adelaide. After they married, Jim and Nancy purchased a war-service house on the corner of Harding and Patterson streets in Somerton Park, close to the well-established suburbs of Brighton, Somerton, and Glenelg.

On 10 September 1956, Jim and Nancy welcomed their first child, Jane Nartare, followed on 11 November 1958 by Arnna Kathleen, and, to complete this family unit, Grant Ellis Beaumont was born on 12 July 1961. With three children and a busy family life, Jim sold his taxis and joined the Lincott Linen Company as a sales manager. Even though he needed to stay overnight in country towns, the hours were more regular and, if he worked hard, the money was much better. This job gave him more time to spend with the family.

Both Jim and Nancy were described by many as proud, loving parents. The Beaumont children spent the early years of their lives in Somerton Park, and like any other Australian suburb in the 1960s, it was a magical time of wonder and immense possibility. The suburb you lived in was your universe. Life in South Australia during the 1960s was more carefree and less complicated than that faced by children today. Many have termed this 'the Beaumont generation era'. Jane and Arnna attended Paringa Park Primary School, a two-kilometre walk from their home. In 1966, Jane was entering Year 5 and Arnna Year 4. The school was small in class size compared to its neighbouring schools in Brighton and Glenelg. There was one class per year level. Grant was four and remained at home in the care of his mother.

***

There was much to explore for children who lived around the beachside suburbs south of Adelaide. A sixteen-kilometre stretch of foreshore ran from Semaphore to Seacliff. All were working-class family suburbs, many with immigrants who had arrived only a few years earlier from the UK, Italy, Greece, and Germany. The beachside suburbs close to Somerton Park were dotted with an array of Victorian buildings, historic pubs built at the turn of the century, several jetties, and an array of pristine beachside parks. The jewel in the crown was the city of Glenelg, which was a major hub of commerce and leisure and still is today. This piece of coastline faced the Gulf of St Vincent with Kangaroo Island at its entrance, which kept these beachside suburbs sheltered from the occasional choppy seas and strong currents. The foreshore was calm, flat, and inviting. Seaside towns were well suited to recreational pursuits, with numerous parks and grassed areas. This provided an ideal community environment for children to spend summer days at the beach without parental supervision. This is unheard of today but was the norm in the 1960s.

Jane, Arnna, and Grant's favourite beach was Glenelg, with its expansive pristine lawns of Colley Reserve sweeping down close to the water's edge, the flat, calm sea gently lapping the shoreline. Glenelg Beach and Colley Reserve during the summer school holidays were crowded with excited, noisy, energetic children running in and out and under the sprinklers, playing tag and hide-and-seek, or flicking each other with wet-tipped towels.

Another popular beach location in the summer months was Brighton beach and pier, five kilometres south of Glenelg, which was also brimming with excited children and teenagers. Capable beachgoers performed somersaults or acrobatic stunts off the pier, but for the less coordinated came the sting of the water five metres below. Scores of kids barely able to swim would dog paddle to keep themselves afloat. The jetty had neither lifeguards nor water-safety signs. It was a chaotic situation, difficult to fathom in today's environment, but this was a child's life in the 1960s.

A child's life in the summer holidays was all about spending time with friends, and breakfast was a rushed job: toast with Vegemite® followed by a bowl of Kellogg's® Corn Flakes, Vita Brits®, Rice Bubbles®, or the poor man's porridge—semolina. They would then head out through the door with these words from their mother embedded in their brain: 'Be home before the streetlights come on.' Other than that, the day was yours.

Each day presented unlimited adventures. For children armed with their imagination, anything was possible. Kids congregated with their friends in the local streets or parks to discuss plans for the day. Riding bikes to the beach or the Adelaide Hills, building a treehouse, or meeting up at the local park could all be on the agenda. Every suburb had a playground, with hours spent on monkey bars, swings, buck-a-bouts, jungle gyms, seesaws, and roundabouts. These recreational parks would be deemed hazardous by today's standards due to a lack of any safety measures. No rubber matting, guardrails, or protective covers. You might say it was a time when playgrounds were potentially deadly, but plenty of fun.

The day offered so much, with only eight hours to fit in all the adventures. Building a cubby house in the backyard was a regular occurrence. For the more adventurous, treehouses were constructed at the local creek or in open farmland never too far away using a collection of wooden planks, old milk crates, and tyres, coupled with wooden boxes and sheets of cardboard, all pieced together with a child's ingenuity. Construction of billycarts required a trip to the local rubbish tip, where children would fossick for old pram wheels, broken bike parts, and discarded wooden planks and boxes. What immediately followed were soapbox-cart races in the local streets. Neighbourhood children and, at times, parents raced, none wearing helmets, much less knee or elbow guards. One does wonder how children came out of the 1960s unscathed, apart from the odd lingering scar on the knee and elbow.

Groups of youngsters on bicycles ventured many kilometres into the foothills of Adelaide. These foothills were dotted with freshwater creeks, swimming holes, and expansive farmlands where one could spend the entire day swimming, fishing, and catching yabbies or tadpoles. So far from home, and yet lunch was always close in the form of the orange, apple, peach, almond, and nectarine trees for which South Australia is well known. One's thirst was always well quenched with clear, clean drinking water from the creeks.

Children and teenagers followed the river Torrens winding its way through the Adelaide hills—meandering through forests and farmland and cutting through the Adelaide CBD—and ambling on its way through the sparseness of suburbs to the sea. Nothing was cemented in or fenced off, and no 'Trespassers Prosecuted' signs blocked the way. Children enjoyed a Huckleberry Finn-style lifestyle. Rainy, grey, wintry days did not stop them. These were spent indoors with friends building a bedroom cubby house with Mum's clean sheets, with pillows and blankets attached from bunk to bunk. Playing indoor games such as Monopoly®, Snakes and Ladders, or Mouse Trap® also took up many hours, as did piecing together model cranes, toy cars, LEGO® buildings and Meccano® pieces.

Train sets and Scalextric® cars were also popular—soap added to the tracks made for awe-inducing spinouts, thrilling boys no end. Young girls compared their Barbie® dolls' new outfits, spending hours hosting dress-up sessions. This might be considered sexist today, but the 1960s were a very different era.

If not venturing into the foothills or down to the beach, Saturday morning interschool sport was popular—netball, softball, Australian Rules football, cricket, or soccer. Paringa Park Primary School, where Jane and Arnna Beaumont attended, would compete against primary schools in the local area—Oaklands Park, Dover Gardens, St Leonards, Ascot Park, Brighton, Glenelg, Warradale, and Stuart's school, Darlington.

With Saturday morning sport completed, groups of friends visited the local bakery or lolly shop. A favourite pastime among the children was scrounging up loose change to spend. At times, children discussed what they might buy should they ever find themselves with a pound note—how rich they would be! The pound note was the Holy Grail and only seen in your mum's purse or your dad's wallet. Its buying power was immense and brought with it a real wow factor.

The rest of the afternoon was taken up playing with friends; riding bikes, scooters, and tricycles; kicking the football; shooting netball goals; or playing backyard cricket. Children enjoyed hopscotch, red rover, red light–green light, tag, skipping rope, hula-hoop, quoits, marbles, playing cowboys and Indians, making bows and arrows, and everyone's favourite hide-and-seek.

Unlike today, youngsters were allowed to ride on the bus to the movies, beaches, or into the city, alone. Kids could buy cigarettes for their parents from the local shop—by today's standards difficult to fathom—and freely purchase fireworks for the annual Guy Fawkes (Cracker Night) celebration in November. Children had no idea who Guy Fawkes was and why this day was celebrated, but buying a plentiful amount of fire-crackers together with matches to terrorise the neighbourhood was a must. Most children were quite inventive, concocting a more powerful cracker by binding them together with tape or rubber bands, and placing smaller explosives in metal garbage bins or down drainpipes to amplify the explosion to frighten the neighbours. Considered irresponsible by today's standards, this was the norm in the 1960s. As children, much fun was to be had. Rainy days or sunny days were all the same for children back then.

Primary school was disciplined and regimented, with manners, respect, and courtesy insisted upon. Children would not speak unless spoken to. Each school employed a part-time Religious Instruction teacher. Classes were broken up for Religious Instruction and divided along denomination lines: Methodist, Baptist, Presbyterian, Catholic, and Seventh-day Adventist. Lack of church attendance was frowned upon, with the local priest or minister paying a home visit to remind one of their duties to the Almighty.

The school morning always began with the class standing for the national anthem and pledging allegiance to the Queen. One did not question authority. The cane and open-hand smacking were regularly employed by teachers. Several teachers smoked cigarettes in the classroom—with the odour of the lighter fluid wafting through.

School children were encouraged to read regularly, utilising the education department's SRA reading laboratory, still used extensively throughout South Australian primary schools.

Jane Beaumont was already reading from the highest colour category, which was well above her age group and featured smaller text and longer, more intricately woven stories. Most teachers set aside a half-hour in the afternoon to read the children's favourite fairytales. Pupils eagerly awaited this storytelling by gathering on the mats placed at the front of the class. They listened intently to their teacher's words, painting magical worlds filled with fascinating mythical creatures and worlds of kings, queens, fairies, pixies, elves, and goblins. Among favourites were Enid Blyton's *The Magic Faraway Tree*, CS Lewis's *The Lion, the Witch and the Wardrobe,* and Roald Dahl's *Charlie and the Chocolate Factory*. While the teacher quietly read to the class, pupils would on occasion drift off to sleep, only to be woken by the clang of the bell to end the school day. As CS Lewis, British writer and theologian, once said, 'Some day you will be old enough to start reading fairy tales again.'[5]

While children spent most of the day outdoors, there was the occasional time spent indoors watching the black-and-white HMV® television—if indeed you had one. TV channels started transmission in time for the midday movie. Popular TV shows included *Lassie, Zorro, Texas Rangers, Rin Tin Tin, The Little Rascals, Robin Hood,* and the Japanese imports *The Samurai* and *Phantom Agents*. Adelaide had its own children's show every weekday afternoon: *The Channel Niners* with Ian Fairweather and Glenys O'Brien, featuring Bobo the Clown.

Children spending time indoors was discouraged by parents. When Nancy or Jim Beaumont were home, Grant, Arnna, and Jane were sent to play outdoors in the fresh air—the same request from most parents to their children in the 1960s.

If you think Uber Eats® is new, think again. The 1960s was also a time of home delivery, usually to the kitchen door. Bakers and the milkman arrived each morning and the grocer several times a week. Doctors made house calls, and the ice-cream van was ever-present in the summer months.

Adelaide in the 1960s had a few special organised annual events that residents eagerly looked forward to. At the Royal Adelaide Show, staged at the local showgrounds, South Australia would put on an impressive display of farmers' produce and parade prized livestock. Other highlights included the wood-chopping championships, dog and cat grooming awards, and show-jumping finals, to name but a few. Numerous pavilions displayed the best of South Australia's farming produce, handicrafts, and horticulture.

For children, all this paled in comparison to the show bag pavilion, the be-all and end-all for adolescents in the 1960s. No other building mattered. Youngsters saved their money all year to buy as many show bags as possible. Mum's favourite would be the Cadbury® or Darrell Lea® Chocolate, but the kids went mad for the Hoadley's®, Life Savers®, Bertie Beetle®, liquorice, Cherry Ripe®, Eta® Peanut Butter and Kit Kat® bags. Children and parents returned home tired and weary after a long day. Once the kids unloaded the contents of each show bag across the bedroom floor, they were ready for bed, leaving mums and dads across Adelaide to relax in front of the TV and delve into their treats. Mr and Mrs Beaumont were one such set of parents.

Another major event many enjoyed was John Martin's Christmas pageant. John Martin & Co (known colloquially as 'John Martin's') was South Australia's leading department store in the 1960s, located on North Terrace, arguably Adelaide's most prestigious street. Thousands of excited families eagerly awaited the Christmas parade each year. The parade culminated with the final float, Santa's Christmas sleigh steered by his reindeer to his magic cave located inside the John Martin's department store. Here, children lined up waiting for their turn to sit on Santa's lap surrounded by his helpers.

Early January was followed by the annual family holiday. Stuart's family, like the Beaumont household, enjoyed their yearly caravanning holiday. By today's standards, the word 'caravan' should be used lightly. A 1960s trailer? A roundish plywood box with a sink and mattress? But, for many children, this was their moving castle on wheels.

For the summer holidays, some families travelled interstate, meandering along the majestic Great Ocean Road connecting South Australia to Victoria, stopping to take in the breathtaking ocean views from the jagged clifftops. This picturesque, rugged coastline road made its way on to the seaside towns of Torquay, Barwon River, and Geelong. Holidays enjoyed at the caravan parks were spent outdoors playing with other children. Great new shiny friends were plentiful. These childhood holiday memories last a lifetime.

If not away caravanning, then visiting Glenelg's Colley Reserve in the evening was popular. Adelaide is well known for its stifling summers with temperatures regularly reaching the high 30s °C, or 100 °F in the old scale, and remaining that way for several days. Families from across town would venture from their homes to the foreshore of Glenelg seeking a respite from the suburban heat. The sweeping, expansive lawns of the reserve, coupled with the cool evening breeze, gave a reprieve from another 'Adelaide stinker'. As the sun set beneath the distant horizon, the coloured lights—green, orange, yellow, and purple—were strung along the Glenelg beachfront, which was host to the Colley Reserve sideshow, the age-old sound of the organ music emanating from a turn-of-the-century merry-go-round.

As the sideshow came to life, so did Colley Reserve. Hundreds of families would stake their place on the lawns to lay out their blankets and unpack their picnic baskets. Inside would be a metal tea or coffee thermos with coloured metal tumblers, alongside a Bobo the Clown cordial bottle coupled with a mum's favourite homemade triangle sandwiches and lamingtons. The Salvation Army band took their rightful place in the rotunda still located in the centre of the park to this day. As the band commenced, the melodies and ambience were complimented by the soft, calming lights strung from pine tree to pine tree surrounding the reserve.

A child's life in the 1960s was truly awe-inspiring—carefree, magical, uncluttered, and full of wonder.

For the Beaumont family, this all tragically changed on 26 January 1966. Jim was not to know that he would see his children for the last time the day before, on Tuesday, 25 January, when he dropped Jane, Arnna, and Grant at the beach in the morning. He stood at a distance, watching them spread their towels before going for a swim, comfortable in the knowledge they were safe.

He then left for a long drive north to Snowtown for sales calls. The lasting image he had of his children was them smiling as they waved goodbye to Dad—an image that would break anyone's heart. The following morning, Nancy Beaumont stood at the front gate and waved goodbye to her children as they walked around the corner to the bus stop to set off for their morning at Glenelg beach. It was the last time she would see her children.

Chapter 2:
What Happened That Day

The abduction of a child is a tragedy. No-one can fully understand or appreciate what a parent goes through at such a time unless they have faced a similar tragedy.[6]

—John Walsh

On Australia Day 1966, Adelaide was experiencing a heatwave. The hot, dry northerly winds blowing down from the northern deserts of South Australia hit the city and beaches like the open door of a blast furnace, with the thermometer reaching 42 °C or 107 °F.

The Beaumont children woke early, excited at what the day might bring. Arnna and Grant ran into their parents' bedroom, waking their mother, Nancy, by jumping up and down on the bed. Both children were joyfully pestering her to allow them to go to the beach. Even though Jane was an early riser, she was not necessarily the first out of bed, as she usually read part of her current book—in this case, *Little Women* by Louisa May Alcott—before joining her siblings in bothering their mum. They had spent time at Glenelg the previous day and wanted to go back. The start of a new school year was just around the corner, and that day was one of the last opportunities to enjoy the school break at the beach.

Nancy understood their excitement, but she realised from the early morning that the day was going to be oppressively hot. By 8 am, the barometer showed signs that the high thirties would be reached by midday. She was not keen on the children walking or riding their bicycles to the beach in such heat; Glenelg was 2.5 kilometres from their home at Somerton Park, and even though the children had ridden their bikes there in the past, they would not be doing it that day. If Jim had been home, he would have been happy to take them, as he had done the previous day, but he had just returned to work after a summer holiday break, and he needed to make sales calls in country areas north of Adelaide and had stayed overnight.

Nancy was not an avid beachgoer, and she had housework to complete. In the back of her mind, she knew that Grant, Arnna, and Jane would eagerly persist, eventually driving her up the wall. Added to this was the thought of three bored children inside the hot house. Arnna and Grant were also making a little mischief for Jane, cheekily repeating to their mum, 'Jane's got a boyfriend! Jane's got a boyfriend!' Nancy didn't pay much attention to this talk or the insinuation that Jane might have a childhood infatuation with someone at the beach. She was more concerned with how she was going to keep three hot, bored children from driving her crazy in the house.

Nancy relented and allowed them to venture to the beach to swim for a short time, even though in the back of her mind was the feeling she should go to the beach with them. She insisted they take the local bus and be home by lunchtime. Nancy gave Jane approximately eight shillings and sixpence—enough for the bus ride to and from Glenelg and to buy lunch for them all.

Jane placed this money in her beige clip purse, which she packed inside her blue airline-style carry bag along with three towels: one small blue towel and two with the same pattern of yellow, black, green, red, and white stripes. Also in Jane's bag was a paperback copy of *Little Women*. She wore one-piece pink bathers with pale green shorts and tartan canvas sandshoes with white soles.

Arnna wore a one-piece red-and-white-striped bathing suit with tan shorts and tan sandals. She sported a bright orange hairpin in her hair.

Grant wore green-and-white bathers under green cotton shorts and red leather sandals. He did not wear a singlet because they were only going to be at the beach for two hours. According to an article in the Adelaide newspaper *The News* on 2 February 1966 titled 'Calls Pour In', when the detectives spoke with Nancy, she said, 'Grant didn't have a singlet or T-shirt as I thought they would be home in a few hours. I know what little ones are like. They would not be bothered with underclothes.'[7]

The children left home shortly before 10 am. Nancy stood at the front gate of their house on the corner of Harding and Peterson Street to wave them goodbye. The children walked fifty metres, then turned ten metres left to the Diagonal Road bus stop, where they caught the local red-and-white Worthley's bus, which began its rounds from Seacombe Gardens five kilometres up the road. This trip was a ten-minute ride to Glenelg. Little did Nancy know this was the last time she would ever see her children.

Jane, Arnna, and Grant alighted the bus at the corner of Moseley Street and Jetty Road. As they hopped off the bus on the busy main thoroughfare of Glenelg, they bumped into their postman, Tom Patterson. 'It's the postie!' an excited Jane exclaimed.

Tom delivered their mail in the morning and afternoon, riding his trusted postman's bike. The 'postie' was an integral part of the neighbourhood in the 1960s, and most children knew theirs by name.

A brisk hundred-metre walk took the children across Jetty Road, the main thoroughfare to Colley Reserve and the beach, according to eyewitnesses: a seventy-four year old lady with her partner sitting on a park bench, along with another younger lady and her young daughter standing close by. They had a clear twenty-metre unobstructed view of the children. They stated Jane, Arnna, and Grant placed their belongings close to the water's edge before running into the shallows, where they were splashing one another for some time. Jane's best friend Jenny, when interviewed by Stuart Mullins in 2017, said that she accompanied Jane to Colley Reserve on many occasions in summer because Grant couldn't swim. Jane made sure he only went up to his belly button. The witnesses then watched the children run up from the water's edge to lay their towels near two pine trees in a quiet corner of the foreshore hidden by the sailing club and the sideshow.

As well as the previously mentioned witnesses, there was a younger man with his family from Broken Hill, an outback mining town in New South Wales, who was in Adelaide with his family to attend the cricket test at the Adelaide Oval between Australia and England starting that Friday. All of these witnesses had noticed a man lying face-down on his towel watching Jane, Arnna, and Grant run up from the beach and dash over to the sprinklers to wash the salt water off. When the children returned to their towels, Grant and Arnna walked over and began to talk and laugh with the man; Jane soon followed. He did not beckon them; they went willingly and appeared familiar. Grant and Arnna jumped over him, and Jane flicked him with her towel. All were laughing and playing happily together, encouraged by this man.

Descriptions of this individual were varied right from the start, which would go on to become a major diversion in the police investigation. The seventy-four year old witness described this man as a suntanned surfie with blond hair in need of cutting. Some members of the media pounced on this, eager to have this uncorroborated information out in the public domain. By the time this reached the papers, they emphasised the detail of the unruly mop of bleached blond hair and further described him as a young surfie-type beachcomber. This description of a younger man still permeates the media today, even though other eyewitnesses corrected it three days later.

However, the initial search and investigation by the police and detectives were based on the original description of the man seen with the children, and as long as they and the general public were looking for a long-haired surfie-type, the individual who abducted the Beaumont children would go undetected.

One of these witnesses, the young man from Broken Hill, stated that the man seen with the Beaumont children had fair to light-brown hair that was combed back and was not in need of cutting. Another witness added that this hair was brushed back and parted to one side.

The agreed-upon description of the man seen playing with the Beaumont children that day was aged between late thirties to early forties, tanned, with a thin-to-athletic build, and light brown brushed-back hair with a wave in it and parted to one side. His height was six foot to six foot one, and he was wearing blue bathers with a white stripe down either side—the same colours as the nearby Henley Beach Surf Life Saving Club. He appeared to be a well-groomed, clean-shaven man with a long face and high forehead, and he spoke with an Australian accent.

By Friday 28 January, the *Adelaide Advertiser* sketch artist Peter Czarnecki was collaborating with detectives from the Glenelg police station. The man from Broken Hill, the elderly lady, and the younger lady who was at the reserve with her daughter on Wednesday all confirmed that a sketch done by Peter resembled the man seen with the children. Police then emphasised to the media on Monday 31 January that the man had light brown, brushed-back hair, and that the man's hair was not long, blonde, and in need of cutting, as previously reported in Adelaide news broadcasts on TV and radio from Thursday 27 to Sunday 30 January.

This man seen at the Colley Reserve was *not* in his early twenties or a mature teenager. The original description of the man was never correct, despite being repeated multiple times in parts of the media over the ensuing decades.

Eyewitnesses also noted the man had with him a towel, which he was lying on, and a shirt and trousers, which he had placed on the park bench next to where the elderly couple were sitting. This was only about five metres from where the eyewitnesses were located. According to their witness statements, no wallet, carry bag, or car keys were spotted.

The eyewitnesses said that after the man had spent time playing with Jane, Arnna, and Grant, he approached the elderly woman sitting on the park bench a few metres away from where they were all playing. Also close by was the younger lady with her daughter and the Broken Hill family. All were close enough to hear the man speaking. The elderly lady thought the man asked, 'Did any of you people see anyone with our clothes?'

When asked why, he stated, 'We've had some money taken.'

The other two witnesses nearby believed the man said, 'Has anyone been messing with our clothes? We have had our money pinched.'

The agreed-upon final account was 'Has anyone been messing with our clothes? We have had our money pinched.'[8]

After this interaction, the man returned to the children. What concerned the sets of witnesses was the man's use of 'we'.

The curiosity of the witnesses was further aroused when they witnessed the man dressing the children. On hearing this, Nancy Beaumont was astonished, for several reasons. Both Nancy and Jim had warned the children on many occasions over the years not to talk to strangers. Also, Jane and Arnna had been capable of dressing themselves for years.

The witnesses, Nancy and Jim Beaumont, and detectives could not understand why this man felt the need to assist the children with such a simple task as pulling shorts up over swimmers. Even stranger to Nancy and Jim was the idea that their children appeared comfortable with him doing so. The man certainly appeared to have their confidence. He appeared nice, caring, attentive, and concerned. He did not appear to be a 'dirty old man' or someone who posed a threat. To Jane, Arnna, and Grant, he was not a stranger.

A female eyewitness stated that the man and the children were still chatting on the lawn just before noon. At about 12.05 pm, the man picked up his towel, trousers, and shirt and walked north toward the Colley Reserve changerooms with the children following, Jane carrying her blue bag and the towels. However, it now appeared Jane had no purse, as this seemed to have been 'pinched' by the so-called thief. The direction they walked with the man was the opposite direction to the children's bus stop, and this was around the time they were supposed to head home.

The female witnesses saw the man enter the changing sheds at about 12.10 pm, and both stated Jane, Arnna, and Grant waited outside for him. It was also stated that the children were not seen walking back along the reserve and did not return to where they had been playing.

The last known sighting of the Beaumont children was about 12.25 pm to 12.30 pm at the iconic Wenzel's Bakery in Moseley Street, just off the main thoroughfare of Jetty Road and across the road from the children's bus stop. The Beaumont children were not with the man, and they did not appear to have their towels at Wenzel's, nor Jane her carry bag.

The shop assistant at Wenzel's knew the children well because they regularly visited the popular bakery. The assistant said Jane bought one pie, five pasties, six finger buns, and two large bottles of fizzy drink—paid for with a one-pound note. The assistant found it unusual as Jane had never paid with a pound note previously, only in coins of shillings and pence. This pound note Jane paid with was a significant amount of money in 1966. The average weekly wage was eight pounds, so this amount of money equated to a day's work—by today's standards, around 140 dollars. This amount of money was a significant amount of cash for Jane or any other child to have. The question has been asked for decades: who was wealthy enough to give a hard-earned one-pound note to children they hardly knew?

This one-pound note was a pivotal piece of information to detectives in 1966 and has been ever since. So the questions are: Where did Jane get it? Who was wealthy enough to part with a hard-earned one-pound note to a young girl? After spending this money at Wenzel's Bakery, the Beaumont children were never seen again, as if they had just vanished off the face of the earth.

While the children were at the beach, and unknown to Nancy Beaumont, an abduction was unfolding. By mid-morning, Nancy visited a neighbour for a cup of tea and to catch up on gossip. Just before noon, she left on her trusty bicycle and rode to meet the children at the bus stop. When they did not arrive, she believed they might have missed their ride due to having too much fun at the beach.

Back at home, friends of Nancy and Jim had popped over to say hello, and all the while, Nancy kept a close eye on the time.

She was expecting the children to walk in the front door around 1 pm, the time the next bus arrived. By 2 pm, the children still had not come home, and Nancy started to get very anxious indeed. Her friend offered to drive her to the beach, but she thought the children might have walked back from Glenelg and she did not want to miss them. So, she felt it best to wait for the 3 pm bus. However, just before the bus arrived, Jim pulled up in the driveway unexpectedly. He was returning home early from Snowtown, and to greet him was distressed Nancy stating, 'The children have not returned home.' Jim assured Nancy that if anything untoward had happened, they would have known about it by now. Outwardly, Jim was showing calmness. Inwardly, he was just as concerned as Nancy.

Jim was immediately out in his car driving the streets of Glenelg, hoping to spot his children. He parked his vehicle and walked the side streets and over to where the children had played the previous day, frantically searching, but there was no sign of them among the large crowd of people on the beach and at Colley Reserve. Jim then drove back to the house to pick up Nancy, and they drove around the streets of Glenelg and adjoining suburbs for several hours. With no sign of their children, they headed to the Glenelg police station at approximately 5 pm.

Detective Constable Mostyn Matters was confronted by a distraught Mr and Mrs Beaumont reporting their children missing. Mos was part of the team headed up by Detective Ron Blight with his subordinates Matters, Lloyd Brand, Peter Tremalick, and Peter Vogel, forming the Criminal Investigation Branch (CIB) at the Glenelg Police Station. Initially, the police presumed that the children would turn up shortly, that they might have stopped in at a friend's house or simply lost track of time. An abduction never entered their minds.

By 5.30 pm, however, a patrol car that was sent to the Beaumont residence to check the house and talk to the neighbours radioed in to report that they had not located the children. If there hadn't been before, there was now a collective realisation among the Glenelg detectives that the Beaumont children were indeed missing and possibly in grave trouble.

Mostyn Matters, commonly known as Mos, is the only living detective who was present at the Glenelg station on 26 January 1966, and he still has vivid memories of that fateful day and the weeks that followed. When speaking with us, Mos said the initial meeting with Nancy and Jim Beaumont left him and the other Glenelg detectives mentally scarred for the rest of their lives. To Mos and the team, one child missing was one child too many. As Mostyn said, when meeting both of us in 2010, 'We were all family men with young children, and the thought of losing them, coupled with dealing with a deeply distressed Mr and Mr Beaumont, shattered us all. Neither I or [*sic*] the other detectives had ever encountered such a situation.'

They all kept asking the same question over and over: How could three children just vanish? It was very unlikely they had all drowned or together had encountered a misadventure. One maybe, but three? Surely someone was holding them against their will and a phone call from a kidnapper would be received requesting a ransom or something similar. Matters remembers the team working well into the early hours of the morning, with Ron Blight, the lead detective, on the phone constantly with the CIB in Adelaide. Mostyn to this day does not remember his boss without a cigarette in his hand and a cup of coffee close by.

In the days that followed the disappearance, the police station was inundated with well-meaning members of the public lining up wishing to speak with detectives. For days on end, there was a line of people that stretched over 100 metres winding down the footpath. Matters and the team had only one phone line into the police station, and it ran hot day and night. All accounts that were deemed to be credible needed to be written down by the officers and then typed up. There were only a few typewriters to share.

When Mostyn Matters was being interviewed by journalist Frank Pangallo for *Today Tonight*, Adelaide Mostyn said, 'We were just a small outfit. We were doing our best, but we could not possibly interview everybody. It was just impossible, nothing was really organised like it should have been.'[9]

The team worked tirelessly up to sixteen hours a day with some, at times, sleeping at the station. They became agitated by a throng of local interstate and international press camped on the footpath and road outside morning, noon, and night. Any police officer seen walking the shopping precinct of Glenelg was accosted for an interview in the hope of an exclusive. It did appear any snippet of newsworthy information—whether fact-checked or not—quickly made its way to radio, TV, or the front page of the papers. Some of this information was not correct but went to print anyway before it could be corroborated. The most annoying thing for police was the description of the man seen with the children that hit the press: a beachcomber surfie with bleached blond mop-topped hair in need of cutting. To this day, Mostyn still gets annoyed that this characterisation is used in the media.

In an *Advertiser* article on 2 February 1966, an individual stated that 'Jane, Arnna, and Grant walked south behind the Pier Hotel Glenelg toward their home at Somerton Park'.[10] This sighting was corrected later by detectives who ascertained that the children seen were not the Beaumonts, but it still did the rounds in the media for years, further muddying the waters.

A newspaper headline—'New Sex Attack Fears' on *The News* 29 January front page[11]—further sowed fear into the mindset of the South Australian public.

Further headlines included 'Chase after three children in car', 'Hectic chase through the Eastern Suburbs' (*The News* 31 January front page headlines[12]), and better still, the *Adelaide Advertiser* of 11 February—'A secret search for the bodies of the Beaumont Children is being made by Victorian Police on four small islands near Port Phillip Heads'[13].

Years later, Mos Matters made a telling comment to us: 'We really did not know who we were looking for. We had so little quality information. It was as if the children just disappeared off the face of the earth.'

The whole team was shattered. Ron Blight was a worrier at the best of times and was known to chain-smoke. Many believed this disappearance exacerbated his already existing health problems. Mostyn said to us that, even though Ron Blight was outwardly giving hope to the public and Nancy and Jim Beaumont, Blight, Mostyn, and the rest of the team were thinking these children had already met their fate not long after meeting the man. They may have been right.

We now have knowledge the detectives didn't have in 1966: child abduction and murder statistics from a 2006 study conducted by the Criminal Division of the Washington State Attorney General's Office state that, of abducted children who are murdered, around seventy-six percent are killed within three hours of being taken. Also, in seventy-four percent of the missing children homicide cases studied, the child murder victim was female, and the average age was eleven years old.[14]

Mr Beaumont's anxiety was further heightened by the knowledge that his children were frightened of the dark and were never out at that time by themselves. The reality of what might have happened began to sink in. Jim spent the evening and well into the early hours of the next morning searching the foreshores of the beachside suburbs and back streets in a patrol car with constables, a loudspeaker attached to the roof blaring, 'Have you seen three children?' But they needed more help, and this came very soon.

Ron Blight alerted the Adelaide CIB of the gravity of the situation that was unfolding, and it sent thirty extra police officers to Glenelg to assist in the search, which went into the early hours of the morning. Over the following days, and with the help of the public and Jim Beaumont's old taxi colleagues, they scoured the foreshores and sandhills of the surrounding beaches and the back streets. They searched the main thorough-fares of Glenelg and nearby suburbs. Neighbours walked the different routes the children might have taken home. As word spread, more information hit the media; radio and television gave regular news updates. Officers were sent to search the family home in case the children had returned and were hiding. One local Glenelg resident who lived in Augusta Street in 1966 told Stuart Mullins they remembered scores of police officers searching local residential gardens for what he believed would be any discarded children's clothing or other items. Police also retraced the bus route the children took and the different directions they would have walked if they missed their ride.

The policedoor knocked local residences, checked back-yards, and spoke to local bus drivers. They checked interstate bus and train movements and set up roadblocks.

The abduction of three children was unheard of, not just in Australia, but around the world. The police, press, and public alike were asking who could be so brazen as to commit such a heinous act in a crowded location in broad daylight. Not only were South Australian detectives left scratching their heads, but so too were interstate and overseas criminal investigators and the media. Ron Blight and his team worked tirelessly, leaving no stone unturned in their investigation

Mrs Beaumont was questioned by detectives to ascertain the correct timeline and exact descriptions of Jane, Arnna, and Grant. The information was immediately sent out through news bulletins locally and interstate. With her children missing, Nancy became so distressed that she required sedation.

As word spread over the next few days and weeks, teams of volunteers again combed the sandhills of the beaches and surrounding foreshore. The Police Emergency Operations Group was called into the search, with five boats from the Sea Rescue Squadron searching the Patawalonga Boat Haven in Glenelg, which they had drained and searched. They scoured the local seas for any floating remnants of the children. There was a thought that Jane, Arnna, and Grant could have been victims of a mis-adventure. They might have dug a sand cave that had collapsed on them or ventured too far into a seaside stormwater drain. Mr Beaumont, with assistance, continued the search and refused to rest until his children were found; however, the parents' worst nightmare was unfolding. As Mostyn Matters stated, 'This was sheer heartbreak, watching both Jim and Nancy unravel.' This disappearance emotionally affected many people. The detectives at the station were never the same. They never shook the memory and vision of these distraught parents. And all of those detectives who have since died went to the grave with a feeling of ill-deserved guilt that they could have done more.

Like Mostyn and the team, Australia was in a state of disbelief and shock. Three children missing without a trace was unfathomable. Jim Beaumont gave a press conference on the morning of 27 January saying that someone must be holding his children against their will. Sadly, he was right.

Chapter 3:
The Sorrowful Years

How do you mend a broken heart?
Sometimes you can't.

—Stuart Mullins

We have enjoyed many talks with Mostyn Matters about the weeks, months, and years that passed after the children's disappearance. His accounts, insights, and commentary are enlightening and indeed invaluable. Mos's heartfelt emotions can sometimes get the better of him when he recounts the collective grief experienced by many regarding those tragic days.

Coupled with Mostyn's recollections, Stuart also had the opportunity to meet and speak with Peter Vogel (who has since passed away) more than ten years ago. Peter, like Mostyn, was a detective stationed at Glenelg that fateful day in 1966. They spoke of the frustration of not being able to pinpoint a suspect and the irritation at the lack of assistance from Adelaide CIB to help out at the Glenelg police station—that there was only a small team of detectives at Glenelg and they found it very difficult to keep up with the amount of information coming in from a well-meaning public. Investigating the crime itself, meeting with people, and taking and correlating their statements was time-consuming.

Over the next days and weeks, they had compiled boxes of notes and statements that were indexed and stored. Bill Hayes, a former detective in the Major Crime Squad in the 1980s, could attest to this. At one point he was given the task of looking through the boxes of information stored regarding this case. As Bill recollects, he immediately realised the enormity of the task at hand. One would require a team of detectives to sift through the amount of stored information. This was not a job for one person.

As mentioned in Chapter 2, it did not take long for the detectives working at the station to become frustrated with the multitude of media camped outside the station day and night wanting 'that scoop'.

Both Mostyn and Peter said to Stuart in 2008 over a cup of coffee in Glenelg, 'We needed to be guarded, careful in what details they released to the public. There was a process when investigating cases, and information, where possible, had to be corroborated to avoid giving false hope to the parents and also to the concerned community.'

The media and the public needed to make sense of it all. They required a rallying point, and the Glenelg police station quickly became that focus. When further speaking with Mostyn and Peter, they explained that the main Adelaide media outlets were, overall, professional to work with but were still in need of 'that scoop' and would go to great lengths to secure one, corroborated or not.

The abduction of the Beaumont children was the biggest crime news story in Adelaide and arguably still is today. Alan Whiticker's *Searching for the Beaumont Children* places this all in perspective: 'The Beaumont case was heartbreaking, but the cold hard fact was, a scoop on the investigation was worth thousands or more copies to a newspaper's circulation.'[15]

The public inundated the police station with phone calls to report perverts hanging around the toilet blocks of Colley

Reserve. They were genuinely fearful that there was a sex-crazed maniac on the loose. Hence, this was truly the day Australia lost its innocence forever. The team of detectives followed up with a comment to journalists: They were clutching at straws.

Worse still, one newspaper got hold of Nancy and Jim's Harding Street address and printed this in the paper. So, a beeline was made to their home at Somerton Park, where media contingents and nosy onlookers gathered for days on end outside their house, which further added to their distress. In the Adelaide *Sunday Mail* newspaper article of 31 January 1966 headlined 'Sex Crime Now Feared', Jim Beaumont spoke with a reporter, saying, '[Nancy] cries all the time and the doctor has to give her sedatives. If I could give my life right now for my kids to be returned safe and sound I would … and no questions asked.'[16]

The CIB in Adelaide oversaw the operations shortly after the children went missing and was headed by Inspector Noel Lenton with second-in-charge Alex Palmer, while the team at Glenelg, led by Ron Blight, continued to interview the general public, trying to piece together the events of the day. Despite the massive searches and doorknocking of local residences, not a skerrick of physical evidence had been found. Alerts also went out to train and bus stations locally and interstate, but there was still no trace of the children.

Again, when speaking with Mullins in 2008, Mostyn Matters and Peter Vogel agreed that this abduction was baffling, Mos saying years later, 'Who could be so damned brazen to abduct three children, let alone from a crowded reserve in broad daylight!' This type of abduction defied logic, not only for Mos and Peter but also for the general public. Also frustrating to the team was the fact that Noel Lenton was still treating it as a missing-persons case. It was evident to the team at Glenelg, however, that this was an abduction.

To add to the team's exasperation, Adelaide CIB waited twelve months before they released the information regarding Jane being given a pound note by the man at the beach. To many, withholding such a vital clue from the public was unforgivable. When Mullins spoke to Mostyn in 2010 at his local Adelaide residence, he asked, 'Why would the Adelaide CIB withhold such vital information from the public?' Mostyn replied he could only have a guess that those in charge wanted to keep an ace up their sleeve. For example, if someone contacted police saying they had the children, the detectives could move the narrative to money and await this individual's response. However, had this information been released just after the disappearance, it just may have well changed the course of this case. To this day, Mostyn's exasperation at this omission was noticeable to both of us.

As the media interest started to wane, one news outlet tried a new angle. They contacted Dutch clairvoyant and parapsychologist Gerard Croiset, who had had some success tracing missing persons. However, his success rate hovered around fifty percent, which would be no better than guessing. Bringing him over from Holland was in part bankrolled by Adelaide real estate tycoon Con Polites, for whom Nancy Beaumont worked at the time, and the Adelaide Dutch community. Mostyn's view, when speaking with us years later, was that bringing Croiset to Australia turned the investigation into a circus. It did, however, reignite interest from the public, which unfortunately also included eccentrics and oddballs with their outlandish visions of what happened—coupled with an array of mediums, religious fanatics, mystics, diviners, prophets, and plain 'wackos', as Mostyn likes to describe them. Many did not go to the media; instead, they directed their attention and visits to the Glenelg police station. At the same meeting over a coffee at Glenelg in

2008, both Mostyn and Peter said to Stuart, 'You could have written a book about these characters.'

Mos and the team were not supporters of Gerard Croiset and thought the whole escapade was a complete waste of time. This view was shared by Adelaide CIB and the South Australian Government. When Croiset arrived, he was met by a large contingent of media, as expected. He familiarised himself with the case and met Mr and Mrs Beaumont and inspected the family residence and the Colley Reserve area. A short time later, he led the media and police to a factory warehouse in Paringa Park where, he said, the children were buried at a factory under the flooring. A dig ensued, but nothing was found. The media dissipated and the clairvoyant flew home.

The detectives from the Glenelg station became known as the go-to officers for any information, which regularly included wild theories and speculation by members of the public. One narrative had the children taken overseas by white slavers; another, years later, was a possible sighting of the trio living as adults overseas; and another, abduction by religious zealots. Others accused the postman Tom Patterson of being involved. Some sections of the local community even turned on Mr and Mrs Beaumont, with rumours spreading that one or both parents were involved. However, Jim and Nancy had been interviewed as part of an investigation protocol and found to be in no way involved. Another man presented himself to the station proclaiming to be Jesus Christ; Detective Sergeant Ron Blight had pointed out that he could not walk on water.

The team kept Jim and Nancy regularly informed, but the Beaumonts were forced to endure unsolicited home visits by random people who had a theory to share. Jim and Nancy were always diplomatic and courteous, but their patience must have run thin, as well as their emotional and physical wellbeing.

The fabric that was binding the two together was fraying at the edges.

In the following few years, another detective, Stan 'Tonner' Swain, took over the investigation as Chief of Homicide. He quickly gained the reputation that he perpetuated: that he was the man to solve the case of the missing Beaumont children. His ego was well known, not just by the officers around him but also by his family, and his dogged focus ended up destroying his marriage and his relationship with his children. He was noted to be a charmer and a relatively convincing talker, but also headstrong, traits that helped him climb the police ranks. However, like many, he became obsessed with the case, which led to his judgement and decision-making capabilities being called into doubt. Swain became known for following and investigating misleading or erroneous information, for not adhering to police department procedures, and for being deceitful. These flaws would eventually be his downfall.

The final straw for Jim and Nancy Beaumont, and the beginning of Stan Swain's undoing, came in the form of what became known as the 'The Dandenong Letters'. In 1968, Stan came into possession, through Jim and Nancy Beaumont, of a letter supposedly written by Jane saying she, Arnna, and Grant were all well and were with a nice man in Victoria, and asking them to meet at the Dandenong post office. The letter mentioned that the media was not to be involved. Stan was convinced this letter was genuine, despite Arnna's name being misspelt and the handwriting not matching Jane's. However, not to be deterred, Stan filled Nancy and Jim with hope, optimism, and anticipation and got them involved. Unknown to his superior, Noel Lenton, they all made the trip to Victoria—but the media got wind of his escapade and the story broke. When it all unfolded, this letter was found to be a cruel hoax. The man and the children did not turn up, only press reporters. Jim and Nancy Beaumont were so shattered and disillusioned by Stan's deceptive behaviour they never gave another public interview.

Though Jim and Nancy's hopes gradually faded, the public interest in their private tragedy never did. Many have asked what happened to Mr and Mrs Beaumont after they stopped speaking with the media. Mostyn Matters and Ron Blight had cemented a friendship with them both, with either Jim visiting the station hoping for a positive update, or both Matters and Blight stopping in at the family home. Mos noted that Nancy kept the children's bedrooms as they were that January day in 1966, and their bikes could still be seen in the backyard. However, the not knowing and the lack of credible leads weighed heavily on the shoulders of both parents, and the constant media attention and scrutiny took its toll.

Over time, Jim stopped frequenting the station, and he and Nancy's relationship slowly dissolved into divorce in the early 1970s, and they sold their Harding Street home. Even though they separated, Nancy and Jim remained friends.

In 2018, Des Bray, who was the head of the Major Crime Investigation Branch, was quoted by the South Australian media as saying, 'We will always do anything humanly possible to locate the Beaumont children and take them home to their family. I don't think there's anybody in the country who doesn't want to find the Beaumont children.'

Mostyn and Ron did visit Jim after this, but their talks dissipated with the march of time and as Mr Beaumont became more reclusive. According to one popular local tradesman who would carry out small jobs for Jim, Chris (not his real name) said:

> He kept to himself but every Saturday for decades could be found having a drink and a bet at a local Glenelg South pub on the Broadway. Jim's stay was short and [he] regularly left with a six-pack of beer, which he would consume by himself at home.

Chris said that, for years, Jim could be seen sitting under the rays of the morning sunshine in the front garden of his apartment.

Around 2014, Mostyn visited Jim at his residence to discuss his thoughts on Harry Phipps. Although Jim was then elderly and in failing health, he respectfully listened but gave Mostyn the impression he was tired of it all, that he could not bear to have his hopes raised then dashed yet again. Perhaps not surprisingly, the decades of false leads had torn away the last semblance of belief he may have had that his children would return home. However, he had kept abreast of developments regarding Phipps over the years and was very appreciative of the work Mostyn was doing and wished him the very best in his endeavours. Chris also paid Jim a visit just before the second Castalloy factory dig in early 2018. The Castalloy digs will be explored in more detail later in the book. He stated that Jim was very appreciative of the work being carried out by us and was in good spirits. In 2018, Jim moved into an aged-care facility.

A few people who knew Nancy said that after the sale of their Somerton Park home, she moved into an apartment in Glenelg North, a short walk to the Jetty Bar in Glenelg where she was a regular for years. At times, when drinking a tad too much, she was offered a room upstairs free of charge—gladly given to her by the publican. She was described as chirpy and enjoyed many a beer and some time on the poker machines. However, her advancing years, coupled with her drinking, caught up with her and she moved into an aged-care facility in Glengowrie around 2010.

In 2013, Mostyn Matters and his wife Diana visited Mrs Beaumont at the nursing home. Nancy was pleasantly surprised and happy to see them both. They described Nancy as bubbly and animated. Mostyn took a back seat to Nancy and Diana as they happily gossiped, but he was happy to see that Nancy was all right. At one point, she paused to show Mos and Di a small photo of her three children tucked snugly into a locket she was wearing. Both commented on how happy they looked, and Nancy agreed, stating they were lovely children.

What struck Mos and Di was the small size of her room and the stark surroundings, with no TV or radio. However, overall Nancy was in a happy place, and that was enough to leave a lasting positive impression on them both. Mostyn felt relieved; over the years, he had formed a deep bond with Nancy and Jim, watching as their marriage dissolved under the weight of the unimaginable pain and suffering of losing their much-loved children. Nancy passed away in 2018 aged ninety-two at an aged-care home in Glengowrie, never knowing the fate of her children.

The abduction and disappearance of Jane, Arnna, and Grant Beaumont tore at the heart and soul of South Australia for decades. It greatly affected the team at Glenelg Police Station, as well as family, friends, neighbours, and even Tom Patterson, the postman. Tom delivered the mail to the Beaumont home days, weeks, months, and years after the children went missing. He was never again greeted with the words, 'Hey, it's the postie,' nor would he see Jane, Arnna, and Grant's smiling faces as they ran out to the post box to collect the mail after hearing Tom's trusted postie's whistle. He told Stuart Mullins and Mostyn Matters when they met in Glenelg in 2008 that the neighbourhood was never the same. A degree of melancholy hung ever-present in the air for years. At times, he would catch either Nancy or Jim in the driveway as he delivered their mail, but he was at a loss for any appropriate words to use apart from a smile followed by a 'good morning', but it was difficult not to see their sadness when their eyes met. Tom said to Mullins, 'There is not a day that goes by I do not think of their smiling faces.' As Mr and Mrs Beaumont and some other Somerton Park residents moved away and were replaced by new families, the recollection of what had occurred in 1966 slowly became a fading memory of what had once been.

Jim and Nancy Beaumont have lived a nightmare for decades. They waited for over fifty long years for answers. Sadly, for Mrs Beaumont, they never came. This was a mother's worst nightmare: no closure, no burial, just unrelenting grief. She spent her life living in the hope that someday her children would return, while enduring a heartache that cannot be imagined. Yet despite her years of longing, Nancy passed away without ever finding out what happened. Now she is finally at peace and reunited with her loving children, Jane, Arnna, and Grant, while their father Jim Beaumont still lives and waits in hope.

Chapter 4:
Three Journalists

Journalism is a craft that takes years to learn. It's like golf. You never get it right all the time. It's a game of fewer errors, better facts, and better reporting.[17]

—Ben Huh

W hen evil the likes of Harry Phipps strikes, as we cover in detail in the following chapters, it leaves behind a trail of devastating emotional and physical carnage and destruction. These predatorial paedophiles destroy not only the hopes and dreams of countless children but also their suffering parents. This abuse adversely affects extended family members, relatives, friends, neighbours, and work colleagues, the local community, and, in this case, the entire state and country. This emotional scarring endures, and no amount of time can erase the feelings of profound regret and heartache.

The media, love them or loathe them, have always displayed a compassionate understanding when speaking with Nancy and Jim Beaumont. No-one needs to explain to them, nor the entire nation, the parents' personal grief, pain, and the total sense of loss and bereavement they have gone through. It is an emotional torment that has continued for a lifetime—unwanted travelling companions, a dark, foreboding, ominous figure that has remained ever-present by the parents' side until Nancy Beaumont's recent passing.

You will recall that Mr Beaumont was called Jim when in the army and continued to use that name until after his children were abducted. Some time later, he had reverted to his birth name Grant, likely as a tribute to his lost son. Several face-to-face interviews with Jim and Nancy were secured in the first few years after the children went missing. One such interview was conducted at the parents' Somerton Park home by Ken Anderson, Doug Easom, and Brian Francis. These journalists worked for *The News* which, in its time, was arguably Adelaide's leading newspaper publication. However, it sadly no longer exists.

The interview encapsulated a most poignant moment in time and was an insightful discussion that gives a great understanding of the parents' mental anguish, regret, sorrow, and grief. It compassionately recounted the heartbreak and suffering both parents had endured up to the time of this article and have continued to endure through the many decades that have followed, broken only by the death of Nancy Beaumont.

Ken, Doug, and Brian also articulated Nancy's description of each of her children—their distinct characters and personalities. She gave a heartwarming yet amusing and even comical account of a moment with a young Grant that stuck in her mind during those trying times when, for a fleeting moment, a wry smile may have just made its way to the face of Mrs Beaumont.

Also, both parents opened up about the love that the whole family had shared at that brief moment in time—a love and a bond that would endure no matter the time that passed. A bond that not even death could break, nor that evil could take.

In one part of the interview, Nancy's mental torment can best be summed up in her words to the journalists. She blames herself for her children going missing. She outlined an emotional burden that no-one should have to bear. The authors have included her quote when speaking with the journalists to allow the reader to be able to understand the mental suffering experienced by Nancy:

> I do blame myself for not having been with my children that day. Very much so. No-one will ever know how much. If ever it gets a bit cold and you don't give your kiddies a cardigan or a coat, and they catch a cold, you blame yourself for their cold. And that's how I feel as a mother. No matter how many ifs and buts, you have to live with the fact that I didn't take my children to the beach that day and I am in the wrong. No-one will make me feel any differently about it.[4]

As one journalist present said, 'No words can describe the compassion with which Jim Beaumont hears out his wife's anguish.'[4]

And there was a positive rapport developing between the journalists and the parents. This allowed Nancy to open up about the pain, intense grief, and confusion about what to say and how to act with friends, acquaintances, Jim, and vice versa. She said, 'The children's birthdays are remembered of course and quietly between ourselves. At times we do not mention these celebrations in case of upsetting one another.' Nancy went on to say, 'You are always hedging your bets. You don't want to pull the other down. Because of not wanting to distress the other. One starts to cry, and the other follows.'[4]

To us, both parents seemed to be walking on eggshells, trying desperately not to cause any further unwanted, and most certainly unneeded, stress.

Ken, Doug, and Brian also paint a picture of life just before the children disappeared and immediately after. The family home appeared to be social central pre-26 January 1966. There were many visits from Paringa Park school friends who would regularly visit after school to play with Jane, Arnna, and Grant. Nancy said:

> We had a fairly busy social life and always had neighbours and friends pop in to enjoy a cup of tea, a social beer and of course some local gossip. However, this all changed after the children disappeared. People didn't pop in as much as they used to.[4]

Neighbours and work friends who were close could not face Nancy and Jim without feeling that they would become emotional.

If they did, they would be terrified of what they might say to avoid upsetting the parents and themselves. Others are lost for words. What does one say and act like when confronted by a situation that very few people have had to face in a lifetime? In the end, the visitor numbers dwindled and Nancy and Jim suffered alone.

However, Mr Beaumont informed journalists at the time of the interview that 'detectives over the last two years have been exceptional in their relentless investigations and he [was] immensely grateful for this'. There were regular visits from them, and he considered Detective Sergeant Ron Blight a good friend.

Overall, Jim mostly kept himself busy by doing an enormous number of sales calls for Lincott Linen. On the weekends, when he was home, he pottered about the garden and tinkered with the car. Nancy kept herself busy cooking, gardening, or cleaning—

anything to keep her mind active and distract her from the living nightmare that her life had become. However, when it came to cleaning, there were two rooms she could not bear to enter. Arnna and Grant's shared bedroom and Jane's. Nancy knew that entering would bring a flood of tears.

Nancy and Jim did go out socially, just needing to have some time to mingle with others and to feel normal. However, when they were recognised, people would become unsure of what to say, perhaps even a bit standoffish. It was like swimming in a goldfish bowl.

Both parents were candid with the journalists and spoke of having nightmares about how scared the children would have been—alone, afraid, frightened, and crying, wanting to go home to be with Mum and Dad but unable to. Jim recounted a story to one of the correspondents about these feelings. This had been brought home to him and Nancy in June 1966, six months after the children went missing. They were travelling north to the outback, Eagle Hawk Station near Broken Hill, what you would term today as Crocodile Dundee Country.

They needed to get away from the commotion for some peace. When their caravan became bogged, they spent a night in the middle of nowhere in the Australian bush in the freezing desert's overnight temperatures. Jim recalled:

It was pitch black and very cold. A very bad experience. Not knowing if help would come. We knew how lost we felt. That's the time you think about things. And we were adults. Just imagine how frightened the kiddies would have felt.[4]

One journalist asked Jim and Nancy what they thought might have happened to the children. They both said that they had no proof; however, they felt that Jane, Arnna, and Grant may have accepted the offer of a ride to Somerton Park and got into a car. They would have done that thinking they were coming home, but the car didn't stop. They fully understood that this was only a theory, but to them, it was the most plausible answer.

If a journalist had ever ventured to ask the question of what might have occurred *after* the children's abduction, this surely would have been met with an indignant silence. The very thought of the answer to this question is so horrible that the majority of people would dare not think about the fate of the children. More so, this question may have crossed the mind of some less-than-ethical journalists at some point in time, but thankfully, they never asked the question.

Mrs Beaumont also added she could not understand how her children would walk away with this individual—having been warned time and time again to not speak to strangers. However, as we saw in Chapter 2, the media and the public were focusing on who they believed this individual was: a sex pervert, sex maniac, 'weirdo', or deviant, all of which made terrifying front-page news banners but were far from the truth. Jane, Arnna, and Grant did not walk away with one of these monsters. They walked with an individual who was everything the kiddies believed a nice man should be but, in reality, was a wolf in sheep's clothing, a devil disguised as an angel. Did they already know this man?

The journalists also asked, 'Do you think time is on your side?' Their response is enlightening. 'Everything is on our side as long as we haven't found any trace of the kiddies. They are still alive somewhere.'[4] According to the journalist, the parents were still hoping that one day Jane, Arnna, and Grant would return home.

On another occasion, Jim was being interviewed by journalist Ron Berryman of the Adelaide News when he said:

This disappearance is a complete mystery. I don't understand it. I cannot think of another place to look. My kids will be crying their eyes out. It's like a nightmare. Now I know what other people go through when their children go missing. Now it's happened to us.[18]

Both fondly spoke with the three journalists about each of the children's characters and personalities. However, the interview mood brightened when Nancy recounted the novel way Grant ate his favourite lunch: a fritz and tomato sauce sandwich cut into triangles. Fritz was usually sold as a thinly sliced luncheon meat, very popular for South Australian school children's sandwiches.

Grant's favourite place to eat these was on the backyard swing with his mum feeding him bite-sized pieces as the swing rocked backward and forward. They had this routine down pat. Every fourth forward motion, Nancy would pop another piece into Grant's mouth. She knew this was naughty and not the best way to teach your child appropriate eating etiquette, but it made for fun memories and was loved by little Grant. This beautiful account in amongst dark clouds may have just brought a slight chuckle from Jim. Further speaking with journalist Ken Anderson in the same interview, he said of his son, 'Grant was a little mischievous and cheeky at times but full of life. He adored his older sisters and would follow them anywhere.'[4]

Jim and Nancy also spoke fondly of both girls, who, despite their very different personalities, got along well and were inseparable. Arnna was always polite, respectful, and very energetic. She enjoyed school but was more an outdoors girl. Arnna wasn't as intellectually gifted as Jane but had a big, bright personality all of her own. She wasn't an avid reader like her bigger sister but had a great imagination. She was a great little singer and loved dressing up and play-acting in the early evening in front of the family. These two were close and loved each other's company.

On the other hand, Jane was the mother hen, and both Arnna and Grant looked up to her. She was highly intelligent, studious, articulate, and an avid reader with a fantastic memory. She also excelled at school. Her father considered her a born leader and could see her as becoming a journalist or a politician. She was always helpful around the house, assisting in preparing the evening meal or bathing and dressing Grant. Jim understood that he and Nancy mentioned Jane a lot. This is because she was mature for her age and the second set of hands to Nancy. Both parents could have a reasonable young-adult conversation with her.

However, as this interview took place, there were clues hidden in the conversations that indicated their marriage was faltering. Their divorce several years later appeared to be the culmination of a convergence of factors beginning at 5 pm Wednesday, 26 January 1966 when the realisation that the children hadn't come home had set in.

When Nancy spoke with the journalists, she said Jim was away most of the week working for Lincott industries—visiting clients in the South Australian countryside and as far away as Broken Hill, a large mining town in far west New South Wales—leaving on Monday morning and returning Friday evening. With only a day and a half to spend together and without the raucous noise of playful children, the quiet became deafening.

Nancy said it was terribly hard to still live there with the children's rooms left as they were, continually reminding Nancy of what could have been and what they had lost. The memories lingered, but their playful laughter had not. It appeared to become too much for Nancy, who spoke about wanting to escape with Jim to the USA or some other place far away. On the other hand, Jim found solace in caravanning in the countryside, and he, like Nancy, dearly missed their children.

She also spoke on numerous occasions in this extended interview with the same journalists—Ken, Doug, and Brian— about this, stating, 'Children are a big part of what makes a happy marriage. They bind one together. Without them, what do you have? I still love Jim very much, but I'll never get used to not having the children here in a million years.' Nancy had admitted that she was very lost and could not fathom why the children were just taken from her without rhyme or reason.

There have been many words spoken over the ages regarding the wonder of being a parent. There is nothing like it as those who have experienced this can understand. The responsibility of having this small person loving you and being reliant on you brings out the best in most of us. Feeling that close bond develop between parent and child where they almost become one is indeed one of the wonders of nature and something that you could never experience with anyone but your own child. Can there be any better feeling than this immeasurable depth of love for your child?

Having one child taken would tear at the very fabric of a stable, loving family. Having three taken would be unbearably devastating. This is what happens when evil strikes. Who could blame either Nancy or Jim for going their separate ways? And in the end, their separate ways they eventually did go.

What Ken Anderson, Doug Easom, and Brian Francis achieved in this interview was to bring to life a heartfelt yet tragic story. Not from hearsay or the opinions of others. They went straight to the source—Nancy and Jim Beaumont—in an honest, understanding, and caring manner. The result is a sincere, warm, and profoundly touching account that tugs at the heart and soul. This was journalism performed at its very best.

Chapter 5:
Jane's Best Friend

Some people come into our lives and leave footprints
on our hearts and we are never, ever the same.[19]

—Flavia Weedn

Many stories have been written over the years about the Beaumont children, some sweeping and generalised, others closer to the truth. However, none are as profoundly personal as that of Jane Beaumont's best friend, Jenny.

For three consecutive years, Jenny and Jane sat next to one another in class at Paringa Park Primary School, not far from the seaside suburbs of Somerton Park and Glenelg. She has fond memories of their time spent together at school and playing in their local neighbourhood. Their final year together— unknown to both at the time—was grade four. Their classroom, like many in the 1960s, had wooden desks arranged in regimented rows with the pupils facing a large chalkboard. On one side were the week's spelling list and times tables; on the other side a list of selected pupils to act as lunch, milk, furnace, and ink-well monitors. Next to the blackboard hung a large map of the world, highlighting the extent of the British Empire. Above the chalkboard, there was a framed portrait of Her Majesty Queen Elizabeth II.

Jenny and Jane loved sitting next to each other, though at times they were a little too talkative, giggly, and mischievous, but nothing so notable as to cause their teacher to put them on detention. Jenny recalls Jane saying to her, as the last days of the 1965 school term were drawing to a close, 'Let's try and fool the new teacher for next year by sitting next to one another to see if they try to seat us at separate desks, having heard about how talkative we can be.' Both would giggle when she said things like this. Jane was wickedly playful at times, coupled with an innocent devilish attitude.

Jenny described her best friend as very intelligent and more mature than her young age suggested. Jane was an avid reader, having a vocabulary well above her years. Sometimes, when Jenny had difficulty understanding an English or maths problem, Jane was available to assist her and would patiently explain the how, why, and what of any particular dilemma Jenny had.

She remembered Jane as an outgoing, bright, bubbly kid with an effervescent, positive personality. Jane had a creative, intuitive, and imaginative mind. Many times, without notice, Jane would laugh out loud as she had envisaged the humorous side of what was unfolding before others did. Her laughter was infectious and could brighten the dullest of days.

Jane wanted to be a journalist and was desperate to write. Her head was stuck in a book on many occasions, hence her range of vocabulary and grasp of the written word. She wrote descriptive, illuminating, and beautiful stories and loved to read them, or passages from the current book she was perusing, to Jenny. She was in love with Robert Louis Stevenson, who wrote *Treasure Island*, and Daniel Defoe, author of *Robinson Crusoe*. When Jane fervently read these fascinating stories of adventure to Jenny, her passionate, expressive delivery and range of emotions coupled with her use of descriptive prose captivated her friend. Jane was always eager for feedback, often stopping mid-paragraph to ask, 'What do you think so far?' Jenny always replied with a thumbs-up, enthusiastic for Jane to continue. To Jenny, Jane wasn't just an ordinary school friend—she was her best friend.

Jenny vividly remembers these times spent with Jane in the 1960s—a time of freedom, fun, and adventure. Jenny recalled being a latchkey kid: a child who returns home from school to an empty house or is often left at home with little parental supervision because their parents are away at work. Jenny's mother had mental-health issues—later diagnosed as a personality disorder—and was not always available. Her father had passed away several years earlier. Jenny said Jane, Arnna, and Grant were also often left to their own devices, as were many other children of that era as their parents were off at work. So, one would come home from school to an empty house.

Jenny had never met Mr and Mrs Beaumont, even though she had been to Jane's house on numerous occasions. Likewise, she could not recall that Jane had met her mother. Children in the 1960s were independent, resourceful, resilient, and self-reliant. Jenny remembers having a house key in her pocket, and Jane kept hers inside her trusty beige clip purse. Other than that, the world was their oyster.

Children saw their parents early morning and early evening for dinner. They had a list of chores to do, and most had this routine down pat: making one's bed, placing the milk bottles out on the porch, and preparing dinner before Mum and Dad arrived home—mashing the potatoes, burning the sausages, peeling the peas from their pods, boiling the carrots, setting the table and, later, washing the dishes.

Being a latchkey kid meant that you were independent. For Jenny and Jane, this also involved acting as a parent to their siblings. Or in Jenny's case, to her mother. Jane was the custodian of Grant and Arnna. Jane and Jenny would also do a lot of the housework—shop, prepare food, pay bills, and, in Jane's case, bathe her little brother Grant. This responsibility bound them together. They recognised something in each other that was different from their peers. They never resented the way their lives were because they never realised that other children didn't do the same things.

Jenny was always impressed by Jane's moral compass, which was more advanced than her young years would have suggested. She knew right from wrong and believed in fairness, treating everyone she met with kindness. Jane was always respectful and showed a conviction rare in such a young girl. She was well liked, reliable, trustworthy, caring, and honest. She did not have many friends, but the ones she had were special to her and she treated them as such. Jane was a positive influence on all she met, making most kids feel special.

One of Jenny's favourite memories was standing on the back-axle platform of Jane's tricycle, riding around the neighbourhood. Being quite uncoordinated, she would lose her balance when hitting a pothole, falling off and landing on her bottom, which was greeted with howls of laughter from them both. Several times, Arnna would also ride along, trying to keep up with them. They would always include Arnna. She was a happy-go-lucky little girl and a pleasure to have along. Jane loved both her siblings very much, and it showed. They had much fun together, never wanting summer to finish.

They had the freedom to do most things, but these two had more freedom than the typical 1960s child. Jenny and Jane would sometimes walk kilometres to and from each other's houses. Jenny described the Beaumont house as very austere and always closed up, with the curtains drawn. When at Jane's residence, they would head straight into her bedroom to listen to the newest hit songs on the radio, finish homework, or quietly read.

Jane was more interested in literature and movies than in boys. Both girls would travel with Grant and Arnna to the local cinema located on Jetty Road, the main thoroughfare of Glenelg. Grant would sit on Jane's lap and, nine times out of ten, he would go to sleep. If Jane had to go to the bathroom, Grant would sit on Jenny's knee. Jane would also talk to the people next to her at the movies. She was always curious and quite the conversationalist. Contrary to popular belief, she was not shy; in fact, she was quite outgoing and very polite.

Jane was a mother figure to Arnna and Grant and would do anything for them. Jenny fondly remembers the Beaumonts as very well-behaved children, and Arnna and Grant never crying or whining. They just were happy, outgoing kids, their cheerful disposition well documented in the many photos taken of the children in the early 1960s. Along with Mr and Mrs Beaumont, Jenny's world fell apart on 26 January 1966, the day South Australia and the nation lost their innocence.

Jane and Jenny had taken the bus many times to Glenelg together. Jenny knew the route that Jane and her siblings would take; it was a ride they had taken many times together. After paying the driver, Jane would have sat Grant and Arnna up the front near the driver rather than down the back because all the teenagers sat there. A trip to Glenelg from their bus stop was ten minutes. They would have alighted on the corner of Moseley Street and Jetty Road fifty metres from Colley Reserve. Jane would have carried Grant on her hip down the steps of the bus with Arnna close by her side. Jane would give both specific instructions, 'Hold my hand, Grant,' and he would move closer to hold Jane's hand as they crossed the busy intersection.

Grant looked up to Jane as a mother figure and would follow her instructions. He was a dear, sweet little boy. Arnna was a little bit more flippant, cheeky and playful. She loved playing dress-ups and was more suited to being an actress in her older years. She was a little girl full of energy and adventure but always looked to Jane for guidance and instruction.

Once at the reserve, they would have laid out their towels, and then all three would have run down to play in the tepid, calm, turquoise waters of the Spencer Gulf. Jane would have told Grant, 'Don't you get your belly button wet, or I'll get cross at you.' Arnna would have frolicked around in the shallows as she wasn't as keen on the beach as Jane and Grant. After their dip, Jane would have taken them up to the reserve and dried both off. Jane always dried Grant first so he didn't get cold. They would have sunbaked, built sandcastles, and run excitedly under the sprinklers shrieking while being sprayed by the water soaking the parched lawns of the reserve. If Jenny were with them, both would have had a long discussion while strolling along the foreshore with Arnna and Grant following, Grant complaining they walked and talked too much. He just wanted to play at the water's edge, and Arnna would happily play in a world of her own.

Jenny has thought about this day many times. So many scenarios have played over in her mind for decades. If she had been there instead of at her grandmother's house, Jenny could have discouraged Jane, Arnna, and Grant from going with this man. She could have reminded them, 'Don't talk to strangers,' or she could have been at Jane's house that morning and they all might have done other things with the day. If only she could have done something. Jenny has felt helpless all these years.

Jenny remembers sitting in front of the TV at her grandmother's house when a news bulletin flashed across the screen in the early evening. Jane, Arnna, and Grant Beaumont were missing. A feeling of bewilderment enveloped her, not comprehending how anyone could simply vanish. It was all surreal. Jenny was crying as she and her grandmother tried to grasp the magnitude of what was happening. News on TV and radio was relaying updates. Photos of Grant, Arnna, and Jane continually rolled across the screen. Panicked thoughts swirled around Jenny's mind. *Silly Jane, where are you? I want my best friend. Please call and come home.*

How could Jane, Arnna, and Grant disappear? How could someone have taken them? It was not like Jane to play games. She was resourceful and far more mature than her age; surely, they had been waylaid or had an accident. They would not have gone off with anyone they did not know. If by slim chance she did, Jane would tell someone. She was a smart, sensible girl and would have found a way of communicating if she could have. Jenny remembers Jane as being so protective of Arnna and Grant she would not let anyone touch them. The longer this went on, the more Jenny's anxiety became apparent. She was shedding many tears, coupled with sleepless nights at not being able to share her grief or her sense of distress with anyone.

This drama was unfolding so that quickly she had a difficult time contemplating that her best friend had vanished. What made matters worse was that Jenny had returned home from her grandmother's to be met by an indifferent attitude from her mother. All she could say was, 'You were lucky you were not with her.' Maybe her mother, like many, believed that the children had run off and would turn up soon.

She has lived with these memories for over fifty years, her emotions at times getting the better of her. She remembers the Patawalonga Estuary being drained and then dragged. A clairvoyant was flown over from Europe, and a Brighton factory was pinpointed as the burial site and excavated. She believed, as did many, that she would find what happened to them. It was only a matter of time.

Along with a classmate, Jenny was interviewed at the start of the school term, only a few days after the children went missing. The headmaster stood at the doorway of their classroom—a foreboding sight for any young child—and instructed Jenny and her friend to follow him to the library. Of course, all the other children thought they were in big trouble. The headmaster did not inform either of them why they were singled out, but they had already guessed.

The classmates were introduced to two gentlemen wearing dark suits and sitting at a table. Once they were introduced as detectives, the principal left. There were no teachers or parents present, just the two girls and the men. The detectives explained what they wanted to talk to the girls about. One detective asked a lot of questions about Jane's habits. Was there anyone that Jenny thought Jane might have met? Did she have a boyfriend or someone she was regularly meeting at the beach? Jenny told the men that Jane was too busy looking after her siblings and just being a happy-go-lucky nine-year-old. She had no boyfriend. The meeting was intense. Both girls were quite nervous and worried and found this experience nerve-racking, which further added to Jenny's anxiety and distress. The detectives appeared desperate for answers and perplexed by the events. Even for a nine-year-old, this was plain to see. The only thing that Jenny could come up with was that Jane would not have gone with a stranger willingly. Both girls felt dispirited at not being able to give these detectives anything of substance.

As the weeks went by, Jenny was still expecting Jane to turn up at school without missing a beat and sit next to her. Sadly, this was never to be. Paringa Park Primary School students were all talking about the disappearance. Jenny would catch the children's gossip, which upset her, but she didn't have anyone to talk to about her feelings. There wasn't the counselling or parental guidance available that we have today. She felt utterly vulnerable, becoming quite reflective regarding the disappearance, regarding losing her closest friend. All this has produced quite a bit of angst over the years.

Many times, Jenny has thought deeply about what might have occurred at the reserve that day. Jane was smart enough to know if she was putting Arnna and Grant in danger. If someone were forcefully trying to take Grant or Arnna, Jane would have followed, trying to help. She would have defended her siblings by putting herself in harm's way. She would have put up a fight, screaming and yelling. She was smart enough not to have gone with anyone unless someone had tricked her, and tricked she clearly was. Jane was not a silly girl. She was simply no match for a cunning predator.

Over the years, Jenny has read many articles stating that the man would have been easily seen and recognisable at Colley Reserve—articles usually penned by people with no experience of Colley Reserve in the summer holidays in the 1960s. Colley Reserve at this time was extremely crowded, Jenny recalls. The children and the man would have blended in with the masses. There were thousands of children at the beach all day and well into the evening. There was no reason to notice them.

For many years, Jenny has pondered the 'what ifs', readily awaiting any new information on the children's disappearance. However, no material had piqued her interest until the publication of *The Satin Man: Uncovering the Mystery of the Missing Beaumont Children*. The scenario outlined in the book, of Harry Phipps being involved in the disappearance, strongly resonated with her. Watching, listening to, and reading the media for the past few years, she believes that Bill Hayes and Stuart Mullins are on to something substantial. Hence, she has spoken out, stating:

> If the boot had been on the other foot, Jane would have been sitting here; she would have, without a doubt, committed to helping find the answer. Jane would have been determined to find an outcome because she had an excellent moral compass and was a loyal friend.

Our investigation into Harry Phipps, which is set out in detail in the following chapters, has solidified Jenny's belief that he is the man most likely to have abducted and killed her best friend. Jenny has asked herself why Jane would have followed this man. For her, the eyewitness reports stating that the man let it be known that his and the children's money was taken are key. Jane, she said, didn't lose anything. With her money stolen, the whole scenario changes. Jenny believes Jane would have been worried that Arnna and Grant did not have anything to eat for lunch and had no bus money to get home. It was too hot to walk home, and poor Grant did not have a singlet or T-shirt. Jane would have also been concerned she would be letting her mother down and would be regarded as having been irresponsible.

Jenny believes that Jane may have known the man from previous visits to Colley Reserve or indeed as a local. He offered to buy them lunch and gave them some money when at his home. A one-pound note Jenny in 1966 had a wow factor for Jenny, as it would have for Jane. She would have felt obliged and taken the money to buy lunch at Wenzel's Bakery for her siblings. She would have walked to the man's house, collected the one-pound note, taken her sister and brother to

Wenzel's Bakery, and then returned with the change. There was no way that Jane would have deviated from their Colley Reserve routine unless something significant had occurred— and it had.

Jenny is also sure that Jane, Arnna, and Grant would not have gotten into a car. Detectives at the time and in the decades since have ruled out a car for many plausible reasons. Jenny, like many professionals, believes the only other explanation is that the children followed the man to a house very close by. She cannot help but sometimes think of how the children met their fate. These events all weigh heavily on Jenny. This abduction has changed her life in many ways. She has a lot of interaction with her grandchildren, and she has never let her own children come home to an empty house. Her life experience has taught her to be careful. The unanswered question that still haunts her is that asked by the general population: What happened to the Beaumont children? Jenny, like many, is desperate to know the answers, even after more than fifty years. Tragically, Nancy Beaumont died without ever knowing what happened to her beloved children, and Jim is now in an aged-care home, which makes it even more crucial that the truth be found and told.

The children had all their unrecognised potential brutally taken away—Jane, Arnna, and Grant's optimism about what the future might bring. Photos of their smiling faces have radiated throughout the decades, regularly reigniting that melancholy feeling of what childhood was and still means— reminding us all to love our children and one another. Jenny believes that had their roles been reversed, Jane would not have forgotten, and she would not have given up. Jane would be doing something about it, and now so is Jenny. After fifty-plus years, she knows we cannot let time get in the way, especially for Jim and Nancy Beaumont, for the memories of all five Beaumonts.

Keeping this story alive is very important. For someone to have harmed Jane, Arnna, and Grant still upsets Jenny greatly. Like a lot of South Australians, she does not believe we will ever be able to move on until we find out what happened to the Beaumont children.

Chapter 6:
All Roads Lead to Harry Phipps

Monsters don't always lurk in the shadows. Sometimes they hide in plain sight.[20]

—Belle Aurora, *Raw*

O ver the decades, several suspects have been put forward and investigated by the South Australia Police Major Crime Investigation Branch, with all, bar one, coming to a dead end. In 2006, an individual was put forward who has stood head and shoulders above all other suspects over the past five decades. This individual is Harry Phipps, a man of wealth and standing in the community, a millionaire whose vast property portfolio included Castalloy, a large factory located in North Plympton with the front office facing the main thoroughfare of Mooringe Avenue, and which produced an array of parts for the Australian automobile industry and household products the likes of cooking pots, saucepans, and frying pans.

The company also carried out casting work for the Adelaide City Council, most noticeably the Victoria Square Three Rivers Fountain in the CBD. Phipps also owned an array of residential properties around Adelaide, including his main Glenelg residence, located on the corners of Augusta and Sussex Streets, a property at Flagstaff Hill, and a holiday house at Goolwa, a coastal town located seventy-six kilometres from Adelaide at the mouth of the Murray River. He also owned another property on Sussex Street, next to Isola, one on Kincade Avenue across from the back of his Castalloy factory, and a house located in Cygnet Terrace, Kingston Park—the suburb next to the seaside location of Seacliffe. In all of these real estate locations, Phipps had access and control.

Phipps was a man with connections to the church and the state and was an individual who came into police focus in 2007, three years after his death, following the publication of Alan Whiticker's book *Searching for the Beaumont Children*, the first definitive account of the event. The release of the book ignited a media frenzy, and wayward and outlandish accounts abounded full of rumour and gossip. Many calls were received from well-intentioned members of the public providing their proposed explanations and suspicions about the case. Others used the opportunity to release pent-up emotions, highlighting the poignant effect this disappearance still has and the emotional attachment the Australian public has to it. Not long after this book was published, Whiticker received a telephone call from Angela Fyfe (née Phipps), who was formerly married to Harry Phipps' eldest son, Haydn, advising Alan that she had read the book and became concerned with some information that she had become aware of. What she said to Alan dramatically changed the course of this tragic tale. Angela presented an extraordinary possibility: that her former husband's father, Harry Phipps, may have been involved in the children's abduction. She described him as a person of wealth, power, influence, and standing in the community—part of the Adelaide upper establishment, However, behind the walls of his Glenelg mansion, according to his now deceased son Haydn, Harry exhibited deviant sexual behaviour based around alleged paedophilia and a fetish for wearing and making women's satin clothing.

Angela Fyfe lived in Queensland in the 1990s and was married to Haydn Phipps for ten years from the early 1990s to the early 2000s. Angela and Haydn met at a cafe in south-east Queensland where they both lived and worked, Angela as a clinical nurse and Haydn for a short time in real estate. Even though she felt he was troubled, she couldn't put her finger on the cause. She saw a tender side to him and found him intelligent.

The pair could talk for hours about world events, and for a time they were happy. As the years went by, their marriage became turbulent due to Haydn's growing dependence on alcohol and prescription medication. His behaviour grew more erratic over the years, with mood swings becoming more apparent and frequent. At times, Haydn fell into a deep depression and suffered from anxiety attacks. Angela had found it difficult to sleep in the same bed as Haydn because his sleep pattern was one of constant restlessness. There were many occasions Angela needed to wake Haydn as his head was buried face-down in his pillow making loud, panicked, muffled groaning noises, and he was hypervigilant if touched while he slept. Angela's suspicions were validated when she finally spoke to her husband about his erratic behaviour and sleep patterns. A few years into their marriage, Haydn made a startling admission: he told her he had been sexually abused over many years by his father, Harry. Angela had no doubt Haydn was telling the truth. She had worked with victims of sexual abuse while employed in correctional facilities and was well aware that only a small percentage of the people who say they were sexually abused as minors are lying.

Angela appears to be correct as, according to child sexual abuse statistics on the Darkness to Light website, only between

4% and 8% of individuals who say they were sexually abused as a minor are not being truthful.[21]

According to the study *False Allegations of Sexual Abuse by Children and Adolescents* by Mark D Everson, PhD, and Barbara W H Boat, PhD, only one in twenty children who say they were sexually abused as a child are lying.[22]

Even though Angela believed him, she was also well aware that Haydn had a brother, Wayne, four years his junior, with whom he shared a bedroom at the time of the alleged abuse. She asked Haydn whether his brother knew of or witnessed the abuse, to which Haydn replied that, in his opinion, he did not. This sexual abuse—according to Haydn when speaking with us, and his former wife Angela on different occasions over the years—nearly always occurred in the early hours of the morning, when Haydn would hear the swish of satin rubbing together moving ever closer to his and Wayne's bedroom door.

Wayne was a newborn when this sexual abuse began. The sexual abuse finished when Haydn was fourteen years old and Wayne had barely turned nine. It's more than likely that at 2 am in the morning, a very young Wayne was sound asleep and unaware, as these types of predators ply their sexual deviant behaviour by stealth. As we have seen over the decades, if a paedophile can fool adults close to them, fooling a child would be easy.

However, this deception of adults was most notable with the conviction of the Australian former iconic entertainer Rolf Harris on sexual abuse charges. This brazen abuse was mostly directed at minors, and even though these assaults were carried out most of the time in plain view, the public and workers around him appeared unaware. These sexual assaults occurred between 1971 and 1984, directed at seven girls, including a thirteen-year-old audience member on the BBC TV programme

Saturday Superstore[23], an autograph-hunter as young as seven or eight,[24] a blind woman, and a disabled woman.[25] On the 4th of July 2014 at Southwark Crown Court London, Mr Justice Sweeney sentenced Harris to a total of five years and nine months in prison. When passing the sentence, the judge said to Harris, 'You have shown no remorse for your crimes at all.'[21]

Like Phipps, Harris also hid in plain sight for decades under the disguise of respectability, generosity, and kindness, always hiding his true motives. After the sexual abuse of Haydn stopped, the question has been asked of us, could Wayne also have been abused? Only he can answer this question.

Angela did not know Wayne well and kept her distance from the family, which she described as dysfunctional. This was corroborated by Mullins when speaking with some former neighbourhood locals and some former senior Castalloy factory managers. Haydn stated to both of us that he protected his younger brother and threatened to kill Harry if he ever touched him.

Angela stated to both of us that one reason she had very little contact with the family was that she and Haydn lived interstate in Queensland. However, she did state that some discussions took place between she and some extended family members regarding Harry's deviant behaviour when she realised her husband may have been sexually abused. Following her discussions, it appears Harry's deviant sexual proclivities were well known by some.

None of this surprised Angela. Being a clinical nurse, she understood the grooming process of young children by the stealth and secrecy with which paedophiles apply their trade. Masters of deception, they fool many an adult, making children easy prey. Angela asked Haydn if he had told anyone else of the abuse. He had not. Who would have believed him?

Harry was powerful, wealthy, and influential. What hope did a child have?

Around the same time that these matters surfaced, Angela watched a TV documentary with Haydn on the disappearance of the Beaumont children. During the program, unexpectedly Haydn exclaimed, 'I believe my father had something to do with that.'

'Surely you don't think your father could have done something like that?' Angela had replied.

Haydn then made a chilling comment: 'They are in the pit.'

She asked what pit he referred to—the car pit at the family home in Glenelg, used to service vehicles?

Haydn replied simply, 'The sandpit,' and then changed the subject.

Angela did not connect the dots until she read Alan Whiticker's *Searching for the Beaumont Children*. When she considered the information set out in the book combined with Haydn's comment and his mental state, alarm bells went off. Could her former father-in-law Harry Phipps have been involved in the abduction of the Beaumont children?

Angela had valid reasons for her concerns. She had already concluded that Harry Phipps had sexually abused Haydn. This concern was amplified by the recent conversations between some Phipps' relatives regarding whispers of sexual abuse in the Glenelg residence, during which, Angela alleged, Harry Phipps' second wife Elizabeth called her and asked, 'Is it true the boys were abused?'

Angela replied that she didn't know for sure and could not make an assumption regarding the younger brother, only that she believed Haydn may well have been. Angela also informed us that she had discussions with other family members about Haydn's alleged abuse and Harry's sexual proclivities and satin fetishes, which Angela stated they were all aware of but only discussed in private.

Adding to all of this was the physical description of the man seen playing at the beach with the Beaumont children. When considering photographs of Harry taken in the late 1950s and early 1960s, Angela realised that the description fitted him. She also knew that Harry was an avid swimmer at Glenelg.

What further perturbed Angela was the fact that Jane Beaumont was given a one-pound note by the man that they had met that day. The police regarded this one-pound note as a pivotal piece of evidence in 1966, and have continued to do so ever since. She knew through speaking with family associates, a former friend of Haydn's, and some relatives of the Phipps family over the years that Harry was known to tip in and hand out pound notes to Haydn and his friends. Angela had also gleaned the tipping of pound notes by Harry to wait and bar staff from Haydn and a former senior manager from the Castalloy factory she met. Mullins backed this up by interviewing some former senior Castalloy Managers who stated Harry was known as the man about town and would always tip waiters and service staff, usually in pound notes. In turn, the staff would give Harry their undivided attention.

This tipping in one-pound notes in the 1950s continued until only a little over two weeks after the abduction on 14 February 1966 when pounds, shillings, and pence were replaced by dollars and cents. The tipping habit, the regular chatter amongst relatives regarding Harry's deviant sexual behaviour, Harry's physical description from the 1960s being eerily similar to the description of the man seen with the children that fateful day—when Angela put all of these together, the alarm bells rang.

Also concerning was the location of Harry Phipps' home in relation to Colley Reserve, a mere 190 metres in direct sight of the Reserve. His residence was also 200 metres from Wenzel's

Bakery, where the children were last seen. However, Harry was not known to be a customer of Wenzel's Bakery. According to Haydn, Harry's go-to bakery was the Orange Spot Café 220 metres north up Sussex Street to the main thoroughfare of the Anzac Highway.

The fact that Harry engaged in a satin fetish and sexually deviant behaviour had become apparent over the last decade, as we had met and spoken to numerous individuals and couples who could corroborate the information Angela had passed on. Also, there was an email trail between Stuart and several of the grandson's former friends in September 2014 talking about Harry's 'no-go Saturdays' and being given money and told to 'fuck off' on the 'special days'. This was further backed up when Mullins received another set of emails. In June and August 2016 between relatives discussing their concerns regarding Elizabeth's behaviour and Harry's deviant ways. It did appear this was well known and discussed in family circles.

With all this in mind, Angela posed the questions that are now being repeated by many professionals and the public alike. For four decades, could we have had an undetected predatorial paedophile living so close to Colley Reserve—a man who flew under the radar, camouflaged by a cloak of respectability—responsible for the abduction, sexual abuse, and murder of the Beaumont Children?

In order to create a clear picture of Harry Phipps, researcher Stuart Mullins, with the assistance of Angela Fyfe, began the arduous task of identifying and contacting people who had known the man. This included immediate family, former friends, relatives, and acquaintances of the extended Phipps family and retired Castalloy factory managers and workers.

What Stuart soon found was that Harry Phipps' public persona was the polar opposite of his private life. He was an upstanding, successful businessman, well known in the local area, and a father hated passionately by his son Haydn and the subject of family rumours regarding his sexual proclivities. He believed the adage 'Where there is smoke, there is fire'.

From as early as 2006, Mullins went on a long and, at times, frustrating journey where he clocked up many hours on the road and earned many frequent flyer points. He sourced Harry Phipps' birth, death, and marriage certificates, his will and information about his real estate assets, club memberships, and the Castalloy factory that he built from scratch. After painting a clearer picture of Harry Phipps' professional background, Mullins delved into his private life.

After vetting and interviewing Angela Fyfe and finding her to be a reliable, credible, consistent witness, Mullins contacted her former husband's son from his first marriage, Nicholas, in 2008. With his assistance, Stuart finally got to meet Haydn later that year. Then followed meetings with Haydn's former closest friends from the 1950s, 60s, and 70s. From here, as the net was cast progressively wider, it became clear that Mullins had uncovered a hornet's nest of sexual depravity and abuse, much of which was hidden from public view.

As the circumstantial evidence mounted of Phipps' culpability in the disappearance of the Beaumont children more than forty years earlier, Stuart contacted the SAPOL Major Crime Investigation Branch and presented it with his detailed findings in a sizeable dossier which he compiled over two and half years, accompanied by a registered post letter sent in late 2008. Initially, Mullins was in contact with the Beaumont cold case detective, who found his information worthy of some investigation. However, this officer felt no need to meet and interview Haydn Phipps or his former wife, Angela, to ascertain their truthfulness. This task should have been one of the very first things to do, straight out of any detective manual. At this time, in Mullins' opinion, this officer appeared to be cherry-picking who he would talk to, namely Haydn's younger brother Wayne, his third wife Irene, and some selected relatives who did not wish to speak to Mullins. They apparently disparaged Haydn's and Angela's character and alleged that both made up stories to damage Harry's reputation. They claimed that Haydn was delusional and that he and Angela were both after money and revenge as they were left out of Harry's will. Was this detective attempting to direct a particular narrative and, if so, why? This detective also informed Mullins by email in late January 2008 that he would tee up a time to meet Harry's second wife, Elizabeth Phipps. By June 2008, Mullins found out he still hadn't done so. This raised red flags that he was being taken for a fool. It was here Mullins knew he was in for a long fight for the truth—a fight worth pursuing.

Stuart understood SAPOL's Major Crime Investigation Branch had been bombarded over the years with whodunnit theorists, as well as the media regularly requesting interviews or comments when covering new leads and accusing the police of sitting on their hands. Over the four-plus decades, all the leads followed led to dead ends. One can be forgiven for thinking the police, as with many others, privately believed this case would never be solved. In the end, it seemed to Stuart Mullins that his dossier was treated with similar scepticism. This was confirmed when the same officer informed Mullins by phone that he was beating his head up against a brick wall and chasing his tail. He was chasing a tale, and what a tale it has turned out to be.

Mullins, however, was not to be dissuaded and leave things be. He contacted and met former detective Mostyn Matters, who was stationed at the Glenelg Police station that fateful day in January 1966. He looked into the dossier that was presented to him by Mullins and stated: 'If this information is corroborated it's the most provocative, detailed information I have read pertaining to this case.' So, a concerned Mostyn introduced Stuart to his old detective mate Ken Thorsen, former head of the South Australia Major Crime Squad in the 1980s. After Ken gleaned some pertinent information in the dossier, he also stated that 'this information has red flags all over it and you should shake the tree and see what falls out'. Both then recommended Stuart take the information to arguably South Australia's finest and most respected private investigator, Bill Hayes, which he did in late 2008. Before moving into private practice, Hayes spent more than ten years as a detective with SAPOL, at least two of those with the Major Crime Squad, during which time he had been lucky enough to have had access to the official Beaumont dossier. Hayes is known not to suffer fools easily. He is focused, forthright, honest, reliable, thorough, and has an eye for detail. He is intelligent and articulate but also empathetic and understanding. Most of all, he is highly respected by the business establishment, the media, and members of law enforcement in South Australia.

Bill met with Stuart in September 2008 and agreed to look into Mullins' research on the case, but only because he was referred by Mostyn Matters and Ken Thorsen, for whom Hayes had a great deal of respect. Hayes told Mullins that both were well-respected, hard-nosed detectives when in the South Australia Police, where they had brief dealings with one another as detectives in the 1980s. Bill was aware Mos was one of the last remaining detectives who had been stationed at the Glenelg police station in January 1966. Hayes was initially sceptical and left his office door open as he expected it to be a quick meeting, as Bill had heard every conspiracy theory and experienced the frustration of detectives following yet another false lead or becoming obsessed with the case.

Hayes informed Mullins that it had always been his and other detectives' belief that the perpetrator in the Beaumont case was highly likely a local. Transporting three unwilling and distraught children any significant distance in a car would cause more problems than it was worth. Hayes has always gone by the principle of Occam's Razor: the simplest solution is usually the correct one.

What Stuart presented that day had a lasting effect on Bill, who described the information on Harry Phipps as being the most incriminating circumstantial evidence he had encountered. Hayes was always of the opinion that the man seen with the children that day at the beach was not someone wearing a red cape with pointy horns. It was more like a respectable, well-presented, and well-spoken individual such as the type of person Harry Phipps presented. This opinion has only been strengthened by relentlessly working together on this case since 2008, gathering a multitude of corroborated circumstantial evidence linking Harry Phipps to both paedophilia and the disappearance of the missing Beaumont children.

This information was uncovered by us when speaking with some former workers and managers at the Castalloy factory, who spoke of Harry's fractured relationship with his sons. Several senior managers stated Haydn hated his father with a passion and they could not put this down to a workplace issue; therefore, something must have been happening at home. Harry dressed in women's garments and congregated on selected Sundays with like-minded men in the Castalloy canteen. He would regularly meet at a private gentlemen's club in the CBD of Adelaide dressed in women's clothing. Some relatives and Haydn's son's former friends described Harry's satin garments and apparent sexual arousal when wearing these. One relative, who spoke to Mullins, would not let her children sleep overnight at the Phipps residence.

As Harry Phipps' predatory paedophilic nature and deviant sexual traits became more widely known, another two individuals gained the courage to step forward. They believed that now their accounts of sexual abuse, at the hands of this man when minors, would finally be taken seriously.

These accounts helped corroborate much of what Haydn and Angela had reported to us about Harry Phipps. These accounts have been supported by Australian criminologist Dr Xanthé Mallett together with former detective, award-winning true crime author, and crime investigative journalist Duncan McNab.

Also in support of those accounts are Steve Van Aperen, arguably Australia's number one polygraph expert, and Terrance G Lichtenwald, PhD, licensed clinical and criminal psychologist and former forensic examiner from Illinois, USA. All have stated that as far as they can ascertain, Angela and Haydn have been truthful in their recollections of Harry Phipps and Haydn's sexual abuse in their statements to Mullins and Hayes. When speaking with investigative reporter Frank Pangallo from Channel 7's *Today Tonight* program on Wednesday 25 November 2015, Steve Van Aperen stated that Haydn was being truthful in his recollections about seeing the Beaumont children and his sexual abuse but was hiding more.[26]

We believe that if Haydn is being truthful, which he appears to be, then Harry Phipps is now the main suspect in this baffling case. Over the next chapters, we expose Harry Phipps for what he was—a deviant, callous, serial, predatorial paedophile who, on 26 January 1966, was waiting for his unsuspecting prey to arrive at Colley Reserve, and arrive they did.

Chapter 7:
The Making of a Predator

Evil may seem powerful but, it loses in the end.

—Jyoti Patel

To understand the case of the missing Beaumont children, we must look to the man most likely to have abducted them, and indeed we must delve even further back to ascertain what made him the man he became.

Frederick Henry (Harry) Phipps was born on 1 July 1917 and passed away on 17 February 2004 at the age of eighty-seven. He grew up in Glenelg in a house that his father, Frederick William Tomlins Phipps, built and named Isola—the Italian name for Island. It was a large sandstone residence with high concrete walls that encircled most of the property. The backyard had a swimming pool which, according to elderly neighbours who spoke to Mullins over a decade ago, was built in the early 1950s. In the backyard, there were also two garages with pull-down roller doors. There was a large back gate for the cars that led onto Sussex Street. What was noticeable to Stuart, when he inspected the property, was that just to the right of this gate and across Sussex Street was a back laneway that runs directly down toward Colley Reserve, parallel to Augusta Street, where the Glenelg Bowling Alley once was. From Stuart's research with the local Holdfast Bay Historical Society, it appeared that, in 1966, this alleyway passed by the north side of the bowling alley and led straight to the reserve. However, this and some other older structures have since been replaced by apartments.

It is important to state that the current owners of the property have absolutely nothing to do with this investigation and should be left in peace to enjoy their home.

Harry's father, Frederick Phipps, was born in Cape Town, South Africa, in 1887 and later emigrated to Australia. In South Africa, he was a qualified electrical mechanic, but after arriving in Adelaide, he studied at Adelaide University, majoring in geology. At the age of thirty-two, he married Katie (Kitty) Benbow Waters in July 1919. Harry was born out of wedlock, which was a substantial social shame in that era, but it did not seem to faze this unconventional family.

Frederick's interest in geographical surveying took him away from Kitty and their newborn for most of Harry's formative years. Even upon returning home, he was only there for short periods before leaving again on long journeys into the outback of Australia with a team of geologists.

According to relatives of Katie, who have since passed away, the raising of Harry was left to Katie. Katie was disappointed at not having a girl and so raised Harry as a girl for the first few years of his life. Katie was known to dress Harry in garments that appeared to be made of satin cloth, which may have been the beginning of his lifelong obsession with the material.

When Stuart was introduced to Harry Phipps' second wife, Elizabeth Phipps, in 2007 by a former senior employee of Castalloy, he informed her he was carrying out some research on Harry and his Castalloy factory. They met at Isola. There, in the kitchen, Mullins noticed a few framed old photos of what appeared to be a young girl sitting on a tricycle in a frilly white dress. When asked who the photo subject was, she replied it was Harry as a child. This appeared to corroborate what some family associates had said.

According to relatives and friends of the Phipps family who knew Katie well, she was very domineering and demanding, allegedly wreaking havoc in the home, running the household in a controlling, authoritarian way, and she was a strict disciplinarian to Harry in the absence of a father figure.

Harry was schooled at Pulteney Grammar in Adelaide, one of South Australia's most prestigious educational establishments. He was an intelligent student who, from an early age, displayed a business-savvy acumen reminiscent of his father.

At the age of sixteen, he left school and began work as a draughtsman at the Torrensville manufacturing plant of Colton, Palmer & Preston. At night, Harry studied at the School of Mines, an industrial trades college for mining engineering, metallurgy, mechanical engineering, and electrical engineering. His entrepreneurial skills were coming to the fore when he joined Sagar Manufacturing. He designed and produced an innovative grease gun that vastly improved the functionality of the tool. The product sold well, and Harry was elevated to a position of authority in the factory.

Harry, with some work colleagues, decided to open their 'Castalloy' factory in the CBD of Adelaide, making metal castings of bread tins, baking pans, ice-cream tins, lids, and the like. In the early 1950s, these items were very much in demand in the rapidly developing city, and by 1953, the business was becoming too large for the CBD location in Weymouth Street, Adelaide. At this time, they had twenty-three employees. In 1955, with the other two co-founders, John Goodes and Eric Scovell, Phipps decided to relocate to a new site at North Plympton, five kilometres from Glenelg. This was an area the government had designated for small industry, even though this area, in 1955, was square kilometres of rolling sand hills sparsely dotted with a few small businesses and bungalows. Phipps, Goodes, and Scovell saw the potential and so began the construction of the new Castalloy factory.

While transitioning from the CBD to their new property, they commenced supplying castings to the Australian automotive industry, mainly steering housings and brake and clutch master cylinders. They further expanded their client base over the years, producing for Mitsubishi®, Ford®, and Harley-Davidson® and winning many business awards. Due to the success of Castalloy, by the 1960s Harry Phipps had become a millionaire. In 1982, Harry retired as managing director and succeeded Sir Robert Porter as chairman the same year. By 1999, when Harry Phipps ceased his relationship with Castalloy, they were employing approximately 500 people. It was also the year the company was sold to the investment company ION, which collapsed into administration in December 2004.

As Harry Phipps grew into the role of a successful, self-made, wealthy businessman, so too his connections grew—politicians, business elite, senior members of the clergy, and police. He became a member of the exclusive Adelaide Club, frequented by members of the city's refined establishment. Behind these walls was where the real power in the state was wielded by the wealthy and influential members.

When we were speaking to some relatives and former Castalloy employees, many believed it was with these connections back in the 1950s that Harry was able to meet other like-minded men with certain perverse sexual preferences.

Harry Phipps married Olga May Waters from Mount Gambier in 1942 at age twenty-five. They had two children: Haydn, born in 1950, and Wayne, born approximately four years later. Olga and Harry were married for fifty-two years until Olga's death in 1994. Harry's marriage to Olga, according to some relatives, neighbours, and senior managers at the Castalloy factory, was strained, distant, and lacking affection and emotion. Several former senior managers from the Castalloy factory told Stuart Mullins that Olga married for love, but Harry had married to maintain the façade of a happily married family man—a requirement for acceptance within the circles of the Adelaide business elite.

Despite outward appearances, Harry was already plying his paedophilic ways. By 1954, he was reportedly sexually abusing his four-year-old son Haydn and seeking out like-minded men who had a penchant for children and deviant sexual behaviour. Anglican Archbishop John Hepworth—who was abused by senior Catholic clergy as a teenager during his time studying at St Francis Xavier Seminary in Adelaide, leading him to leave the Catholic Church and be ordained an Anglican priest—was already aware of Phipps' name in paedophilic circles.

Hepworth recounted to Stuart Mullins an episode in which he, as a young teenager in the 1950s, sat in the back of a black car driven by a senior clergy member with a well-attired businessman in the passenger seat. As they drove past a boys' school the two men noted the 'tight arses' of some of the schoolboys, with one of the men commenting, 'Phipps would like that one.'

According to *The Advertiser* on 15 December 2010, District Judge Paul Rice said the reason some paedophiles who were members of the clergy were able to prey on the young was that the church had swept their previous crimes under the carpet. They did that with John Hepworth, assisted by sections of the Adelaide establishment. Their continued silence further enabled the predators.[27]

Olga, on the other hand, was a kind-hearted and compassionate mother and a trusted friend. She did her best to provide for and protect her boys, but this was the era of the subservient wife and Olga knew she had no real power. Even though she was aware of Harry's fetishes and deviant sexual appetite, what option did she have? When Mullins spoke to some elderly family associates between 2008 and 2010 who have now passed away or are in care, they recounted some quiet conversations they had with a few trusted friends, but no-one was willing to speak out. To us, Olga had nowhere to go. She was not confident of having any moral or financial support if she did leave Harry. She understood that making ripples would likely leave her destitute and without her children.

Harry was smart enough to know he had a stacked deck, as most paedophiles did in this era. Harry was influential, persuasive, and connected. The repercussions on Olga would have been swift and damaging. In our opinion, it appeared that Olga had no choice, and Harry's true nature was kept hidden. The making of the predator was complete. Harry Phipps was reassured that his crimes would remain undetected, and Olga retreated into a comfortable lifestyle of tennis days and regular afternoon teas with the wealthy ladies of the Glenelg establishment.

Not long after Olga's death in 1994, Harry placed a newspaper advertisement for a maid/cook. Stuart Mullins met with a husband-and-wife team who owned a school garment factory in Adelaide. They employed Daisy Ward, who had successfully applied for the position with Harry and got the job. Daisy told her factory co-workers and the husband-and-wife owners that she had 'struck the jackpot'. She further stated that she was always after a 'sugar daddy' and had finally found one. Daisy told factory owner Gary that 'Harry is loaded'. Gary believed that this would suit Daisy, who had a chronic gambling addiction.

Once she secured the role, Daisy soon married her employer, changing her name to Elizabeth Phipps and taking possession of a Mercedes. The marriage, however, was another sham, but in this case, it was a win-win situation for both parties. Elizabeth enabled Harry with her silence and by playing wife. In return, she inherited the house and land and one and a half million dollars after Harry's death.

The more we delved into the background of Harry Phipps, the more concerned we became with the question of just what makes a paedophile. Is it nature or nurture? Does being sexually abused as a child lead to a life as an abuser? There have been many comprehensive studies carried out on this subject, with differing opinions. There is, however, a growing consensus that the origin is largely biological, and that paedophilia is not a learned behaviour. Dr Fred Berlin, director of the Johns Hopkins Sex and Gender Clinic in the US city of Baltimore, stated in the article 'Preying on Children: The Emerging Psychology of Pedophiles' in the *New York Times* in September 2019, 'People don't choose what arouses them—they discover it.'[28]

In a *60 Minutes* interview, Dr James Cantor, director of the Toronto Sexuality Centre in Canada, stated that we need to rethink the way we deal with paedophiles by making medical treatment and counselling more readily available. MRI scans of adults convicted of sexually abusing children found a dramatic cross-wiring in the connective tissue of their brains, Dr Cantor told *60 Minutes*, and this network does not appear to be appropriately connected. 'It's accidentally identifying things in the environment that should evoke a parental nurturant instinct, but instead, it's provoking a sexual and erotic instinct.'[29]

This appears to be the case with Harry Phipps.

The *New York Times* also reported that if the sexual preferences of teenagers do not mature at a normal rate, they may get stuck on the same-aged boys or girls who first attracted them at the start of puberty.[28] The way Harry Phipps was raised by a domineering mother might have affected his sexual maturity as he grew into manhood.

In the case of Phipps, the other question we asked was 'Could Harry's upbringing have been a catalyst for his predatory nature?' We think so. We have investigated Harry's early childhood and agree, based on these studies, that his satin fetish was not directly related to his paedophilic nature, but it may have been a catalyst. The way Harry Phipps was raised by a domineering mother might have influenced his sexual maturity as he grew into manhood.

The same *New York Times* article also notes that those who are sexually violated are at far higher risk of future substance abuse, depression, persistent traumatic stress, or criminal aggression than they are of becoming abusers, as was the case with his eldest son, Haydn Phipps. As Dr Cantor states, 'A chaotic childhood increases the likelihood of chaotic adulthood, of any kind.'[25]

The study also noted that most offenders deny any sexual abuse in their childhood and that not all people who experience paedophilic urges act upon them. Many know the difference between wrong and right and live a normal life.

According to Haydn Phipps, when speaking with us, Harry had spoken to him in his later years about the abuse and admitted that he hated what he had done but claimed he could not stop. Many cannot until they are caught. Harry Phipps was never caught. Supremely confident, self-assured, arrogant, and ostentatious, he broke the paedophile mould. Age and sex were immaterial when he sought a victim. He was an opportunistic predator, and all were fair game.

Chapter 8:
Circumstantial Evidence

If it looks like a duck, swims like a duck, and quacks like a duck, it's probably a duck.

—Anonymous

In cases involving abduction and sexual abuse, the predator will try to avoid generating direct evidence. Hence the prosecution can rely only on the circumstantial evidence available. The question is then asked: 'When is there enough circumstantial evidence to warrant detectives further pursuing a person of interest?' The quality of the information presented is paramount. Circumstantial evidence relies on inference or interpretation and reasoning of the content presented. Facts set forward imply there is a possible connection between the individual and the crime. Therefore, the more quality information provided, the more focused on a particular person the police will be. Detectives can then establish the likelihood of guilt or innocence through reasoning and common sense to take it to the next step.

Individual pieces of inferred information standing alone would only be one small piece of a larger jigsaw puzzle and would be challenging to use as a basis for any valid judgement.

However, as the amount of credible circumstantial evidence increases, a tipping point is reached. Concerning Harry Phipps, this occurred several years ago as an ever-increasing amount of incriminating information started to paint a damning picture of this individual's probable involvement in the abduction and murder of the Beaumont children. The hypothesis presented by us is a thought-provoking one, but the question should be asked: 'Can you convict on circumstantial evidence alone?'

When speaking with us in 2017, Duncan McNab, former NSW detective, award-winning true-crime writer, investigator, and crime editor for 7news.com, stated:

> The answer is a little tricky. Usually, more quality than quantity of information is required. For example, the location of Harry Phipps' house is compelling, but only after you work out the logistics of the Beaumont case. Many contested criminal cases are driven entirely by circumstantial evidence of varying impact—geography, logistics, ownership of times, and so on. The police need a reasonable cause to suspect to arrest someone, and this requires some compelling circumstances—[this] might be two or three pieces of persuasive information, [or it] might be a pile! Concerning Phipps, it's the latter.

This is where circumstantial evidence can have a distinct advantage over direct evidence. Statements can come from multiple sources that reinforce each other and help form the narrative.

In 2006, both Alan Whiticker and Stuart Mullins: co-authors of the best-selling *The Satin Man: Uncovering the Mystery of the Missing Beaumont Children*, were struck by how close Phipps lived to Colley Reserve. Once Bill Hayes came on board, he too was startled by the proximity of Colley Reserve to the Phipps' residence, as were respected criminologists, investigative journalists, and current and former detectives.

As well as the geographical factor, we considered the psychological profile of Harry Phipps. By speaking to Haydn Phipps, other victims, relatives, business associates, and neighbours, they could identify Harry Phipps' mental, emotional, and personality characteristics based on his past deeds. It became apparent that he was a manipulative, cunning, narcissistic, sociopathic paedophile exuding a superficial charm, with a grandiose sense of self. Thriving on respect and the need to control, he was authoritarian while exploiting others effectively.

Phipps displayed promiscuous deviant behaviour, acting out sexual fantasies, and is an alleged serial child sex offender.

Later in this book, we see that his victims stated that Harry needed to dominate and humiliate, showing a lack of remorse or shame and a distinct callousness and an absence of empathy—blaming the victim for what they 'made' him do. The striking amount of mostly corroborated incriminating circumstantial evidence directed against Harry Phipps is damning. Weaving together the information set out below and in the following chapters leads one to the inevitable conclusion that Harry Phipps abducted and likely murdered Jane, Arnna, and Grant Beaumont.

- Phipps closely matched the final agreed-upon physical description of the man seen at Colley Reserve with the children.
- The man at the beach wore blue bathers with two white stripes, one down either side—the same colours as the nearby Henley Beach Surf Life Saving Club. Haydn Phipps was a member of the Henley Beach Sailing Club, and Harry was an avid swimmer at Glenelg beach and frequented Colley Reserve.

- The man seen with Jane, Arnna, and Grant was described as in his early thirties to early forties, or as one of the witnesses stated, 'middle-aged'. In January 1966, Harry Phipps was forty-eight years old, but corroborated accounts by Castalloy senior managers and neighbours to the Phipps residence from the 1950s to the 1970s stated he looked much younger than his years in the 1960s, then aged quickly in the 1970s.
- Harry Phipps lived 190 metres in direct sight of Colley Reserve and 200 metres from Wenzel's Bakery, where the children were last seen paying for lunch with a one-pound note.
- Phipps was well known to hand out one-pound notes in the 1950s through to the mid-1960s before Australia moved to decimal currency. This information has been corroborated from multiple sources—including two close friends of Haydn Phipps in the late 1950s and 1960s who remembered being given one-pound notes by Harry and told to 'fuck off' from his house on Saturdays, which we discuss in Chapter 12 and is a critical piece of information regarding this case since 1966.
- According to some relatives and former friends, Harry Phipps engaged in deviant sexual paedophilic behaviour and exhibited an overwhelming obsession with making and wearing satin dresses, kaftans, and pyjamas—an uncontrollable fetish that caused high sexual arousal in Phipps when he wore, saw, or handled this fabric. Many were shocked by the number of satin dresses found at his residence, most in shades of lime-green, pink and purple, red, orange, and yellow—darkly reminiscent of the colours worn by the Beaumont children on that fateful day in 1966.

- A former manager at Castalloy in the 1970s told Stuart Mullins, 'A few of us knew that Harry liked to dress as a woman, but it was not common knowledge. Harry was very well-liked and respected, with a loyal workforce, which most would not want to see his reputation tarnished. An old employee, Don (now deceased), whose job it was to come in on a Sunday to light the furnaces, ready for production on a Monday advised that he came in on the Sunday as usual, and happened to go into the canteen, where he came across a group of men who were all dressed up as women having a party.'

- The Anglican Archbishop of Adelaide, John Hepworth (see Chapter 5), knew of Harry Phipps in paedophilic circles in the 1950s and onwards.

- If we believe Harry Phipps' son Haydn, then he is an eyewitness in this case. Haydn stated to us that he saw the Beaumont children in his backyard around lunchtime on 26 January 1966. He described the children down to the carry bag Jane had with her that day. He also mentioned the colours of the towels the children had with them. He was not certain of the colours but believed they were bright colours like yellow or orange. Haydn was surprisingly not too far from the facts. Unbeknownst to most even now, Jane, Arnna, and Grant's beach towels were blue and two had the same pattern of yellow, green, red, black, and white stripes. The final comment Haydn made to Bill Hayes after a lengthy recorded interview was 'They are in the sandpit, Bill'. From that day until the present, Bill had felt sure that Haydn was telling the truth but was holding something back. Dr Xanthé Mallett said, 'I believe Harry's son is telling the truth; it's the best lead this case has had in a long time.'

- It should be noted that Haydn saying he was home for lunch when he saw the Beaumont children might answer the question of who the sixth lunch was for. At Wenzel's Bakery, Jane Beaumont bought one pie, five pasties, six finger buns, and two large bottles of fizzy drink. A lunch order for six. Jane, Arnna, Grant, and Nancy Beaumont, the man and the only other person who appears to be involved—Haydn. By buying lunch for their mum, the children were given a false sense of security, believing they would be driven home by the man. This is conjecture on our part, of course, but was Haydn also in the car with the children? It's worth noting that Haydn could have said that he saw the children in the morning or afternoon, but he saw them around lunchtime, which coincides with the children and the man leaving the beach together and walking to the change rooms just after noon.
- In late 2017, Linda (not her real name) presented damning information to Bill Hayes alleging that Harry Phipps brutally raped her in the 1970s when she was a thirteen-year-old schoolgirl, and this assault occurred across the road from his Castalloy factory in Mooringe Avenue, North Plympton.
- As of early 2019, another credible individual has stepped forward accusing Harry Phipps of sexual abuse that occurred in the cottages onsite at the Castalloy factory with other like-minded men. Bill Hayes is working with this individual.
- A husband-and-wife team who bartended at a private gentlemen's club on South Terrace, Adelaide, in the 1970s recognised Harry Phipps as one of the patrons who, along with other like-minded men, gathered at the club dressed in women's clothing.

- Another husband and wife who were Elizabeth Phipps' former employers were asked to assist in removing loads of colourful satin garments from the house Isola after Harry was placed into care. These items were in one bedroom and a sewing room-cum-basement/cellar. The couple explained to Mullins when he met them that the satin garments were mostly dresses in the colours of pink, lime green, dark green, red, purple, and yellow/gold. They had retained rolls and bolts of satin from Phipps' property, which they kept at their residence and showed Mullins. This satin was put to good use in a local nativity play later that year. As the couple were removing these materials, they described Elizabeth as being distraught, telling them, 'You have no idea what I have got myself into.' Also, when they asked where all the satin garments came from, Elizabeth replied that they were from an ocean cruise they had been on. This did not make sense to either of them.
- Two local tradespeople, who knew Elizabeth as they had completed a few painting jobs for her, were also asked if they could remove loads of satin garments from the attic at Isola after Harry was placed into care. Again, they described a large number of satin garments as mostly dresses in the colours of pink, lime green, dark green, red, purple, and yellow. They had also removed ladies' gloves, wigs, and bras from the attic. When asked where these items came from, Elizabeth replied that they were from the old country, apparently referring to the UK.
- Haydn Phipps' relative said Harry was well known as a dressmaker. The wearing of satin garments was common knowledge with several in the family circle. This cousin saw the satin fetish in action and the change that would

come over Harry when around this material—he had to touch and feel it—and stated that the family had a well-known rule to not wear satin in his home. Rumours were rife among some members of the family circle regarding sexual abuse.

- Friends of Haydn and Haydn's son remember Harry Phipps' 'no-go Saturdays'. On these days, they were not allowed near the house; in fact, on some occasions, they were given a one-pound note to stay away and told to 'fuck off'. Later, they found out these were the days Harry made and wore his satin garments.

- Another family associate, who visited Phipps' house on several occasions, described him as a sexual deviant, experiencing first-hand his sexual arousal when wearing satin. She claimed Phipps would become so aroused that he would spontaneously ejaculate. She noted to Mullins that the stains were quite noticeable. The woman saw two different sides to Phipps: being charming and charismatic, and being a sexual deviant. This individual thought that Phipps' son Haydn was after affection and further believed that something was eating away at him—that he hated his father, but was not sure why. This individual was allegedly threatened twice by other family members to recant her story.

- In 2008, when Mullins met the unit managers of a large beachside apartment at Broadbeach, Queensland, where Haydn resided at the time, they both said they knew Haydn well and that when he drank, he became a mess. On occasions, late at night, he would be found lying face-up on the outside lawn sobbing, dressed in fishnet stockings and women's garments coupled with a padded bra fixed around his chest on the outside. He would also have lipstick smeared across his face. At times, he would rant and rave in his apartment and come downstairs crying and wanting to talk. The managers said it was clear that something was eating at him, but they were not sure what.

Castalloy factory managers who knew Haydn in the 1960s and 1970s stated that he hated his father with a passion. They were unsure why he would display so much hostility toward a parent, though one of these managers stated to Mullins, 'If Haydn was abused, this would answer a lot of questions.' The same Castalloy managers stated that the domineering Harry Phipps and his first wife, Olga, had a frosty relationship and rarely spoke to one another. Two senior managers said their marriage was a sham and one of convenience.

A former friend from Haydn Phipps' teenage years stated Haydn was a heavy drinker, abusive, erratic and exhibited a death wish, and that he vehemently hated his father from an early age. He, too, said that if Haydn had been sexually abused, it would answer a lot of questions.

- In 2007, Stuart Mullins met with Elizabeth Phipps in the family home. When in the basement, Mullins spotted a beige purse that matched the description of the purse Jane Beaumont was carrying the day she disappeared. Once Elizabeth was alerted to the significance, she allegedly threw it away. The initial police report described Jane's purse as white, but according to Jenny, Jane's best friend, the purse was beige.
- Three days after the Beaumont children went missing, Harry Phipps paid two then-teenage boys to dig what they called 'a grave-sized hole'—six feet deep, five feet long, and three feet wide, with straight sides—at the back

of his Castalloy factory. The boys described the whole event as 'eerie'. While they were digging, Harry sat just staring (the boys' words) at them from the driver's seat of his car. Once satisfied the hole was adequate, he paid them in one-pound notes and told them, 'Fuck off, you little cunts, and never come back.'

In 2018, the SAPOL Major Crime Investigation Branch, with forensic experts present, dug up the site, finding only a few animal bone fragments of a cow, sheep, and horse, and a small amount of rubbish. This finding would certainly not warrant a hole of such proportions. This whole episode raises many questions. Who filled in the hole? Why didn't Phipps employ the boys to collect and throw in any rubbish and then fill this hole back in? Who digs a hole two metres deep and then half-backfills it and then only throws in some bones, not a carcass, bones that could have easily been disposed of in a bin. Castalloy had many large bins around the site. Thus they could have avoided having to dig out then half fill the hole, put a few bones in, and then being left to fill in a very large hole. It simply defies logic and common sense.

We have asked how Harry Phipps could be so unaware that this handing out of pound notes could ultimately lead back to him; in the early-to-mid-1960s, handing out such a large sum of money was a rarity. However, without realising, Harry Phipps' calling card was the pound note. It partly defined him. It said, *I am here; I am Harry Phipps; I am successful*. It was embedded in his psychological identity.

Marianne Szegedy-Maszak, award-winning *New York Times* journalist, editor, and writer for the National Alliance on Mental Illness, wrote, 'We are conscious of only about 5 percent of our cognitive activity, so most of our decisions, actions, emotions and behaviours depends on the 95 percent of brain activity that goes beyond our conscious awareness.'[30]

In other words, what we mostly do becomes automatic or subconscious. The other question is, was Harry Phipps unconsciously leaving a trail of breadcrumbs? Was this conscious behaviour, as he was so self-absorbed and smug that he believed that he was above the mere naïve masses?

As Terrance G Lichtenwald stated to Mullins and Hayes in an email on 27 June 2019, 'Considering all this circumstantial evidence, Harry Phipps to me is a serial sexual deviant paedophile and the primary suspect in the disappearance of the Beaumont children.'

Chapter 9:
The Pound Note

You cannot hide from the truth. Anytime you try to
argue with the truth you lose. Anytime you try to
evade it or run away from it, it will find you down
the road.[31]

—Karen Essex

As we've shown, on that fateful Australia Day more than fifty years ago, Jane Beaumont was given a one-pound note by the man that she, along with Arnna and Grant, met at Glenelg beach not long before they disappeared. This event was regarded as a vital piece of information in the case by police detectives back in 1966 and has remained so ever since. As officers at the Glenelg Police Station asked in 1966, which has been reiterated by South Australian detectives and the media alike over the years, who was wealthy enough to hand over a hard-earned one-pound note to children they supposedly hardly knew?

Author Bill Hayes, who grew up in the United Kingdom, remembered his weekly wage as a youth in the 1960s as two pounds a week. The Australian adult wage was eighteen pounds a week and a lot less for working teenagers. So, a pound note represented a significant part of a weekly wage—not an amount of money that an individual from middle-class employment would easily part with, especially to give to a child.

Those who enjoyed their childhood in 1960s Australia will remember the 'wow factor' of having a pound note. Imagine the reception of a child of that era being lucky enough to be given one from a parent, even to hold. Their first reaction would likely be to excitedly wave this crisp green bill around in the air. This amount of money equated to several buckets of sweets (lollies) together with a multitude of ice creams, cream-filled pastries, and fizzy drinks. Instant friends would appear, and for a short time, the holder of the note would be the king or queen of the castle.

Jane Beaumont, though mature for her age, would likely have been the same. She, Arnna, and Grant were no match for the lure and the thrill of receiving a pound note. Dr Xanthé Mallett stated, in her book *Cold Case Investigations,* 'When children are taken by a stranger the most common tactic is to lure the child into a car with the promise of money, sweets or to see some puppies or kittens, anything that might appeal to a young child.'[3]

This type of enticement did not go unnoticed by Haydn Phipps' teenage friends in the 1960s, who to this day distinctly remember being given a pound note each by Haydn's father to, in the words of Harry Phipps, 'fuck off' from the family house on his 'special no-go Saturdays' when Phipps wanted to engage in his clandestine activities. These youths would happily oblige and spend the afternoon at the Colley Reserve enjoying their new-found wealth at the local sideshows and fun fair. When Mullins spoke to Haydn and two of his former friends several years ago, all clearly remember being given a pound note on numerous occasions, mentioning how much this was to have at the time. If teenagers in the 1960s thought the pound note held a 'wow factor', what did Jane, Arnna, and Grant think? How would they have reacted to being offered one? This man at Colley Reserve had their undivided attention, and he knew it.

So powerful was this pound-note information in the Beaumont case that it sent a shiver down Stuart Mullins' spine, as it had done to many others over the years, including Bill Hayes, Alan Whiticker, former South Australian detective Mostyn Matters, and Ken Thorsen, the former head of the South Australia Police Major Crime Squad, along with experts such as Dr Xanthé Mallett and award-winning investigative journalists Duncan McNab, Graham Archer, and Channel Nine Australia *A Current Affair*'s Brady Halls. This information is regarded as a vital clue in the abduction and disappearance of the Beaumont children. Yet, the public in 1966 was unaware of this detail. The South Australia Police did not release this crucial piece of material to the media for a year; it made front-page headlines in *The News* on 25 January 1967, reported by journalist Michael Coward:

NEW CLUE REVEALED BY POLICE
'The three missing Beaumont Children who left their Somerton Park home with 8/6 in silver in their pockets bought their lunch at the Glenelg Cake Shop with a pound note.'

The journalist goes on to say that this new clue was revealed exclusively to the newspaper.

'This handing Jane a pound note is a significant component of this case.' Coward went on to say that this compelling lead had also baffled law enforcement officers in Australasia and aroused worldwide interest. Detective Sergeant Ron Blight at the Glenelg CIB also stated to this journalist, 'How the children got the pound note is the intriguing question.' Together with then-detective William T Cook, who was involved in investigating this crime, Blight stated that the pound note might hold the key to the mystery.[32]

To us, this statement made by Detective Cook regarding the importance of the pound note rings true; indeed, it may well be the key that unlocks the door to answering the question, 'Did Harry Phipps abduct the Beaumont children?' We believe that when this information was finally released to the public, the consensus from police and the public alike was that the children received the pound note at the Colley Reserve from the man with whom they had been seen playing. We will show in a further chapter that this may not be correct and that the children appeared to have received this money from a residence close to Colley Reserve. Jane, Arnna, and Grant had highly likely followed the enticement of a pound note to buy lunch dangled by this pied piper, who led them to his lair.

The decision to withhold this vital information for a year was not made by the Glenelg detectives. The investigation was controlled by Police Headquarters in Adelaide, meaning the dissemination of material, as well as decisions about what was released and what would not be released regarding this case, came from there.

When Stuart Mullins met with Mostyn Matters and Peter Vogel—the last two remaining detectives who were stationed at Glenelg on 26 January 1966—more than a decade ago in Glenelg, both had outlined their frustration and annoyance that this information had not been released to the public immediately. They had lamented effectively being 'muzzled' by Police Headquarters. They realised that the decision to hold back the information relating to the pound note had essentially cut off a piece of vital information to the public of South Australia. However, there was nothing they, as local detectives, could do about it; their hands were tied, and crucial time was lost. With the passing of a year, people move on, and interest waned. Others thought that if the disappearance had not been solved by then, what assistance could they possibly be?

We ask, why wasn't this significant information released to the general public twelve months earlier, especially if, as we have seen, police at the time understood its significance? Detectives at the Glenelg police station had been conducting intense investigations behind the scenes, and they wanted this information immediately released but were denied the opportunity.

Mostyn Matters and Peter Vogel could produce only one reason: the CIB wanted to keep an ace up their sleeve. As Bill Hayes said, the withholding of certain pieces of information regarding serious cases was not out of the ordinary and, in fact, could be a vital investigative tool. The media and the public at times only receive information that detectives deem necessary to be released at that time—information that will not jeopardise the ongoing investigation of an individual. In addition, as previously mentioned, it is a handy tool when speaking to suspects; if, for example, a suspect was to mention the pound note when it had not been made public, the interviewing officers would know that this person had just dug a hole for themselves. It follows that a suspect's knowledge of the pound note, or indeed anything that was not common knowledge or released to the media, could only indicate some involvement on their part.

Overall, in this case, the detectives' hands were tied. Without a fully informed public, an essential piece of the puzzle could not be identified and inserted in place. In hindsight, this was a crucial shortcoming on the part of the police but was almost understandable in the circumstances.

Another possibility that might explain why this information was not released could be that there were others involved in this crime. How else could one person possibly control three inconsolable, frightened children? Firstly, with the enticement of a pound note for a short period of time, but then what? This line of thinking delves into the once-unmentionable rumour of an exclusive high-end paedophile ring of like-minded individuals of influence operating in South Australia; abusers of children, depraved individuals who may have included members of the clergy, influential businesspeople, senior members of the legal profession, and politicians. The very mention of such people being active and organised paedophiles in that era was deemed too far-fetched to be believed. Unfortunately, as we now know, it is not far-fetched at all.

Regarding the abduction of the Beaumont children, we argue that it was wrong to withhold information that was deemed to be significant to this case. The giving of a pound note to the children was indeed a crucial component. The immediate release of information to the public could well have had a positive effect. Of course, it could have led to some individuals coming forward to present erroneous pound-note theories, but these could have been promptly discounted after brief questioning. However, other information not deemed erroneous would at least have been written down and names taken and indexed. Imagine, for one moment, if one of Haydn Phipps' friends heard this piece of evidence and stepped forward, or indeed some workers or managers at the Castalloy factory informed police detectives that Harry Phipps was known to hand out pound notes. Others may have connected more dots. Not only did Harry Phipps hand out pound notes: his physical description was similar to the man seen with the children, he was a regular swimmer at the beach, and he resided in close proximity to Colley Reserve and Wenzel's Bakery. Of course, this does not make Phipps a killer, but it could have been a starting point for questions to be asked, and at the very least his name would have been catalogued. Detectives cannot usually solve cases alone; they require input from many sources—most importantly, the public. Bill Hayes stated that many serious crimes are solved by information generated from the general public and informants.

As we have noted, there are many cold cases worldwide that have been recently solved or reopened by detectives reviewing files and with the assistance of social media. We see examples of police bringing to justice individuals who committed heinous crimes in some cases several decades earlier. These include the serial predator Joseph James DeAngelo, who became known as the Golden State Killer. DeAngelo was identified, tried, and convicted in 2018 of a multitude of murders and rapes across California between 1973 and 1986.

There is also the case of Australian Chris Dawson who, as a result of the 2018 podcast *The Teacher's Pet*, stood accused of killing his wife Lynette in 1982. Dawson had recently faced a murder trial to decide guilt or innocence. Since writing this chapter the trial of Chris Dawson has concluded in a finding of 'Guilty' and Dawson is in custody awaiting sentence. Like the Beaumont case, this crime was decades old but has been solved and justice done. Also like the Beaumont case, Dawson was convicted entirely on circumstantial evidence.

Other cases have been reopened, and with the benefit of better-educated police officers, improved crime-scene protocols directing the collection and collation of evidence, increased and thoroughly reliable forensic tools becoming available along with better-trained, more knowledgeable, better-equipped, and better-resourced detectives, we are seeing great results in the ever-increasing and regular successes in clearing up cold cases. At times, when revisiting cold cases, we can find that during the initial investigation, individuals had been named and catalogued but overlooked in the investigation carried out decades before. The same could be said for Harry Phipps: if the information about the pound note had been released when this detail first came to light in 1966, the outcome might have been different.

This is not to say that Harry Phipps would have been seriously looked at as a suspect in the Beaumont case. This was, as we know, the 1960s, and the public was of the view that this abduction was the work of a 'dirty old man' or 'scruffy sex pervert' or, according to the press at that time, a longish blond-haired beachcomber, not a well-to-do businessman of high standing in the community. Irrespective of whether he was a regular swimmer at Glenelg beach or handed out pound notes, or any other of the compelling pieces of circumstantial evidence, Phipps was unlikely to be considered a serious suspect. Back then, one phone call from Phipps to the 'right people' would be all that it took to place the detectives back on the leash. Would this happen today? In our opinion, it would not.

However, this was the 1960s, when wealth and power put a man on a pedestal and rendered him untouchable. If Harry Phipps' name and some circumstantial evidence had been known and catalogued in 1966 and if Phipps were alive today, things would have been very different. Detectives revisiting him would not be swayed by his connections or wealth when trying to solve this cold case. He would have to answer some very pertinent questions.

Even at this early stage, we believe to have presented compelling circumstantial evidence linking Harry Phipps to the abduction and disappearance of Jane, Arnna, and Grant Beaumont. Although all the points of circumstantial evidence so far do raise eyebrows, it is the handing out of pound notes by Harry Phipps that stands out like a zebra in a field full of horses.

Of the six suspects in this matter named over the many years since this terrible event, Harry Phipps is the only individual known to hand out pound notes. Add this to the amount of initial circumstantial evidence against him, and you have the makings of a perfect storm.

Chapter 10:
Geographic Profiling

*Sometimes the best hiding place is the one
that's in plain sight.*[33]

—Stephenie Meyer

One of the factors in the disappearance of the Beaumont children that has puzzled SAPOL detectives and the public alike since January 1966 was the complete lack of physical evidence and a clear suspect.

Missing children was not a common occurrence. Sure, there had been cases of marital disputes where a spouse would flee with their child, or a youngster reported missing only to return home several hours later due to losing track of time. However, detectives were not prepared for anything of the magnitude of what unfolded that day.

In the 1960s, the police force in each state was somewhat insular and worked independently. They did not have the technology to share information readily; the compilation of statistics was in its infancy. They relied on good old-fashioned doorknocking and patrolling the local area, and on the community coming forward with information.

Many people believe that this case will never be solved, which for many years seemed entirely plausible. Geographic

profiling has emerged as one of the most important developments in crime analysis and investigation in recent years. Cold
cases that remained unsolved for many years are being actively
investigated, with several crimes solved. Stuart Mullins and Bill
Hayes believe that the disappearance of the Beaumont children
will be no different. This tool, when utilised effectively, makes
it abundantly clear that the individual who abducted Jane,
Arnna, and Grant Beaumont highly likely lived close to Colley
Reserve.

Geographic profiling is a criminal investigative tool
that analyses the locations of a connected series of crimes to
determine the offender's most likely place of residence, place of
work, social venues, and travel routes—these are known as their
'spatial patterns'. As Colin Johnson, professional geographic
profiler with the UK's Serious Organised Crime Agency, states:

> This technique works because criminal behaviour is not
> random. They follow the same lines: motivation, opportunity,
> mobility and perception, and based on four main principles;
> routine activity, rational-choice principle, least-effort
> principle and distance decay.[34]

Julien Chopin, Stefano Canneppele, and Eric Beauregard
published a study in November 2019 on extra-familial sexual
homicides and their spatial mobility. 'The study combines the
location of the crime scene and the offenders' and victims'
residences in mobility crime triangles.'[35]

The findings reveal that most of the homicides fall within the
categories of offender mobility and total mobility. Their results
show the validity of the distance-decay function, with over
seventy percent of homicides occurring within ten kilometres
of the offender's residence. It appears that under certain circum-

stances, sexual murderers perceive their surroundings as a safe place to commit a homicide.[36]

What is also noteworthy to us are the words 'crime triangle'. This is what we have in the Beaumont case from where the children were playing at Colley Reserve to Harry Phipps' house to Wenzel's Bakery. As true crime author Alan Whiticker noted many years ago when speaking to Brady Halls, a journalist for Channel Nine's *A Current Affair* television programme, this is the crime's Bermuda Triangle.[37]

Criminologists use this method to try to explain criminal behaviour. Combined with paedophilic profiling evaluating the common characteristic of a paedophile, we have the perfect storm. At the time, the detectives would have been completely unaware of the concept of geographic profiling. This technology in the 1960s was only in its infancy with the FBI in the United States. Therefore, what law enforcement at the time couldn't know was that Harry Phipps ticked all the boxes: geography, proximity, familiarity with the crime scene, psychological traits, and paedophilic behaviour.

Just imagine for one moment that detectives had available this investigative tool in 1966. Harry Phipps would have been one of the first individuals visited by detectives. Whether he would have been brought to justice is another matter. Another critical component of profiling has been the introduction of a 'jeopardy surface', which is essential to this case. Kim Rossmo, PhD, states, 'This methodology, used in geographic profiling, analyses locations connected to a series of crimes to determine the most probable area in which the offender lives.'[36]

This method interprets data relating to time, distance, and movement to and from the crime scene. Used effectively, law-enforcement officials can identify an area where a criminal most likely resides.

We used this technique to significant effect when evaluating the abduction of the Beaumont children. Having stood on the corner of Sussex Street and Augusta Street outside the former residence of Harry Phipps, what was chillingly apparent was how close Phipps' residence was to Colley Reserve and how easy it would have been to lure these children away.

Dr Xanthé Mallett did the same a decade later in 2017 and noted her agreement in her book *Cold Case Investigations*, 'I stood on the pavement outside the main suspect's house looking towards the beach and understood how easy it would have been to coerce those children away.'[3]

Duncan McNab stated to us in late 2017, when filming for the true-crime documentary, *The Beaumont Children: What Really Happened*, that standing on the corner of Augusta and Sussex Streets outside his house for the first time, a chill literally ran down his spine.

We considered witness statements and the psychological profile of the suspect, as well as studying the demographic data and inspecting the crime site and undertaking a hands-on study of streets, pathways, and the shopping precincts of Glenelg. We met with current and retired detectives on the case and people who knew Harry Phipps. We were interested in the distinctive patterns relating to the suspect.

There are many studies of the spatial behaviour and patterns of sexual offenders by criminologists. Generally, findings indicate that sex offenders do not travel far to assault or abduct their victims. Like an animal in the wild, they hunt their prey on their patch of turf, comfortable with their familiar surroundings.

Disposing of any evidence—or, tragically, bodies—would be in familiar territory. Surprisingly, when Stuart secured information regarding Harry Phipps' real-estate assets mentioned in Chapter Four, he found that all but one property was in close proximity to Phipps' home or the Castalloy Factory.

Was this crime opportunistic or planned? Based on the offender's and children's behaviour, the latter seems most likely. This individual was already lying, settled on the grass well before Jane, Arnna, and Grant arrived and laid their towels close by. The children all played under the sprinklers the man watched and planned. By the time the children walked over and started to play with him, their money had been taken. From this point, he knew how this abduction would play out.

In our opinion, Harry Phipps saw vulnerable potential victims, not innocent, fun-loving children. When sexually aroused, the consequences of his actions become secondary to him. This suspect exuded supreme confidence and superficial charm, knowing he would have anonymity within the large crowd assembled at Glenelg beach and Colley Reserve on Australia Day.

Had Phipps now graduated to the next level after allegedly sexually abusing his eldest son for many years? Had the abuse well run dry when Haydn was old enough to fend off his father? Did Harry's deviant sexual appetite need to be fed? As perverse as this sounds, we believe Phipps was living out his graduation ceremony at Colley Reserve in 1966. At the time, this abduction of three children was in a league of its own—until 1966, the abduction of multiple children, never to be seen again, had never been reported anywhere in the world.

This crime site was not random. Criminologists state that offenders locate and target victims near their permanent residence—they mostly frequent locations where children are plentiful. Colley Reserve in the summer school holidays was such a place. This reserve was his hunting ground. As we know, Harry Phipps was born and lived in Glenelg all his life. His

Castalloy factory was an eight-minute drive from his residence in Augusta Street to North Plympton. He was comfortable with his familiar surroundings, where later we will see his predatory skills used once again. Professionals term this 'distance-decay function'.[38]

According to Mike O'Leary's journal article 'Modeling Criminal Distance Decay', the further away from the regular activity space an offender is, the less likely they will engage in a predatory criminal activity.[38]

Canadian environmental criminologists and geographic profilers Paul and Patricia Brantingham suggest that crime sites and opportunities are not random. There is an emphasis on the interaction between the offender's mental map of spatial surroundings and the allotment of victims. This interaction was occurring at Colley Reserve within Phipps' environmental comfort zone. Brantington and Brantington reiterate that the criminal act is most likely to occur relatively close to the location of the offender's home or workplace. They further state, 'As the success rate increases, there will be a burgeoning sense of confidence to seek his prey further from home and to travel a greater distance.'[39]

However, an offender's comfort zone can vary substantially depending on the individual's place of employment, lifestyle, and upbringing. Harry Phipps never travelled far. He grew up in Glenelg. His work was his life at Castalloy, five kilometres away. It is unlikely Phipps would have developed a comfort zone outside the Adelaide inner suburbs.

As we asked over a decade ago, could this abduction be that simple that the abductor was always living in clear sight of Colley Reserve under our collective noses, hidden behind the façade of a respectable businessman?

Chapter 11:
Characteristics of a Paedophile

Evil at times comes disguised under the cloak of respectability wearing a business suit.

—Stuart Mullins and Bill Hayes

A paedophile is not and never was a dirty old man. They have always been hidden in clear sight as the kind uncle or aunt, swim coach, scoutmaster, schoolteacher, nice next-door neighbour, or a member of the clergy. To the outside world, they are charismatic, caring, understanding, charming, engaging, and amiable. However, under the mask of respectability, they are ultimate manipulators. Scheming, shrewd, cunning, and deceptive. To them, a child is fair game and adults are mere pawns to be manipulated.

Adelaide in the 1950s, 1960s, and 1970s was a bastion of societal order with the Anglican Church at the centre. Religion played a significant part in politics and business. The general population knew their place in society based along religious denomination lines, wealth, and standing in the community, and stayed within their convictions and beliefs with rigid conformity.

On face value, Adelaide was an orderly, God-fearing society. The underbelly, however, was unchecked paedophilia.

Parents in the 1960s told their children when travelling to the beach or out for an adventure to watch out for 'dirty old men'. A choice of words used more to describe a harmless individual to be ridiculed and derided, which disarmed the child's notion that this person could physically and mentally harm them for the rest of their lives.

A child's idea of a paedophile was a dishevelled, scruffy-looking hobo—easy to pick and avoid. Well-meaning adults who used this terminology were leaving the door wide open for the scoutmaster, uncle, aunt, swimming instructor, member of the clergy, or the friendly next-door neighbour to walk right in. In the majority of cases, paedophiles are known to their victims.

Children and adults alike unquestioningly trusted authority figures, which allowed paedophiles in the 1960s to go about their business unabated and unfettered. Once the abuse had taken place, they were protected by 1960s community norms. *Children should be seen and not heard. Children should keep quiet and respect their elders. The nail that sticks out gets hammered down. Keep your head down and your nose to the wheel.* Until the 1980s, the molestation of minors was a reality that existed mainly under the radar. With no-one to believe them, no-one to speak to, children suffered in silence.

Paedophiles left a trail of life-altering carnage in their wake. Many of them went undetected, as Harry Phipps had. Like many of his type, they knew well that any who did speak out would not be believed. The paedophile's sociopathic personality manipulates those around them into thinking they are upstanding members of the community, with friends and family unwittingly supporting this wolf dressed in sheep's clothing. As Judith Lewis Herman, Professor of Clinical Psychiatry at Harvard University School of Medicine and author of *Trauma*

& Recovery—The Aftermath of Violence From Domestic Abuse to Political Terror, wrote:

> To escape accountability for their crimes, the perpetrator does everything in their power to promote forgetting. If secrecy fails, the perpetrator attacks the credibility of his victim. If he cannot silence them absolutely, he tries to make sure no-one listens.[40]

Through intensive investigative journalism, government inter-vention, and a more enlightened, better-trained police force over the past three decades, the extent of child sexual abuse has been laid bare. Long gone are the days of hiding behind wealth or connections.

Australia's Royal Commission into Institutional Responses to Child Sexual Abuse highlighted widespread cases of systematic child abuse at the hands of the clergy.[41]

The investigative journalists of the *Boston Globe* highlighted the same. This sanctity of the church, held in high regard and sought for guidance and advice, was, in fact, a hive of paedophilia. Senior clergy members were made aware of the problem and ignored it. Both investigations highlighted paedophilic priests being moved from one diocese to another only to abuse again. People entrusted with children's care took advantage and changed their lives forever.[42]

As Alex Gibney, American documentary film director and producer, states, 'The Church must be all-powerful. You discover these horrors within institutions because predators find ways of hiding in plain sight.'[43]

What happened to Haydn Phipps and others at the hands of his father was no different. People were complicit in their inaction, their silence allowing this sexual abuse to continue unabated. Paedophiles were assured adults would not speak out, shackled by the chains of conformity, conventionality, and docility.

The turning point for many in Australia and Britain over the past few decades was the news that Rolf Harris was a sex offender. Not good old Rolf Harris? Australia's beloved export to the UK. A real Aussie character. A qualified teacher, talented musician, singer-songwriter, composer, comedian, painter, and lovable television personality warmly welcomed into the living rooms of many Australian and British households in the 1960s, an all-around good guy… and a predatory paedophile. The realisation that Rolf Harris was a paedophile shattered long-held beliefs and perceptions of what made a paedophile. The paedophile is not a dirty old man; he looks and acts like you and me. Rolf Harris was convicted and imprisoned for indecent assault of underage teenage female victims. Did he show any remorse? No, they never do. He has written a song accusing his victims of being after his money. The predator does not stop. They will continue to hunt and abuse children, increasing their tally until they are stopped.

For Australians and the world, more was to come as the walls were tumbling down. The prevalence of child sexual abuse was becoming shockingly alarming. No-one was immune, no-one was above the law—not entertainers or politicians, the clergy, the businessman, the schoolteacher, or the scoutmaster.

A Rolf Harris moment occurred in Australia with the naming of television's loveable sitcom dad Robert Hughes as a paedophile. Likable, charming, mischievous Hughes had the looks your mother would love. *Hey, Dad!* was a rating bonanza, a witty, feel-good TV sitcom for all the family. However, while this show was at its peak, Robert Hughes was sexually abusing his young stage daughter Sarah Monahan.

In her adult years, Sarah accused Hughes of sexual abuse, which was supported by fellow cast members. He denied the accusations. However, more was to follow. Hughes' niece claimed that he had also molested her. Hughes' daughter rejected the allegations and questioned why the accusations were not raised earlier.[44]

The same question was asked by some family members regarding Harry's older son Haydn Phipps when he said his father sexually abused him. According to the *Herald Sun* newspaper of 14 June 2017, Sarah Monahan did speak to the NSW Police about the abuse but was told by an investigating detective, 'I have tried to get this guy, but every time I do, someone covers for him.' And by having someone cover for him, he was allowed to continue the violation of children. Fellow *Hey Dad!* actor Ben Oxenbould claimed he was passed over for TV work after supporting Monahan against Hughes.[45]

It is a vicious circle, with the perpetrator having many adults supporting their impeccable character while deriding the abused as lying, or being after money, notoriety, or revenge. As stated in *Trauma & Recovery: The Aftermath of Violence* by Judith Herman, MD, Harvard University School of Medicine, 'All the perpetrator asks is that the bystander do nothing. He appeals to the universal desire to see, hear, and speak no evil.'[46]

In April 2014, *ABC News* wrote that Hughes was found guilty of two counts of sexual assault, seven counts of indecent assault, and one count of committing an indecent act. He was sentenced to ten years and nine months' imprisonment.[47]

Hughes was charming, friendly, and likable—he was also manipulative and used his position of power and influence. He looked for opportunity and insisted on secrecy. Paedophiles appear like any other member of society. Some paedophiles, as with Harris and Hughes, offer rationalisations or excuses that enable them to avoid assuming responsibility for their actions. They show no remorse or emotion. Many blame the child for being sexually provocative and alluring, or they maintain that they are 'teaching' the child about 'the facts of life' or 'love'. Many believe they have done no wrong.

In '11 Known Facts About Sex Offenders', researcher for SACS Consulting Investigative Service Timothy Dimoff provides a frightening statistic based on United States research: male offenders have an average of 150 victims each.[48]

Gerald Francis Ridsdale, an Australian Catholic priest, was convicted of sixty-five counts of child sexual abuse against children as young as four between 1993 and 2017.[49]

Over the past six decades, society has experienced many examples of paedophiles who escaped the long arm of justice because they died before facing the full force of the law. English DJ, radio, and television personality Jimmy Savile was awarded an Order of the British Empire and later a knighthood. He had a reputation for eccentricity and flamboyancy, which camouflaged his true nature. He was a TV star at the top of his game in the UK, but rumours of his sexual deviancy swelled. Allegations were made in the 1960s, 1970s, and 1980s. On each occasion, Savile's public-relations team went into overdrive. The few victims who did speak out alleging this man sexually abused them were discredited, disbelieved, and dismissed. His legal team used the usual paedophile defence: the victims were after Savile's money; they wanted publicity and notoriety. All this was a warning to others. Savile was influential, wealthy, and connected. Speak up—be shot down. People with standing in society were placed on a pedestal and deemed incapable of such heinous acts. Savile was one of them, a sign of the times. Savile's dark side was exposed only after his death—hundreds of allegations of sexual abuse were made against him. His victims ranged in age from five to seventy-five. Most of this abuse occurred when Savile was visiting children's hospitals and aged-care facilities in the name of charity. It is alleged that one of his favourite things to do at the hospital was to get the keys to the morgue. It is unthinkable why he wanted them.

To this day, many are dumbfounded how this abuse could have occurred under their watch. So many hospital staff, and on occasions members of the media, were present. Surely Savile would have been seen in the act, or someone would have known. However, paedophiles are incredibly cunning. Predators feign emotions, energised by the control they wield over their flock. They are devoid of emotions apart from feeding their self-gratification. They know precisely how and when to act; they are chameleons acutely aware of their surrounding environment. They hunt by stealth, lurking in the shadows, watching and waiting for a moment to strike. Many are sociopathic by nature and lack a sense of moral responsibility or social conscience. In Savile's case, he was a generous financial benefactor to the hospitals. Where he would also ply his predatory, deviant trade.

More recently was the conviction and jailing of the Australian former CEO of Bega Cheese, Maurice Van Ryn. The sixty-four year old is currently serving a sentence of more than thirteen years for the abuse of nine boys and girls between the ages of eight and fifteen, plus an extra twelve months after further review.[50]

This further highlights that paedophiles cast their shadow across all levels of society, from the wealthy and connected to the CEO to the factory worker. You cannot pick a paedophile on looks or the way they present or their standing in the community. Many people struggle to accept that well-groomed, wealthy, connected individuals could be sexual predators. As American author and public speaker Tucker Max put it, 'The devil doesn't come dressed in a cape and pointy horns. He comes dressed as everything you ever wanted.'

Predatory paedophiles never recognise the rights of the child. They see their self-serving behaviour as permissible and will continue to hunt until they are stopped. Their victims are mere instruments to be used and discarded. These predators blame the children for their arousal. They lack shame, empathy, regret, or remorse. The end justifies the means; they let nothing stand in their way. Instead of friends, they have victims and unwitting accomplices that they use as fodder. These accomplices intentionally or unintentionally do the predator's bidding, publicly exclaiming the person's virtues, perfect character, and record. A predator's cunning and deception has no bounds. They have not only groomed the child but the family, relatives, and community. So, it is often the person we would least expect who is the wolf in the flock of sheep.

In later chapters, we will see that there are commonalities between the stories of abuse told by Haydn Phipps and 'Linda', who came forward at the end of 2017 and accused Harry Phipps of raping her as a thirteen-year-old schoolgirl. Both Haydn and Linda described Phipps as having a lack of emotion after the rape. They were made to feel responsible for his actions.

When Haydn first spoke with Stuart Mullins many years ago, he described how he was puzzled and bewildered when his father attended morning breakfast acting as if nothing happened the previous night—as if it were business as usual, asking Haydn how school was going or informing Olga about work or what time he expected dinner. He showed no emotion, no inkling that what he was doing was wrong or that it had even happened, just an air of arrogance. In Mullins' eyes, Haydn's mannerisms indicated he was still haunted and indeed perplexed by his father's complete lack of guilt. Linda, whose story is outlined in Chapter 16, was no different. She too has been emotionally scarred for life by

Harry's sheer callousness. She remembers him standing up after the sexual assault and brushing the dust from his trousers, saying, 'See what you have done? You got me all dirty.' His thoughts were about him, not Linda, who he left lying in the dirt raped, grazed, bleeding, and sobbing having just lost her innocence in such a brutal manner.

Paedophiles have many of these traits in common; making the abused feel responsible is part of the paedophile's ammunition. For decades, sexual predators plied their trade with impunity, knowing full well that the child would rarely tell anyone of their ordeal for fear of not being believed. The few who did speak out were belittled and derided—in some cases, made to apologise to their abuser for telling lies. Later this predator would exact their sexual revenge on the child.

However, there is one factor that works against the paedophile: eventually, their victims will grow up and recall the events that occurred and might expose the predator. This is exactly what has happened with Harry Phipps. In recent years, the small protest of support for him has fallen mute due to the overwhelming circumstantial evidence. As more victims of child sexual abuse come forward, public sentiment has changed. The victim is now believed over the predator.

As Chrystine Oksana writes in *Safe Passage to Healing: A Guide for Survivors of Ritual Abuse*:

> Violators cannot live with the truth: survivors cannot live without it. There are those who still, once again, are poised to invalidate and deny us. If we don't assert our truth, it may again be relegated to fantasy. But the truth won't go away. It will keep surfacing until it is recognised. The truth will outlast any campaigns mounted against it, no matter how mighty, clever, or long. It is invincible. It's only a matter of which generation is willing to face it and, in so doing, protect future generations from ritual abuse.[51]

Chapter 12:
Follow the Money

The best place to hide something is in plain sight.
Things that are hidden out in the open are the most
difficult to see.

—Prairie Johnson, *The OA*

During our extensive research and investigation, and on gaining a further understanding of how this abduction unfolded, we came to the conclusion that the individual who abducted the Beaumont children highly likely resided within a 300-metre radius of Colley Reserve. Following are the clues that, when considered in the broader context of the event, make it clear that it is likely a local predator was on the prowl on 26 January 1966, and that predator appears to have been Harry Phipps.

The man was not seen swimming.

Eyewitnesses who were at Colley Reserve before Jane, Arnna, and Grant Beaumont arrived said the man was already lying on his towel. At no time was he seen swimming. His hair was described as neatly brushed back and parted to one side, which appears to indicate he had not been in the water, as brushing back one's hair after a swim is simple enough, but parting to one side without the use of a mirror is a little more difficult. If this man was not at the beach for recreation, what was he there for? The simplest solution is usually the best. If this man arrived after the eyewitnesses, it would be interesting to ascertain if there was any mention from the witnesses in the original detectives' reports of which direction he may have arrived from.

His arrival time.

If the man arrived before the eyewitness, he may have already gone for a swim; however, indications are that he appeared to be at the reserve for only one purpose. The answer to the question of when this man arrived at Colley Reserve may well be hidden in the myriad boxes of statements taken and stored at the head-quarters of South Australia's Major Crime Investigation Branch.

Travelling light.

The man seen playing with the children at the beach that day was travelling light.

Eyewitnesses stated the man had with him a towel, a pair of trousers, and a shirt. No carry bag, wallet, or car keys were spotted. If this man lived a few kilometres from the beach, one could expect a carry-bag of some sort. His car keys and wallet could have been in his trouser pockets or placed under his clothes. However, none were seen.

The staring.

The same eyewitnesses stated to the detectives when interviewed that the man watched the children arrive at the Glenelg beachfront and then frolic in the water. He then watched the children run up from the beach to where Jane, Arnna, and Grant placed their towels, about ten metres behind and slightly to the side of where the man was lying. Noticeable again to these eye-witnesses was that this man watched the children run over and play under the sprinklers and then return to where they had laid out their towels.

A pre-arranged rendezvous?

Arnna and Grant teased Jane on the morning of January 26th by excitedly telling their mother repeatedly, 'Jane has a boyfriend,' presumedly meaning at the beach. There appeared to be *someone* at the beach that these children knew. This appears to be the case, as once the children returned to their towels and dried themselves off after playing under the sprinklers, Grant and Arnna walked over to this man, not the other way around. Grant began jumping over him, and Arnna started flicking him with her towel. A short time later, Jane joined in. According to witnesses, they were all conversing, laughing, and having a fun time, as if they knew one another.

As Australian criminal investigative analyst Kris Illingworth stated in a recent critique she sent to us outlining how this abduction may have unfolded:

> This man targeted these children because they were unac-companied by an adult that day. His playful behaviour and the responding behaviour of the children as they interacted together at the Reserve is suggestive of them having had some prior contact. Not necessarily in any significant way but having simply 'met' on an earlier occasion.

Please note Kris does not say this individual is Harry Phipps; she is just stating how she believes the abduction took place.

We believe this meeting could have been a pre-arranged rendezvous. The children were present at the reserve the day prior, when Jim Beaumont drove them to Glenelg in the morning to drop them off for a morning at the beach, where he watched as he waved goodbye and Jane, Arnna, and Grant headed over to their normal spot at Colley Reserve. The area the children were playing at appeared to be a regularly frequented location, according to Jane's best friend, Jenny, whom we meet later in the book.

'Our money has been pinched.'

We have asked many professionals, including investigative journalists and former and current South Australian detectives, where Jane Beaumont received the one-pound note she used to pay for lunch at Wenzel's Bakery. All said, 'From the man at Colley Reserve.'

Yes, she received a one-pound note from the man, but not at the reserve. Let's not forget that after playing with the children, the man approached eyewitnesses. An elderly couple sitting on the park bench where this man had laid his clothes stated that the man had asked, 'Did any of you people see anyone messing our clothes? We have had some money pinched.' The younger witnesses—the man and his family and the mother and daughter—believed he said, 'Has anyone been messing with our clothes? We have had our money pinched.' The final consensus reached when all were interviewed by detectives days later was that the man said, 'Has anyone been messing with our clothes, as we have had our money pinched.' Therefore, the children with the man left the reserve with no money.

By asking two sets of eyewitnesses, we believe that he was showing concern and empathy, further gaining the children's trust—all straight out of the paedophile's playbook. This child molester used 'our' to reinforce the appearance of them being all together and safe.

We conclude that after raising his concerns with the eye-witnesses, the man returned to the children and confirmed that their money had been stolen. Not once did this man state to the witnesses that his wallet had been taken. In our opinion, there was no wallet. With both the children and this individual now having no money at Colley Reserve, this man was able to connect with the children and further gain their confidence. In turn, and by stealth, he gained control over Jane, Arnna, and Grant.

Follow the money.
The children and the man were all in the same boat. What if his next line was, 'Oh, boy; what can we do? I know—I have some money at my house.' So, Jane, Arnna, and Grant willingly followed him. You might imagine the man saying to the children something like, 'How about a pound note to buy lunch?' If that were the case, he certainly would have had their undivided attention. The children were not in any distress, because they believed that this man was going to help them. He was a knight in shining armour. It could be also assumed if this kind and caring man had money in his pocket, he would give the children some so they could walk to their bus stop and Wenzel's Bakery to buy lunch. By him not having money—or pretending he didn't—the scene of abduction was being set up and played out. We believe the pound note was the bait.

Bill Hayes refers to this child molester as cunning, acute, luring, premeditating, intelligent, charming, and manipulative. It would appear that this unfolding abduction was well planned, and the grooming appears to have commenced days earlier, following predictable predatory stages.

In our opinion, this individual had been stealthily stalking these children, waiting for the ideal opportunity to pounce, knowing who he wanted and how he was going to take them. The stolen-money scenario was the perfect alibi. The offer of a crisp pound note and possibly a ride home after the children bought lunch from the bakery was the ideal bait.

We ask, did he think this through? Did he plan to sexually abuse one or all of the children? Was he going to let them go or dispose of them? Or was he so sexually overwhelmed that receiving erotic gratification outweighed the consequences? If this man was Harry Phipps, as we believe, he was likely aware that he could hide behind his wealthy businessman veneer and connections. Also, in our opinion, Phipps' Castalloy factory was a perfect spot to dispose of evidence. Phipps has been accused of abusing other minors and would well have known, as many paedophiles did in the 1960s, that they could abuse a child over and over, safe in the knowledge that if the child did speak out—which was unlikely—no-one would believe them. But three children? That was another matter. It is unfathomable to think that this individual planned ahead and that these children were never going to return home.

How did the man know that Jane had any money?
The few shillings that Nancy Beaumont gave Jane were put in her beige-coloured clip purse and placed inside her light blue airline-style carry bag. If the theft of Jane's purse was a random act by an unknown perpetrator, how did the thief rummage through the man's clothes and Jane's bag without the nearby witnesses noticing?

To us, there was no mysterious thief, as this man likely looked inside Jane's airline-type bag whilst the children happily ran and played under the sprinklers. This does appear as the only plausible prior opportunity. Once he had Jane's purse, he had control over their further movements. Or, as Kris Illingworth says:

> The 'theft' of money from the children and the man's property is interesting. I don't believe there was any actual theft but rather the man created this subterfuge to gain further leverage over the children. By telling them they had no money, they would feel compelled to go with him for a lift home or to go somewhere with him. The 'theft' of their money effectively stranded them, and not knowing what to do due to their tender years, they fell into his 'care'. [Please see further information regarding a purse in Chapter 24.]

If the children knew their money was taken, why were they playing so happily? How did the man know that their money had been taken without looking into Jane's bag? Because they were unaware until the nice man informed them on their return. To top this off, he showed how concerned he was by approaching the couple sitting on the park bench knowing full well what their response would be. Jane, Arnna, and Grant were now indebted to this kind, empathetic individual. This was just another step in the grooming process, creating a valid reason to lure the children away from safe surroundings.

On another note, and speculation only, what else inside Jane's bag did this man see? Jane's paperback copy of *Little Women* by Louisa May Alcott. This may have alerted him to the fact Jane is a reader and allowed him to use this knowledge to further gain her confidence by talking about this well-known, much-loved story with her.

Hence, they happily followed him, safe in the assumption that this man was their knight in shining armour. This individual was, however, cold and calculating and incredibly brazen—it is no small feat to take three children. This was immaterial to him; sexual gratification overrode all logic. We ask the question as many readers would. Why would this man want to be seen in broad daylight?

Kris Illingworth further explains in a well-articulated written critique she sent to us recently how this abduction likely unfolded at Colley Reserve:

> This man doing all this quite openly in a busy, public place in front of witnesses indicates he felt confident that his appearance and his behaviour would not raise suspicions, either by the children or nearby witnesses. If he was to later be identified and spoken to by Police, his behaviour, and importantly the children's, could be put forward to show nothing untoward could have occurred. The offender devised, implemented, and exploited this strategy.

This is backed up by Dr Xanthé Mallett.

> This was all about power and control and a very bold brazen thing to do. It's no small feat to take three small children from a very public place. It was someone very confident, charismatic, but also a cold calculating person. He had to win them over and if he looked scary they would not have gone with him.[52]

As we point out, this man and the children would not stand out in the crowd of thousands of beachgoers. The children were comfortable in the man's company and followed this nice-looking, well-groomed man, never bringing attention to themselves

The distinctive colours.

The man helped dress Jane, Arnna, and Grant, which all the children appeared comfortable for this man to do, before they all walked north up Colley Reserve to the change rooms. On hearing this, Nancy Beaumont was astonished—Jane would never allow anyone to dress her, even if it were just putting on her shorts over her bathers. When speaking with detectives at the station several days after the abduction, Nancy was astonished, stating, 'Jane would never allow anyone to assist dressing her—not even me.' Nancy reiterated this when speaking with journalists from *The News* on Wednesday 21 February 1968.[53] This activity begs the question to be asked; did the children already know Harry Phipps?

However, experienced paedophiles are charming, manipulative, caring, and engaging. He had these children captivated. On a side note, why did this man feel he needed to assist the children to dress? All they had to do was pull up their shorts over their swimmers, a very simple task even for Grant.

What is important to consider at this juncture is the difference between what parents know of their children's behaviour compared to their behaviour around other children and in the company of others. Children can be quite different outside the home environment, especially when they are around their friends, classmates, teachers, or other adults without their parents around. According to Jane Beaumont's best friend, Jenny, Jane was not a shy girl. She was inquisitive, intuitive, articulate, talkative, and intelligent. When speaking with Mullins in 2018, Jenny said she often witnessed Jane strike up conversations with strangers—adults and teenagers alike—who, for example, might be seated next to her in the cinema in Glenelg. She was quite the conversationalist. We believe that if this man Harry Phipps picked up on this, he may well have been happy to indulge her and make friends.

We speculate that this touching and feeling of the children as he helped them dress is crucial; not only may have he been attracted to them, but their coloured apparel may also have been stimulating: Jane's one-piece pink bathing costume with light green shorts, Arnna's red-and-white striped bathers, and Grant's green-and-white striped bathers with green shorts.

When speaking to us on occasions between 2008 to 2014, Haydn Phipps stated Harry's favourite satin colours were pink, lime green, dark green, red, orange, yellow, and purple—darkly reminiscent of some of the colours the children were wearing. When around this type of coloured material, he felt compelled to touch it. These colours were further corroborated by four other people who saw the many colourful satin dresses Harry made. Criminologists, detectives, and profilers noted the touching and dressing of Jane, Arnna, and Grant appeared to be behaviours of a paedophile well into the grooming process.

This abduction appears to be well planned and carried out. We believe that Phipps had seen and spoken with the children before Australia Day 1966, more than likely the day before when their father, Jim, drove them to the beach, which might explain how the children appeared to know him. According to Jenny, when she spoke to Mullins in 2018, the children only had one swimsuit each, which to her were easily identifiable due to their bright colours. This was reiterated by Jim Beaumont when speaking to a journalist with *The News* on 28 January 1966, adding that what they were wearing that day was distinctive in colour.

When Bill Hayes was interviewed by Michael Usher in late 2017 for the 2018 documentary, *The Beaumont Children: What Really Happened,* he said the way they were all interacting that morning was more like a father playing with his children.

Offer an alternative.

In our opinion, it appears that with no money, there is no bus home and no lunch for the children. If walking home, the children would have been very late. The journey was approximately 2.5 kilometres or 1.5 miles in 40-to-42-degree Celsius heat (or over 100 degrees Fahrenheit). Also, Grant was not wearing a T-shirt and he had already been a few hours out in the sun. This would all have added to Jane's concerns. Being a responsible girl, she felt duty-bound to look after her siblings and to make the right decisions for all of them. She did not wish to let her mother down. Also, Nancy would likely be annoyed that Jane lost her purse. So, accepting assistance from this caring gentleman may have been considered the right thing to do. As Bill said in the Channel 7 documentary, 'If your plan was to entice the children somewhere, to get them away, what better way than to remove their method of getting home and be able to offer them an alternative?'

This paedophile was a local.

It is only speculation, however, in our opinion, what happened to the children likely occurred within a 300-metre radius of Colley Reserve. Why? According to witnesses, Jane, Arnna, and Grant started to leave Colley Reserve with the man just after midday, and the children arrived—without the man—at Wenzel's Bakery at approximately 12.25–12.30 pm. Within this twenty- to twenty-five-minute time frame, the children walked with the man ninety metres north along Colley Reserve to the change rooms, in the opposite direction from the children's bus stop and Wenzel's Bakery. There, they waited for him while he changed. According to one eyewitness speaking with detectives days after the abduction, the children and the man were not seen walking back south along Colley Reserve from the change rooms. If this is the case, then did the witnesses see the man and the children walk in another direction from the change rooms? Directly east across Colley Reserve toward Augusta Street? North-east up to the busy Anzac Highway and beyond? Or directly north to the car park at the end of Colley Reserve? We believe the answer may be hidden in the myriad boxes of statements stored at the headquarters of the Major Crime Investigation Branch.

We also have little doubt the children, with the man, walked at a Grant Beaumont pace from the change sheds at about 12.10–12.15 pm to somewhere close enough to make a stop. They would then leave their towels and Jane's carry bag and be given the pound note, only to arrive at Wenzel's Bakery at about 12.25 pm to 12.30 pm, where they bought lunch. Also, the shop assistant who served Jane did not see them carrying towels or Jane with her bag. Due to the approximate twenty- to twenty-five-minute time factor and logistics involved, they believe the abductor resided very close to Colley Reserve.

The change sheds.
It's also interesting to consider why he led them to the change sheds. In our opinion, he only had a shirt and trousers, which he could have put on at the same time the children changed. Why did they walk to the change sheds? Of course, this could have been as simple as him wanting a toilet stop as nature had called. Or, as Tony Zappia, Federal Member of Parliament representing his South Australian constituents of Makin in Canberra, who has been an important part of this investigation, asked in an email to the authors on 4 May 2021, 'What did this man have that Jane did not? Her purse. The change rooms was [*sic*] a good place to hide this on his body after he dressed.'

Tony goes on to say, 'Isn't it interesting that the one thing that Jane loses ends up being seen at Harry Phipps' residence decades later? [*This is discussed in more detail in Chapter 25*] The change shed was a good place to hide this on his body after he dressed.' Our impression of what this man was thinking of doing was to discard the purse before realising this would have left physical evidence, so he kept it. Bill goes on to state: 'This taking of the purse is consistent with this type of predatory behaviour. Keeping this item as a trophy is a reminder of this individual's kill.'

The use of a car.

Due to the twenty- to twenty-five-minute time factor and logistics in play, we believe the initial use of a car appears implausible. On 30 January 1966, detectives at the Adelaide CIB told Bill Perry, a journalist with the Adelaide *Sunday Mail*, that the official assumption was that the children were murdered and buried within kilometres of the beach.[16] Why? Because in their words, one cannot transport three children any significant distance without being seen. The longer one travels by car, the more difficult it becomes to control the children. The detectives interviewed went on to say that this man would have disposed of the bodies quickly and close by. When speaking with Stuart and Mostyn several years ago, Ken Thorsen stated it was highly likely that the children did not leave the area, adding that in an abduction of this nature, getting the children out of sight quickly and not bringing attention to oneself would be paramount. Taking them any great distance produces its own unwanted problems. Mostyn Matters and Peter Vogel, along with their police colleagues who worked on the original case, believe the same, as do many former detectives that we have spoken to.

The oppressive heat.

Further slowing down their departure if a car was used was the oppressive heat. We assume the car was parked north-east on Colley Terrace or in the car park at the north end of the reserve. The interiors of cars in the 1960s were mostly made up of metal and vinyl. The dashboard was metal, as was the top rear back of the car. Doors had metal trimming and the steering column was made of metal. The front and back bench sets were covered in vinyl. We also assume the vehicle had the windows wound up in 100-degree-Fahrenheit heat and was left in the midday sun. In their opinion, the interior heat of the car would be enough to fry an egg on the front dashboard. Therefore, it is unlikely the children and the man would have immediately got into this car due to the extremely high interior temperature. It's more likely all would have waited for the interior to cool down, further slowing down their departure.

Again, in our opinion, once a car is in play, the time factor blows out. How? A vehicle would likely indicate that this man was not from Glenelg and travelled to Colley Reserve from another suburb. It would simply take too long for this man to drive with the children to his residence outside Glenelg through stop-start traffic, navigating traffic lights and train and tram crossings. He would then have to stop, get out, pick up some money, drive back to Glenelg in traffic and find a parking spot so that the children could walk to Wenzel's Bakery. We have attempted driving several routes and on each occasion, the time blows out. The use of a car is not feasible.

Another bakery.

If this individual is from another suburb kilometres away, why return to Wenzel's Bakery? Adelaide is well known for its myriad of bakeries. Why not stop at one closer to his home?

The Anzac Highway scenario.

Jane, Arnna, Grant, and the man may have walked diagonally north-east across the reserve toward the very busy Anzac Highway. There, they could only turn right to continue their journey along the highway. We have walked this route at a child's pace with rest stops included, keeping in mind the children with the man were walking in extremely hot weather, further slowing their pace.

They would then have waited at a residence a few hundred metres up the highway where the children needed to collect the pound note and then walked back down either Sussex, Nile, Waterloo, Henry, or Byron Streets before turning right onto the busy Jetty Road—Glenelg's main thoroughfare to Wenzel's Bakery. In all of the alternative walking routes, the time taken in each instance ranged from forty to forty-five minutes. In all cases, there was much more chance for the children and the man to be seen. The Anzac Highway alternative is unlikely. See the image pages for an aerial view of the area.

North-east of Colley Terrace.

What could be plausible is the children and the man may have walked diagonally north-east across Colley Reserve to Colley Terrace towards some of the 'terrace apartment boarding houses', as they were known in the 1960s. This may account for why the man travelled light: the children collected the pound note and then walked down Colley Terrace and Jetty Road to Wenzel's Bakery. The time factor suits. However, some of the witnesses did not see the children walk back along this way.

Augusta Street.

Harry Phipps' residence was located on the corner of Augusta Street and Sussex Street, Glenelg. Here we had an undetected, alleged paedophile living approximately 190 metres in direct sight of Colley Reserve.

We have walked from the change rooms directly up Augusta Street to Phipps' residence. Again, keeping in mind the variables, a slow Grant Beaumont walk, due to his tender age, and the oppressive heat combined would further slow their pace. We waited outside the former Phipps' residence for five minutes and then continued to walk down Sussex Street to Jetty Road, turning right and then making a quick left to Wenzel's Bakery. This is the same route the children might have taken decades before. Our journey was nineteen minutes. The time factor fits.

The alley way.

Running parallel to Augusta Street from Colley Reserve in 1966 was a back alleyway that appeared to run from the north side of the former Glenelg Bowling Alley on Colley Terrace east across Durham Street, ending when it meets Sussex Street. This endpoint was directly across from the former Phipps residence back carport gate. Taking this route, the timing factor also fits from when the children and the man left the change rooms at about 12.05 pm – 12.10 pm and then Jane, Arrna, and Grant arriving at Wenzel's bakery at about 12.25 pm – 12.30 pm

We propose that the individual involved in this abduction resided close to Colley Reserve. That person, the authors believe, is Harry Phipps. Phipps would have been able to be at the beach anytime in the month of January 1966 as his factory, Castalloy, was closed during January and would open again in early February. He had the opportunity, the method, and the means to take these children.

A puzzling question regarding the man seen with the children at the Colley Reserve has bothered us throughout our investigation. There is no doubt that there was widespread publicity regarding the abduction of these children and the suspicions attaching to the 'man at the reserve'. It is doubtful that there would not have been a cognitive adult in South Australia that didn't hear the story. We ask, if the man that was seen playing with the children on that day was innocent of any wrongdoing, why did he not come forward and speak with police and eliminate himself from this enquiry? Surely that is what an innocent person would do, isn't it? We are convinced that the man seen with the children at the reserve that day was the abductor and that that person was Harry Phipps.

Above are newly married Jim and Nancy Beaumont

Below are Jane, Grant, and Arnna with Dad in their backyard

Above: Happy times playing in the backyard at their Somerton Park home

Below: Arnna and Jane ready for the school day at Paringa Park Primary School

One of several caravanning holidays. This time along the
Great Ocean Road, Victoria.

Above: A happy Jane, Arnna, and Grant pictured here on Victoria's picturesque Great Ocean Road.

Below: The children spent many a day in the summer school holidays at the very crowded Colley Reserve and Glenelg Beach.

What the children took and wore to the beach.

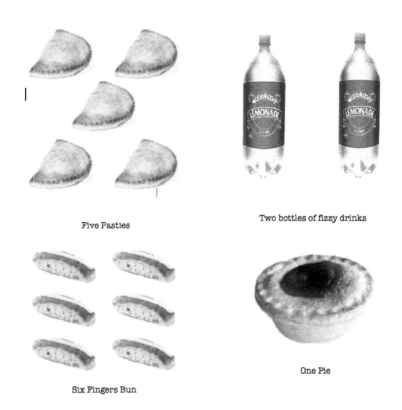

Five Pasties

Two bottles of fizzy drinks

Six Fingers Bun

One Pie

Jane, Arnna, Grant, and the man left Colley Reserve with no money. Yet a short time later, the children are seen at Wenzel's Bakery buying lunch with a pound note. Where did the children receive this wow factor amount of money from in such a short time? Also, they appear to have bought lunch for six. Who is the sixth lunch for?

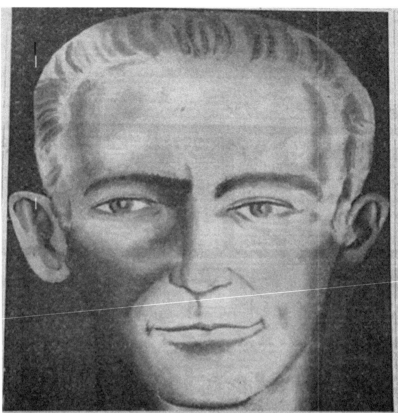

New witness found

"This sketch is as good a likeness as you could get from a drawing."

That is how a Glenelg woman today described this reconstruction (above) by News staff artist John Chizmesya of the face of the man wanted in connection with the disappearance of the three Beaumont children.

The woman had yesterday reported to police that she had seen the man playing with the children the day they vanished.

As a result of her information, an elderly couple to whom the man also spoke at Colley Reserve last Wednesday came forward today.

She said that when the four — the man and three children—approached her and the elderly couple, the elder girl was nearer her.

The woman said the girl looked like Jane.

The woman said the man asked her and the elderly couple: "Have you seen anyone messing around with our clothes? Our money has been pinched."

Det.-Sgt. R. Blight, who is heading police investigations, and another detective today took the couple to the foreshore to reconstruct the scene.

It is understood they used the Chizmesya sketch of the wanted man for identification purposes.

The police were still interviewing the couple when this edition went to press.

The man seen at the beach with the children never had blonde hair. Or bleached blonde hair in need of cutting, as continuously reported in the media over the years. The man had light brown hair and parted it to one side. Brushed back with a slight wave in it.

142

The man's shirt and trousers were placed here

One of the eyewitnesses was sitting here

The children lay their towels about this spot

The man was already lying on his beach towel about here before the Beaumont children arrived at the beach

The beach 20 meters

Harry Phipps house in 1966 where the Beaumont Children were seen after leaving the beach before going to Wenzel's Bakery

Change rooms here

The children arrive at Wenzel's bakery with a pound note at about 12.25-12.30pm

The Beaumont children and the man were playing about here. At about 12.10pm, the children follow the man 90 meters to the change rooms. Where neither the man nor the the children have any money

Jane, Arrna, Grant, and the man all left Colley Reserve with no money. So where were Jane and her siblings given this wow factor pound note from, to arrive at Wenzel's Bakery in such a short period time after leaving the reserve? Who do we know that resided close by and was well known to hand out and tip in pound notes?

143

THE NEWS
ADELAIDE ADVERTISER
THE SUNDAY MAIL

Pervert on the lose   Sex Maniac

Mothers worst fears: some   Children Lured away
crank must have taken them

Sex Crime now feared   Nightmare goes on

NEW CLUE REVEALED

12 months of keeping this crucial piece
on information hidden from the public

The News
Jan 25, 1967

The children receiving a pound note was a pivotal piece of information in
1966 and has been ever since. Yet this vital piece of information was only
released to the public a year later. On January the 25th, 1967.
A travesty in the making.

Jane's last Christmas card given to her best friend Jenny in December 1965

145

Nancy and Jim face the heart-breaking fact that their children are officially missing

Chapter 13:
The Eyewitness

Truth never damages a cause that is just.

—Mahatma Gandhi

Bill Hayes spent a decade as a detective in the South Australia Police Force. He has heard every Beaumont conspiracy theory and felt the frustration of detectives following another false lead that again led to a dead end. He has seen potential suspects brought to light with no charges laid, and the hopes of Mr and Mrs Beaumont and the Australian public yet again being dashed.

SAPOL still receive more calls regarding this cold case than any other, yet no substantial information had ever been received to crack this case wide open—until now. Crucial to the naming of Harry Phipps as a suspect has been the testimony of his oldest son, Haydn, about the ongoing sexual abuse he suffered at the hands of his father, along with his account of seeing Jane, Arnna, and Grant Beaumont in his backyard on that fateful day in 1966.

Over time, Haydn Phipps has gained a negative reputation. According to his second wife, Angela, and echoed by a close cousin, former friends from the 1960s and 70s, and several Castalloy managers that we spoke to, Haydn was an alcoholic with a drug dependency. These people had seen Haydn angry for no reason, at times, displaying fits of rage and temper outbursts. Haydn was also prone to pronounced mood swings and appeared at times to have a death wish. He was unable to hold down a job for any length of time and twice divorced. Added to this, quite a few people who knew him as a teenager and into adulthood stated that he hated his father, Harry, with a passion, his abhorrence clearly visible and for no apparent reason.

With the assistance of Haydn's ex-wife Angela, Bill Hayes located Haydn living in a men's supported-accommodation home on the Gold Coast, Queensland. Angela had initially put Haydn at ease about meeting with Bill, but it still took months of negotiation and encouragement for him to warm to the idea of telling his story, especially to a former police officer, which is not unusual for a victim of child sexual abuse. To convince Haydn to meet Bill, there needed to be a slowly, slowly approach to build trust. This was achieved over many months, after which he finally agreed to meet.

Bill, donning his detective's hat, had already vetted and interviewed Angela, and he was confident that she was reporting the truth as she knew it about what Haydn had confided in her. Bill, as he always has, followed the old police ABC of investigation: *assume nothing*, *believe no-one*, and *check everything*.

On Thursday 18 September 2008, Bill boarded an aircraft to make the two-hour flight from Adelaide to Coolangatta Airport in Queensland, where he finally met and interviewed Haydn, now aged fifty-eight. His first impression was nothing like he expected, given all the things that he had heard about the man. Haydn wasn't a dishevelled shell, an unkept person, a raving alcoholic, or dazed out on prescription drugs. What

Bill found was a tall man of solid build, casually dressed, well presented and intelligent. What was noticeable from their initial conversation was that Haydn Phipps still loved and cared for his ex-wife Angela, as she did Haydn. They were simply unable to live together.

It didn't take long for a rapport to build between the two. Bill found Haydn articulate, personable, and forthcoming with a dry sense of humour. Bill also sensed sadness behind the chitchat, and it became obvious that Haydn was a man carrying a heavy burden. Bill was also aware that Haydn had been abusing alcohol as well as prescribed and illicit drugs and had been receiving professional assistance for mental health issues. Bill's years of experience assured him that Haydn was mentally competent and stable and in a clear-minded state for the interview. Had that not been the case, then the interview would not have proceeded. After a long chat and a cup of tea, Bill was relieved that Haydn agreed to be recorded when speaking about Harry's alleged involvement in the abduction of the Beaumont children.

Bill uses an interviewing technique that he had experience with which had been developed by the FBI to help law enforcement officers ascertain if the interviewee is telling the truth. This is known as the 'adaptive interviewing technique'. The interview began with some straightforward questions. Haydn confirmed he had attended one of Adelaide's most prestigious and premier schools, Pulteney Grammar, the same school his father had attended many years before. Upon leaving, he was accepted at university, where he trained as an engineer. However, he did not complete the degree course and after eighteen months of study, he left to join Castalloy Limited, a company his father owned, as a draughtsman, where he then spent several years. Harry Phipps was managing director of Castalloy for the best part of twenty-three years.

Haydn grew up in an area called Torrens Square in Glenelg, South Australia. The family home, Isola, had originally belonged to his grandfather Frederick Phipps, and his father, Harry, had inherited that home. Haydn lived there for roughly his first nineteen years with his parents, Harry and Olga Phipps. His father—whom Haydn referred to only as 'Harry', never 'Dad'—died in 2004 due to complications arising from Alzheimer's disease and kidney failure. His mother, Olga, passed away ten years earlier. She came from an Irish Catholic background and his father was of a strong Church of England faith.

Haydn said his parents' marriage was a bitter, unhappy one. He didn't think they had any sexual relationship at all. According to Haydn, Harry used to sneak off to another room so he could go to sleep in his satin pyjamas.

Haydn described his father in the mid-1960s as approximately six-foot-one-inch tall with a concave chest, skinny, weak-limbed, and lanky. His hair was blonde or light brown with a slight wave and, to the best of his recollection, he parted his hair on the left side.

Haydn recalled that his father often took walks by himself around Glenelg and Colley Reserve and further south-east to Somerton and Brighton beaches. He was an avid swimmer at Glenelg and a man who was very much focused on himself. The family were always hesitant to ask him what he was doing or where he was going.

Isola was a short distance from Colley Reserve. Just like the Beaumont children, Haydn regularly played at Colley Reserve as a child. It was, and still is, a favourite beachside location for children and teenagers. His father's factory often sponsored running races held at the reserve in the 1970s. A basic 'vegetable and steak' man, Harry would eat pasties from a nearby Orange Spot bakery on the Anzac Highway that he would often frequent.

Haydn went on to say Harry thrived on his notoriety, never going anywhere without his .38 police revolver. This was confirmed by a neighbour and a former senior manager at Castalloy. He enjoyed being 'the man about town', many describing him as a big-noter, self-assured, confident, and exuding bravado. Haydn also knew his father to be violent, especially in the household. As he had once written to his then-wife Angela in 2010, who then forwarded this email on to Mullins:

> You and nobody else knows of the full terror I lived with daily, sometimes minute by minute. I suffered at the hands of this man, my so-called 'father'. I was, ever since I can remember, full of an absolute terrifying fear of him and what he was capable of.

Haydn advised Bill that his father had an emotionally poor upbringing. His mother, Katie, had wanted a daughter but got a son. To compensate, his mother dressed him as a girl until he was approximately five, and his grandmother had made Harry little gowns of satin. His father had admitted to him on many occasions that he had a fetish for women's clothing, saying the satin fitted his body snugly.

Haydn went on to say that his father was an accomplished tailor and would produce countless satin kaftans, dresses, and pyjamas. Harry Phipps would wear the satin gowns at home, and the family would see him dressed this way. Haydn had also seen this when covertly watching his father from the cellar stairs or the entrance to the attic. His father would become sexually excited from wearing this clothing. Haydn saw signs of what he later believed to be Harry's ejaculation stains on the fabric. This arousal around satin had also been noticeable to other extended family members who had quietly spoken to Mullins in confidence, revealing that Harry at times would wear satin kaftans in their presence and they had also noticed these stains, which they believed were caused by ejaculation. They had also spotted some of Harry's dressmaking handiwork in the house, draped over a mannequin Harry would use to make his satin paraphernalia.

Much of this satin garment-making would be done in the attic of the home or in the downstairs cellar. The latter contained a workshop and a large cabinet, built by his grandfather, in which Harry would cram his dresses. Haydn revealed to Bill, 'Having draped himself in satin, Harry would move up to the attic.' Haydn went on to state that this was where his father also stored many of the satin dresses that he made. One could stand up in this attic, which contained a boardwalk throughout the roof space that led to a large, black-painted corrugated-iron room that Harry's father had built. This room contained shelves where satin would also be kept as well as a seating area. The door was sometimes bolted shut.

This description was corroborated by the two local trades-people that Elizabeth Phipps had asked to remove a myriad of satin garments, and many other pieces of women's parapher-nalia from the attic, including a plethora of women's gloves, stockings, and some wigs.

Other corroborators were a husband and wife who were Elizabeth's former employers. They were also asked if they could remove a load of the satin rolls and garments from the basement after Harry was placed in an aged-care home.

Both pairs of witnesses stated to us that there were so many satin dresses, kaftans, pyjama bottoms, and satin bolts that they needed to make several car trips to the rubbish tips to clear all of this clothing out of the house. The witnesses described the satin colours of lime green, darker green, pink, orange, yellow, red, and purple. When Mullins met Elizabeth's former employees at their residence, he was able to see and touch some of the bolts of satin they had kept. Later, the former employees donated this satin to a local church group to use in a Christmas nativity play. When Haydn's grandmother died, Haydn found some of his father's clothing, and his mother, Olga, said to him, 'You found out the secret at last; your father is a queer.'

Haydn advised Bill that he was sexually abused by his father from an early age. This involved acts of violent and full sexual intercourse. Haydn knew that the sexual abuse was about to happen when he would hear the swish of satin brushing together as Harry moved down the hallway, usually in the early hours of the morning.

Haydn would always feel rattled and bewildered just hours later when Harry would arrive at the breakfast table as if nothing had happened. But then again, many child sex offenders are unlikely to feel remorse or guilt for their behaviour. Few, if any, think of themselves as the villain; therefore, there is a chronic tendency toward repetition. Harry Phipps was no different.

Haydn stated to Bill Hayes, when interviewed and recorded in 2008, that Harry's sexual abuse continued until he had reached the age of fourteen. Haydn had joined a local rowing club and became strong and sizeable enough to stand up to Harry. All this came to a head when one evening his father had become angry about some minor issue. He had picked up a plate of food and slammed it into his mother's face with such force that it cut her. So incensed was Haydn by this callous act that he grabbed his father by the hair and dragged him out of the kitchen into the passageway, where he knocked him to the ground and punched him several times, telling his father that he was never to hit his mother again. This event caused his father to flee the house, not returning for days. After that event, Harry never hit his mother again, and his sexual abuse of Haydn stopped.

Many paedophiles are bullies and cowards. They terrorise and intimidate the smaller and weaker because they can get away with it until the abused grow old enough to tell their story and fight back.

Haydn admitted the abuse he suffered had serious effects on him but became more manageable to deal with as he grew older, as more assistance became available where once it had not been. Survivors of sexual abuse are more likely to be believed than they were decades ago. Haydn discussed his abuse with several psychiatrists and also in sessions with a psychologist at a facility dedicated to the treatment of the survivors of sexual abuse.

At this point, it would be fair to ask that if Haydn were lying, then why go to these lengths to seek help? Why keep up this façade? Haydn reiterated to Bill this was not something that he had made up, nor was he delusional. Bill, with decades of experience as both a police officer and private detective, believed him to be recounting events that did occur.

Bill went on to ask whether Haydn had ever known his father to have paedophilic reactions or feelings towards other children. Haydn said that despite what had happened to him, his father's preference seemed to be for young girls. He would become sexually aroused by being around them. Haydn recounted seeing Harry—dressed in his bathing costume and playing in the water at Glenelg and Somerton beaches—rubbing himself up against two young pre-pubescent daughters of family friends. Haydn watched in horror as his father rubbed the girls up and down in front of his body, all the while thinking, *You dirty old bastard.* He had seen Harry becoming sexually aroused, yet neither the children nor their parents seemed to be aware of what he was doing.

Haydn said his father had never discussed any fantasies that he might have about younger girls. Harry would only disclose that he felt shame and horror at the things that he had done. He would say, 'I am so ashamed for what I have done,' but he wouldn't go into detail. These conversations with Haydn started in the mid-to-late 1960s. They would take place when Harry became overwhelmed by his memories and his conscience.

Haydn stated his father would do anything to protect his satin fetish; it was his life, his great passion, and Haydn believed he would do anything to avoid exposure. Haydn had no doubt that if Harry felt threatened by children that he had abused, he would not hesitate to kill them to ensure their silence. He would do anything to protect his precious fetish. Further, Haydn believed that Harry would have no conscience about doing it at the time but he would very likely regret it later, as he used to when memories overwhelmed him. It was his illness, the precious fetish he coveted and loved. Nobody could come into the land of his illness because it gave him an excuse to protect it, no matter what. If Harry couldn't buy you off, he would fix you. As Haydn wrote to his former wife Angela, 'He had absolutely no remorse or conscience for any of this, he never ever did.'

After intently listening, Bill Hayes decided it was time to speak to Haydn about Australia Day 1966, a day of great infamy and shame for the people of South Australia and the nation.

Haydn remembered that day. It was, Haydn told Bill, a very hot and humid day. He came home from his part-time job at a local bowling alley around lunchtime. He and perhaps one of his friends—to the best of his recollection—had gone to the 'cubby house' situated at the rear of the family home. They had been smoking in the cubby, and they could see Harry loading plastic bags into his Pontiac. He guessed that these bags contained some of the satin dresses Harry had made to feed his fetish that he stored for the long term in one of the two cottages that sat on the grounds of the Castalloy factory. This cottage, the smaller of the two cottages, was for Harry's use only—only he had the keys; therefore, no-one else could gain entry to it. It was his 'safe place', where he could keep his fetish material and engage in whatever behaviours that he wished to engage in.

Haydn also said that Harry liked his own time, usually Saturdays, which came to be known as 'Harry's no-go Saturdays', where he insisted on everyone clearing out of the house. Australia Day 1966, although a Wednesday, was one of these days. Olga would be out all day playing tennis with her friends, and Haydn and his brother would also be out of the house.

These 'No-go Saturdays' were the days Harry would engage in his satin fetish. According to Haydn, Harry would be washing then hanging the satin dresses on the line, ironing, or stitching them. On these days, Harry wanted to be left alone. According to Haydn, Harry hated himself for his behaviour. He hated everything that he was doing, but he couldn't stop doing it. He was a mass of contradictions.

Harry's generosity with money was extended to Haydn and his friends, who would be given money to go away—'fuck off' was the usual terminology—when Harry wanted privacy on his No-go Saturdays. The most common amount given was a one-pound note, which they usually spent at the nearby sideshow alley. Haydn reported that Harry could be very generous. If he wanted to get rid of you, he would give you any amount of money you wanted. Harry was well known to hand out one-pound notes and always had plenty of money on him.

These were, after all, the days before credit cards, when cash was king.

As many children who grew up in the 1960s and who are now adults can attest, a pound note to a child or teenager in the 1960s had a 'wow factor'. This was at a time when the average weekly wage for a male adult skilled tradesman in South Australia was fifteen pounds, less for non-skilled labourers. So, for a child or teen to receive such a princely amount of money was very unusual.

Bill's interview took Haydn back to 26 January 1966. Did Haydn know anything about the disappearance of Jane, Arnna, and Grant Beaumont? He replied:

> I was home for lunch—around midday to 12.30. I am not exactly sure, but around lunchtime—from working at the Glenelg Bowling Alley with a friend as pin boys. From the cubby house, I saw them come into the backyard. They came into the backyard, they went inside the house and that's it.

It is interesting to note that the children with the man left the change rooms at Colley Reserve at about 12.05 pm to 12.10 pm. Haydn saw them enter the backyard between noon and 12.30. He could have said he saw the children in the morning or later afternoon. However, as coincidence has it, he saw them between noon and about 12.30 pm, which coincides with all of them leaving Colley Reserve. Haydn then sees the children enter the house, where the front door points down Sussex Street 200 metres to Jetty Road. A short turn right, and then left, is Wenzel's Bakery. The timing of when the children left the reserve to being seen by Haydn and then being seen buying lunch appears to fit.

Haydn said to Bill that the children—whom he now believed to be the Beaumont children, although at the time he did not recognise them—looked to be lost. Haydn described Jane, Arnna, and Grant as being little kids, one shorter than the other two. He said they all had short haircuts and initially he was not sure if they were three boys or girls because they all looked similar. He worked out not long after that it was two girls and a small boy. He went on to note they had coloured beach towels with them; he was not sure of the colours, but they were bright colours like yellow or orange. He later told Bill that the taller of the children had a little 'jiffy bag' over her shoulder, 'like one of those little plastic airline bags that kids would carry at the time'. These comments from Haydn bore strong similarities to what the children had with them that day. Indeed, Jane did have with her an airline-type bag. Also, unbeknown to most, even now, Jane, Arnna, and Grant's beach towel colours were blue and two had the same pattern of yellow, green, red, black, and white stripes.

'They came in from around the front of the house to the backyard, and Harry must have been putting his bloody dresses in the back of the boot of the car and they copped—copped him doing it and I don't know, well—see, a lot, a fair bit of time went past, a fair bit of time went past, like, we didn't really take that much—we didn't pay that much attention to what was going on and we just sort of thought, like, oh, the old prick will take them down to the bloody tram stop or whatever to do—take them—take them home or whatever he'll do and that was it,' Haydn revealed to Bill.

Haydn saw the children talking to Harry, but due to the distance between them, he couldn't hear what was said. Harry appeared to be a bit terse with them but didn't send the children away; instead, he sent them into the house and followed them in. Haydn remembers thinking that Harry was perhaps going in to make a phone call. He doesn't remember seeing the children come out of the house. He said that about twenty minutes after he saw the children talking to Harry, he saw Harry come out of the house and load a few more plastic bags and get into the car and drive off. Harry did not return home for a long time. Haydn recalls going into the house sometime later and finding that the front door had been left open. There was no sign of the children and no disturbance within the house. He hadn't heard any sounds of screaming or shouting while the children were at the house. At this stage, it is also interesting to note that the children's carry bag and towels were not spotted at the bakery by the shop assistant serving them. Were they left in Harry's car or the house? By retaining these items, Phipps was assured of their compliance.

Bill asked Haydn whether he thought at any stage that he should have spoken to the police about what he had seen that day. Haydn responded that he thought about it, but he had watched the way the police and media treated others who came forward about the case—they made 'such a farce of [the] person that was the psychic and all the rest of it and it made them look like such dills and [I] thought no, I'm not going to be shown up as a dill just by saying anything, you know?'

When Haydn was forty years old, he spoke to a psychologist about the disappearance of the Beaumont children and what he had seen that day, but not at length. He also spoke to his former wife Angela Fyfe about the sexual abuse he had suffered at the hands of his father, and that he believed that his father had something to do with the disappearance of the Beaumont children.

Bill spoke with Haydn about the houses at the Castalloy factory site. The smaller of these two houses was where Harry would take his dresses for safekeeping, and only he had a key and access to the structure. He had sewing machines, drafting boards, and sewing tables, as well as many rolls of satin material—which he imported from Hong Kong—to feed his fetish as well as other 'stuff' in there. He used the sewing machines to make dresses and codpieces. The home wasn't his sole workshop when it came to his fetish; when his urges overtook him, he would need to fulfil his desires wherever he was.

Bill asked Haydn if there was a dump on the company property where Castalloy could dispose of its waste. There was—it was over about four acres of the company block, right at the back of the houses. The company would dispose of the sand castings from the foundry into the sandpit/dump, which had a drop of 3–4 metres from the front to the back, and use a bulldozer that was kept on site to flatten the piles of rubbish. According to Haydn, Harry could, and frequently did, drive that bulldozer. He said that apart from sand, they would dump everything in there, that 'it was a shit pit'. When Haydn left the organisation in about 1998, the dump was still there.

During the period of Bill's interview with Haydn, he was able to see changes in Haydn's emotional appearance as he relived and spoke of these things. When relating some of the abuse that had happened to him, on occasion, he closed his eyes as if he were remembering, and the pain was evident on his face. In other parts, Haydn was quite matter-of-fact about what he was saying and seemed sad about other aspects of it. Perhaps surprisingly, he said that what he was telling Bill was unfair— unfair because Harry was not there to defend himself. Despite being subjected to violent physical and sexual abuse of the worst kind by Harry, he was still defending him and speaking about fairness.

At no time during the interview did Haydn exhibit irrational behaviour or anything that would suggest that he was not fully aware of what he was saying. Several days later, upon Bill's return to Adelaide, he received a phone call from Haydn. It was clear to Bill, almost instantly, that Haydn was upset. He asked Bill to discontinue the investigation and to forget everything that he had told him, and he said that since speaking with Bill, the bad dreams had returned. Bill advised Haydn that what had been said could not be unsaid—we were talking about the abduction of three children in broad daylight all those years ago, and that justified the investigation. Haydn made it clear that he wanted no further part in the process.

From there followed a long period with little or no communication with Haydn. Angela stated he would be up and down depending on how he was feeling. We both had heard from Angela, as well as Haydn's son, that he was drinking again and lapsing back into his old behavioural patterns.

During this period, we met with the then-second-in-command of SAPOL's Major Crime Investigation Branch, a detective chief inspector. At that meeting, they outlined their dealings with Haydn and what he had said in Bill's interview. It was an affable enough meeting, and at its conclusion, Bill advised that if the police were to speak with Haydn they needed to do it with great delicacy due to his mental fragility at that time. Bill offered to act as a go-between and to make introductions to ease the way.

Unfortunately, due to the tyranny of distance between South Australia and Queensland, the economic reality was that a police officer from South Australia would not be sent to Queensland to speak with Haydn Phipps, even for a matter as notorious and serious as this was. Instead, Haydn received an unexpected, and apparently heavy-handed, telephone call from a Queensland

Police detective—a call that was disastrous for Haydn and also, for a time, to this investigation. He abruptly ended the call after he was shaken by the officer's manner toward him. He later received a call from the SAPOL detective with whom we had spoken, and on being pressed by the detective, Haydn said that he had 'made it all up'. Haydn later told us that he felt that this was what the detective wanted to hear and that he was so disturbed by the manner of the calls that he would have said anything to make them stop. The detective hung up after he told them this. Mullins also spoke to the detective after this call with Haydn, where he reminded the detective that Haydn was in a vulnerable state and that should have been kept in mind. The detective replied that people with a mental disorder say these things. Mullins challenged her as to how they make this judgement without meeting and spending time with Haydn. It did appear to us this detective may well have got the outcome that they desired as she seemingly would not be told how to do her work by members of the public.

Just after this phone call, Haydn sent an email to his former wife Angela. In that email, he wrote, *Everything I told you about him was the absolute truth! I have been questioned, inter-rogated, tape-recorded, phone-called from Adelaide and had all sorts of ranking officers try to trick me into what I have said-have not said* [*sic*].

He also contacted his cousin after receiving a call from the South Australian detective, saying, 'Who in the fuck does this detective think they are asking me such a question over the phone? I have said all I had to say in my interview with Bill Hayes.' Due to this approach by the detective, it took us two years to regain his trust.

When at last Haydn was willing to once again speak with us, he advised that he had lied to the detective when he said that he had made up the story—he just wanted to get rid of them. But he had not made it up. He had told Bill Hayes the truth. He had told this same story to his son and his cousin as far back as the early 1990s, but no-one had taken him seriously until we had become involved.

In October 2011, Bill Hayes travelled to the Gold Coast and met with Angela Fyfe in the hope of convincing Haydn Phipps to agree to a second recorded interview. She was exactly as Bill had remembered her to be—truthful, honest, reliable, forthright, and trustworthy and asking for absolutely nothing from the process.

Angela had agreed to pick up Haydn and bring him to meet with Bill the following morning. The following day, Angela had, true to her word, gone and picked up Haydn and brought him back to the hotel to meet with Bill. When Angela brought him to Bill's suite, there were two surprises. The first was that Haydn commented that he hadn't believed that Bill was going to be at the hotel; the second was Bill's surprise at how much Haydn had deteriorated since he had last seen him. At their previous meeting, Haydn was sober, clean, well dressed, well fed, and alert. On this day, although it was only around 10 am, Haydn was obviously the worse for wear due to his alcohol intake. He was unshaven, gaunt, and dishevelled in drink- and food-stained clothing. This was a complete 180-degree turn from what he had been at their first meeting.

Bill sat him down and asked Angela to remain in the room because she obviously made Haydn feel safer. After insisting that Haydn have some water, Bill engaged him in casual conversation. Although Haydn was able to easily participate in this conversation, Bill made the decision that he would not, out of respect for Haydn and to ensure fairness and accuracy, record the interview as he had planned. The conversation took place over about thirty minutes, and then Bill decided to get Haydn home because he was rapidly tiring. It is fair to say that the conversation was friendly and left Bill feeling that he had once again been able to establish a rapport with Haydn. The three of them walked down to the front of the hotel and, when Angela went to get her car, out of the blue, Haydn said, 'Are you going to put these bastards in jail, Bill?'

It was interesting that Haydn used the plural 'bastards' as opposed to the singular 'bastard'. Bill explained that if Harry were solely responsible for the abduction and death of the Beaumont children, he could not go to jail because he was deceased. He further explained to Haydn that his and Mullins' desire was to find the children and return them to their elderly parents. The next comment Haydn made was, 'They are in the sandpit, Bill.'

This was a chilling statement made in a clear and strong manner by a man who had been through the wringer and in many ways was still going through it. Again, Bill had no doubt that Haydn was telling the truth as Haydn understood it to be. They were then joined by Angela, and Haydn said no more. That was the last time Bill saw either Angela or Haydn before their deaths.

Neither Haydn nor Angela were ever personally interviewed by police regarding their story in this sad case. A once-in-a-lifetime opportunity was lost. Sadly, this would prove to be the case with several potential witnesses, now deceased and forever silent. This is despite Angela Fyfe sending a detailed email to the Major Crime Investigation Branch in Adelaide. May they both rest in the peace that had eluded them in life.

Chapter 14:

Angela's Letter

Strong people stand up for themselves, but stronger people stand up for others.[54]

—Suzy Kassem

Below is a letter sent in 2016 by Angela Fyfe, Haydn Phipps's ex-wife, to the detective investigating the Beaumont case. According to Angela, she never received a reply, and she has now, sadly, passed away. The way in which this correspondence is written displays an individual who is respectful, articulate, intelligent, empathetic, and understanding. As Aleksandr Solzhenitsyn, Nobel Prize recipient for literature, once said, 'And the simple step of a courageous individual is not to partake in falsehood. One word of truth outweighs the world.'[55]

Dear Jim [not his real name],
Stuart Mullins passed on your email address. My name is Angela Fyfe, previously Phipps. I was married to Haydn Phipps for ten years between 1990 and 2000. My background is as a registered nurse for fifty years working in various community settings including a drug-and-alcohol detox centre in Melbourne and from 2000 until my retirement, at Palen Creek Correctional Centre as a forensic nurse. When I

first commenced work there in 2000, this was a low-security gaol for 60 percent sex offenders and 40 percent mainstream prisoners. In both these settings, I came to understand the impact of child sexual abuse and also to understand the psyche of paedophiles and their different reasons for offending. So, you could say I have experienced both sides of the coin.

Jim, you can feel free to reference-check me if you wish. I understand Stuart has already done this. The management who were there when I was employed is still there.

I initially contacted Alan Whiticker, author, after reading his 2006 book *Searching for the Beaumont Children*, for several reasons stated below in bullet point form. As a Victorian, I knew of the Beaumont murders but had little knowledge of Adelaide at the time of their disappearance, so found the book enlightening. So, by the time I read the book, it started to ring some alarm bells.

I am willing to undergo a lie detector test and am willing to be interviewed by the Major Crime Investigation Branch. I always have been, though I have never been contacted, even though I was apparently the first person Haydn revealed the extent and nature of the abuse he suffered and probably have the most detailed knowledge of Haydn's complex life and Harry's impact on that.

And, contrary to some opinions apparently expressed by a Major Crime Investigation Branch detective that I have heard about but never had said directly to me, I have/had no axe to grind and am frankly not interested in explaining or justifying myself to people about whom I don't care and, in some cases, have never met. My only interest was and is the truth and to possibly bring some closure to the Beaumonts before they pass over. Plus, some vindication for a man who spent his entire life in turmoil due to the house of horror in which he was raised so close to the area of the Beaumont disappearance.

1. Haydn stated to me back in the 90s while watching a program on the disappearance of the Beaumont children, 'I believe my father had something to do with that,' which caught me by surprise. I had a clear understanding of the proximity of Haydn's family's home (Isola) to the beach, Colley Reserve and the pie shop. By reading the book, things started to fall into place. Over the years of our volatile relationship, speaking to Haydn in depth and knowing first-hand Haydn's mannerisms and characteristics and having surmised a great deal about Harry's psyche, Harry's involvement became far more plausible. I felt uneasy and hence called the author Alan Whiticker, though not without some reluctance.

2. Haydn, over the ten years I was with him, was a mess at times, and something was always eating at him. He certainly hated his father, but conversely, as is often the case with abused children, he also loved him and craved Harry's approval. Haydn's mood swings, depressive states, alcohol abuse, and addictions to multiple drugs all worsened over the years as he revealed more and more details of the abuse he had suffered. Many times, over the years, I would have to wake him from lying face down in the pillow in panic mode breathing with difficulty, making muffled distressed sounds and not being able to move and in that mode he was hyper-vigilant/hypersensitive. If I was to touch him, he would react swiftly with a jolt and alarm. This, he later explained, was due to his reliving in dreams that suffocating feeling of his father's body on his during the night. Haydn stated he was sodomised three times per week for eight years.

3. Because of the method of construction (cement interior walls) of Isola, little sound from the street can be heard and no doubt the reverse is true.

4. I knew of Harry's habit of always carrying a money clip with a substantial amount of cash in it—mostly $50–$100

notes at the time I knew him. So, the information regarding the one-pound note was significant to me and as I am pre-decimal I knew few if any children of the Beaumont's' background would be given what was then a quite substantial amount of money. Harry Phipps was known to give this type of money out.

5. I knew what Harry looked like (even though he was aged sixty-five or so when I met him). I could see the identikit picture was a likeness in his brushed-back wavy hair, parted to one side, high forehead and his height. So, the description of Harry to me fitted what was in the book. He was known to be a regular swimmer at Glenelg also.

6. I believed Harry to be a particularly deviant and, in my opinion, psychopathic individual due to my experiences living with Haydn, whom I have absolutely no doubt was subject to sexual, emotional, and physical abuse during his childhood. The psychological game-playing continued all Haydn's adult life while Harry was alive and I have personal knowledge of that. I have had years of experience dealing with both paedophiles and the sexually abused to know Haydn was sexually abused by his father.

7. Henley Beach Club: Haydn was an avid sailor in his teen years with this club. I do not remember him telling me their colours were blue bathers with a white stripe; however, I read the man at the beach had bathers like this. Henley Beach Club, I believe, is the same colours.

8. I was called in the mid-to-late-90s by the second wife of Harry, Elizabeth Phipps, who asked me, 'Is it true the boys were sexually abused by Harry?' I replied, 'How could I know for sure? I wasn't there at the time.' However, Haydn certainly exhibited the symptoms of someone who has been sexually abused.

9. I had discussions with two in-laws who stated Olga, Haydn's mother, would never allow any of their children to sleep at Isola, a fact the in-laws assumed related to Harry's

sexual habits such as his satin fetish. In the context of Haydn's sexual abuse, I regarded this as a significant admission.

10. Haydn would speak to me of Harry's satin fetish, which he learned about from his mother when he was about eleven years old. According to Haydn, Harry was a very clever designer and excellent seamstress, making all his own satin dresses, not so much kaftans and an array of what he termed 'sick' costumes including codpieces. According to Haydn, a copy of the Phantom costume [was] a particular favourite, apparently. Harry had bolts of fabric and several sewing machines at Isola and also at a cottage in the grounds of Castalloy. A few years before his death, Harry made Haydn promise to destroy all evidence of this idiosyncrasy so his reputation wasn't destroyed after his death. Haydn was unable to fulfil this. This was according to Haydn who confided in me.

11. I met Harry on several occasions and was wary of him, great in the public eye quite different in private.

12. Haydn most definitely mentioned the [Beaumont] children and a sandpit. To me, Haydn suggested the children were buried at Isola under sand and then concrete as a pit in the garage had been filled in with concrete in the week after their disappearance. Castalloy's green sandpit was another option mentioned. But Haydn mentioned 'sandpit' as far back as the 90s several times.

13. In 1991, I had spoken to a doctor in Adelaide, a psychiatrist who Haydn had consulted with sometimes and he told me that Haydn had never exhibited any signs of psychosis but was extremely angry and, if I knew anything about the family dynamics, I would understand why and that his anger was justified. Haydn certainly hated his father.

14. Haydn was admitted to Bundaberg psychiatric ward at the time using the powers of the police then subsequently transferred to Prince Charles Hospital in Brisbane at the suggestion of Doctor Williams [not his real name], the only psychiatrist in Bundaberg with the agreement of his

then GP. After this time, Haydn consulted with a number of doctors, psychiatrists and some counsellors. However, Haydn had stated once to me that if he really faced/admitted the truth of the extent of the abuse he had suffered, he would permanently lose his mind. Due to this fear, which I have subsequently discovered is a common fear in abused persons, Haydn never really was able to be free of the horror of his childhood and increasingly was unable to lead a normal life.

As Haydn and I were divorced at the time of Harry Phipps' passing, we had only sporadic contact. I had absolutely no expectations of being included in his will. Harry was also aware I did not hold a very high opinion of him and was never interested in his money. Please note, during my years with Haydn, I tried to have minimal contact with all members of the Phipps family, especially as I became more aware of the truth behind the façade of a happy one. Haydn seldom referred to Harry as Dad or Father. At the time, I was admittedly sceptical, although I believed Harry to be a paedophile; however, not all such criminals resort to murder. Haydn would never have gone to the police believing, as he did, in Harry's power. [Harry] had an Order of Australia and Haydn knew few would take his word against Harry's.

The above is true and as mentioned I would be fine talking directly with you.

Regards, Angela

PS I have met Bill Hayes; feel free to discuss me with him.

Angela has been interviewed several times at length by us. She has also been interviewed and filmed by Channel 7 for *The Beaumont Children: What Really Happened*. Statement-analysis experts, criminologists, private investigators, and investigative journalists present stated that Angela was truthful at all times. Neither Angela nor Bill were contacted by police as a result of this letter.

Chapter 15:
The Polygraph Expert

The only people who are mad at you for speaking the
truth are those people that are living a lie.

—Anonymous

Polygraph examiners are better known to the public as lie detector operators, who conduct polygraph tests, better known as lie detector tests. They aim to determine the receptiveness of an individual taking a polygraph exam. These polygraphs are used by police departments worldwide; however, the results are not admissible in court. In 2011, we approached Steve Van Aperen, an internationally accredited Australian polygraph expert who is sometimes affectionally referred to as the 'human lie detector'. They were aware Steve trained with and examined polygraph testing and behavioural interview techniques utilised by the Federal Bureau of Investigation (FBI) and US Secret Service, to name a few. He has also assisted the police in seventy-eight homicide investigations and two serial killer cases. Steve was well aware of this case, as he provided consultation services to the Victoria Police homicide squad and the SA Police Major Crime Squad. He was well aware of the effect of abduction and disappearance on the Australian psyche. Hence, Steve was very interested in receiving and analysing Haydn Phipps' recorded interview and made himself available to the authors over the years when required. After examining the interview several times, he said:

> There was nothing that I observed or detected in the transcript or the recording in Mr Phipps' responses that indicated to me that he was being deceptive, evasive, fabricating or embellishing his version of events on 26 January 1966.

Steven states:

> When a person lies, they often do so by omission rather than commission. That is, we become evasive when answering a question rather than directly lying to it. This is the selective editing process taking part. In other words, deceptive people will often edit the information they supply, being careful not to divulge information that may implicate them in wrongdoing or deceit.
>
> In many cases, deceptive people will edit themselves out of the story, create distance, avoid providing content and detail and fail to answer questions altogether. During the analysis of an interview, I look for either qualifying statements, avoidance, deflection or blaming a bad or poor memory.
>
> Neurologically truthful people only need to rely on the facts or experiences that they lived through. In contrast, deceptive people need to fabricate, embellish, invent or create a false memory. Overall, lying requires cognitive loading and processing and a very good memory. A deceptive individual takes time to answer questions as they do not want

to trip themselves up. They must remember what they have previously said, which may contradict earlier statements.

Bill and Stuart agree Haydn did not do this. He took ownership of what was happening.

That is, Haydn was reliving what happened that fateful day in 1966. Mr Van Aperen does not dispute the sexual abuse had occurred. Haydn described his feelings and emotions directly and succinctly, which clearly displayed the hatred, animosity, and disdain he harboured towards his father as, in his words, 'Haydn's emotions are in the right place'. Steve has no doubts at all when listening to the 1.5-hour recording that Harry Phipps was a paedophile. When Mr Aperen spoke with Frank Pangallo and was filmed by *Today Tonight*, Frank asked Steve the question, 'How much credence can we place on Haydn Phipps' story?'

Steve replied:

I did not detect any inconsistencies in Mr Phipps' narrative or recollection of events. In those areas where there were any inconsistencies or doubt, they were examined and clarified by further questioning by Mr Hayes. Also, I can only test on factual information. I cannot test on a feeling or thought, opinion, or belief. I can only test on black and white and test on the veracity of the conversation that took place.[23]

Steve stated to Frank after analysing a recorded interview that Haydn Phipps was being truthful, which adds more credibility to Haydn's account. However, Steve believed, as do we, that Haydn was not telling the total truth. He was hiding something which appeared to relate to the children, the Castalloy cottages, and the sandpit. On a side note, Steve asked us if South Australian detectives had met and interviewed Haydn due to the vital information he had. When informed that a detective had only called Haydn over the phone, he was gobsmacked, asking, 'How can this detective make an informed decision by not meeting him and gauging his body language and verbal clues and non verbal clues?'

Also, in November 2015, Haydn's son Nicholas agreed to a polygraph test administered by Steve in front of cameras with journalist Frank Pangallo for Adelaide's *Today Tonight* current affairs programme. Nicholas was also tested on the veracity of his accounts when asked questions regarding living under the same roof as his father and grandfather Harry, and also whether Haydn had ever spoken to him regarding his sexual abuse, and what his father told him about what happened to the Beaumont children.

Nicholas replied that Haydn was convinced that Harry had killed the children and that they were taken to Castalloy, and that his father did speak about his sexual abuse. Nicholas also spoke about seeing a myriad of satin garments around the house and stated that, out of the house and in public, Harry was seen as an upstanding businessman, but he was the most aggressive person you would want to lay your eyes on when the doors were closed in the house. After analysing the results, Steve stated to journalist Frank Pangallo he did not doubt in his mind Nicholas was being truthful about his recollections and conversation between he and his father. In the same year, we were contacted by a lady who introduced herself as Mandy (surname withheld) from Europe, a former uniform police officer before becoming a homicide detective, where she began training with FBI profilers. Mandy had developed such an interest in this field that she had become recognised as something of a pioneer and has been involved with initiatives and developments of new methods and techniques.

Some of the areas involved included missing persons, cold cases, videotaped interrogations, second opinions, coaching interrogators, and text analysis. In 2005, she graduated with the first-ever Master of Criminal Investigation (MCI). She trained in text analyses. With this experience, she returned to university, having decided to study criminology.

In 2019, she became a Registered OSINT Investigation Analysis Expert (ROSIE) and graduated with a Master in Criminology (MSc). Mandy also introduced her colleague Yvette, who ran a private investigation company specialising in statement analysis. After reading *The Satin Man: Uncovering the Mystery of the Missing Beaumont Children*, they became aware of the unsolved case. Both Mandy and Yvette (surnames withheld for privacy reasons) were immediately struck by how close Harry Phipps lived to Colley Reserve and Wenzel's Bakery. They were mindful of distance decay, which reflects that criminals are more likely to commit crimes nearer their anchor point, the home residence, rather than further away, since travel requires time and effort. Due to this, they believed that whoever abducted the children lived close to Colley Reserve. Hence, they said, Harry Phipps ticked many boxes. Stuart forwarded Bill Hayes' recorded interview and Haydn Phipps' former wife Angela's email for their analysis.

Their analysis was impressive and correlated closely with Steve Van Aperen's. Here are some salient points Mandy and Yvette made:

1. 'I could hear the swishing of the satin coming down the hallway.' Haydn is clearly reliving this nightmare scenario and articulating the sounds, the timing and how he felt.
2. Haydn did not use the word *disappearance* during the interview. He calls it a situation or problem. Something he expected to have been solved by the police. Not calling it a disappearance is very plausible if he 'knows' (whether it is true or not) where the children are.

3. Haydn says, 'I didn't think it would go this far to be quite honest with you.' And that it is more likely that something did not go the way Haydn assumed it would go.

4. The number of words Haydn uses talking about seeing the Beaumont Children in his backyard. 'They came in from the backyard', 'They all had the same haircuts', 'They had bright coloured towels, yellows and orange like', 'I first thought they were three girls as they all had the same haircuts', and 'Harry must have been fucking around putting his bloody dresses in the back of the boot of the car, and they copped—copped him doing it and I don't know, well—see, a lot—a fair bit of time went past, a fair bit of time went past, like, we didn't really take that much—we didn't pay that much attention to what was going on and we just sort of thought, like, oh, the old prick will take them down to the bloody tram stop or whatever to do—take them—take them home or whatever he'll do, and that was it'. Haydn appears to be blurring between the two, which may well be due to the time that has passed since the abduction. After using the term 'copped', Haydn accelerates in language. That means that he's jumping over time: 'and they copped—copped him doing it and I don't know, well—see, a lot—a fair bit of time went past, a fair bit of time went past, like, we didn't really take that much. 'This acceleration is something that we often see when it comes to the part when it all went wrong: the crime, the incident itself. This is where his mood changes. Who is the 'we' and 'they' Haydn is referring to?

5. Haydn states, 'We really thought that it would not come this far.' And that the children must have 'copped his father'. It is crucial to clarify who he meant with 'we'. And copped him doing what?

6. Most strikingly are the many times Haydn comes up with the 'open front door' in his statement. He uses passive language, like the front door was left open on most occasions. This is an indication of concealing identity. It's like he's telling us, 'I thought the kids went out by themselves.' This could be at Isola or at Castalloy Mooringe Avenue. The front door of the two houses could be the only way out from the Castalloy property for the children without anyone noticing. Therefore, the front door could serve as an alibi for both Harry and Haydn to say, 'Well, I thought the kids had left by themselves.'

7. Bill: 'Okay. How long were they inside for?' Haydn: 'Um, well, that's when it all sort of rolled into one, you know, like, um, that's it, you know, that's it. It's just they went inside. I don't remember them coming out.' This, *I don't remember*, is often used for something that, in reality, was extremely important.

8. In Haydn's words, 'they are in the sandpit', which appears to be behind the two cottages facing Mooringe Ave at the Castalloy factory. Later, he says, 'They dug the wrong spot', referring to the 2013 dig at the back of the Castalloy factory carried out by the South Australia Major Crime Investigation Branch detectives.

9. The two old houses or cottages on Castalloy property at Mooringe Avenue. This spot is important to him and is mentioned many times in his statement. Haydn tells Bill Hayes the four acres of sand in front of the cottages is a dump. But later, his language around that spot goes from four acres of sand and a drop-off to more profane words: 'shit' and 'hell' to, finally, 'a shit pit'. That implicates that his feelings toward this place have changed negatively.

10. Bill: 'Okay. So, can you tell me any more about Harry's dressing now?' Haydn: 'No, he just continued on a journey, and I think his mother encouraged it. I think she made him the outfits and dresses and encouraged him to be a girl and mix with girls and the whole scene just—his mother was a sick— She encouraged it.' Haydn's description of his father fits the witness accounts in 1966 that the person of interest seen with the kids at Colley Reserve was *dressing* the children, and the kids allowed him to do so. According to Haydn, he and his brother would watch his father engage in deviant behaviour while wearing his satin dresses. His father was not embarrassed, as he didn't know that they were watching him. The behaviour happened in the attic and downstairs, where he had a workshop. 'There was a big X-ray cabinet that my grandfather had built, and he'd stash it full of dresses. He would shoot up the stairs, and we used to be able to watch him, what was going on from the laundry where we had a copper tub. We used to be able to hide in there and watch him and what he was doing.' What Haydn is saying appears truthful due to his use of words that indicate again he is reliving a past event that happened to him. He is speaking from memory.

11. In speaking with Bill, Haydn does remember the fact January 26th 1966 was a 'bloody hot day; as hot as hell', saying to Bill, 'It must have been a hundred degrees.' Why was this day so special that he remembered how hot it was? This day, to Haydn, may have related to a particular activity or sighting. The day must have had significance for him to have said that.

12. Haydn never refers to the incident as a 'disappearance'. He calls it a 'situation', a 'problem', or a 'loss' of the children. One of the striking remarks Haydn makes is 'I never thought it would go this far, to be quite honest with you'. That implies that something got out of hand. But what? He also mentions that 'there has been a lot of enlightenment to him on what happened subsequently'. What enlightenment? Caused by what and subsequently to what?

13. Haydn further advised that soon after coming back from inside the house, Harry 'took off with all his bags in the back of the car. So I just thought he was going down to work with his bags in the car'. To Haydn, Harry may have had something in mind and witnessed this unfold.

    In his interview with Bill, Haydn shows anger towards his father's behaviour when at the beach with friends and their young daughters; 'He'd rub himself with his bathers on up against their bodies and things like that, that's not normal, man. That's just not normal. I hated him for that.'

In conclusion, even though Haydn at times blurred the lines due to the time that had passed, it does appear he was telling the truth about seeing the children in his backyard that day and about being sexually abused. Something bad was going on at the factory. However, this is where he clams up. Steve Van Aperen appears to agree.

Chapter 16:
Another Victim

Childhood should be carefree, playing in the sun; not living a nightmare in the darkness of the soul.[56]

—Dave Pelzer

In late 2017, a cousin of Bill Hayes living in Victoria contacted him with a startling story. This relative had been reading *The Satin Man: Uncovering the Mystery of the Missing Beaumont Children* and found it intriguing. When called out of his office, he left the paperback on his desk, and a female colleague, Linda (not her real name), passed by and noticed the book. Later, she confided to Bill's cousin that she once lived across the road from the Castalloy factory and believed she had pertinent information about the at-the-time unnamed suspect described in the book.

Hayes' cousin immediately got in touch with him, leading to a compelling, yet disturbing, conversation between Linda and Bill. Over the years, we had personally met and spoken to many individuals regarding Harry Phipps. Many could be discounted; however, some struck a chord with them. Linda was one of those people.

Hayes met with Linda at her residence in Victoria. After spending part of a day talking with her, he organised, with her permission, for her story to be videotaped by Channel 7 News for *The Beaumont Children: What Really Happened.* What followed was alarming to Hayes, the film crew, and the investigative journalists present.

Linda grew up in the 1970s in a house directly across the road from the Castalloy factory on Mooringe Avenue, North Plympton, South Australia—a factory that Harry Phipps once owned. Linda, a child of European migrant parents, described the street as basically in an industrial area, with their home being one of the few domestic premises. Linda didn't know what was made or done in the factory. She did know that it was a big factory and she used to sit out the front of her house sometimes and watch the cars go in and out. During the working week, the factories were noisy during the day, but after 5 pm, the streets were deserted. From Saturday afternoon until Monday morning, it was tranquil.

She remembered one particular day in 1979 when she was about thirteen years old, a day that sits embedded in her memory. Linda's best friend lived on Kinkaid Avenue around the corner behind the Castalloy factory. Linda used to run to and from her friend's home regularly after school, which would take two to three minutes, sharing homework or working on assignments set by their teacher. On this particular day, it was daylight saving, which occurs during the summer period in South Australia. The days are long, with the sun setting around 8 pm. Linda was wearing her school uniform, which included a short dress in line with the way high-school girls dressed in the 1970s.

On this particular afternoon, Linda needed to get some information for homework and upcoming exams, so at about 4 pm she ran over to her friend's place. Linda remained there longer than she had intended, and when she realised she would be late she called her mother from a nearby public phone box to let her know where she was. Her mother emphasised the need for Linda to be home before her father returned from work. He was a strict disciplinarian who was not shy about physically disciplining his daughter in a forceful manner that would be considered unacceptable by today's standards. Her mother was frightened of her husband and would not say or do anything that might provoke his anger. Linda fully understood the urgency.

Leaving her friend's place later than expected, she quickly ran around the corner of Kinkaid Avenue, turning onto Streeters Road, which runs along the side of the Castalloy factory and then joins Mooringe Avenue. She didn't like that time of night when everything was shut down and the streets felt eerie.

Running down Streeters Road, she remembered a large tree and a man standing and looking as if he were expecting her. She had realised it was the same man she and her friend had seen on several occasions standing on the corner of Mooringe Avenue and Streeters Road outside the Castalloy offices watching them as they walked to school. Linda would wait for her friend to come down Streeters Road from her home in Kinkaid Avenue in the morning, and they would meet there and go on to school together.

Over about four weeks, they had seen him on ten or eleven occasions standing there watching them. He would wave to them and smile. In her innocence, she took this to mean that the man must know her, so she would wave and smile back. Linda had never seen him come or go from the Castalloy building, but he seemed to be from there.

Recalling the particular night that changed her life forever, she noted that he was wearing dark grey pants and a shirt and tie; he smelled nice and clean. She noticed he had a screwdriver in his hand, which he put into his pocket. She didn't think anything of it, because she was an innocent, naïve teenager in the 1970s, and this was compounded by her upbringing at the hands of her strict European parents.

Upon approaching Linda, the man placed his arm around her shoulder and guided her across the street towards a vacant block of land at the corner of Streeters Road and Mooringie Avenue. The man spoke gently to her, asking how she was, telling her that he had seen her around and that she was a pretty little girl. He was persuasive, but Linda knew that something wasn't right; she was confused because he was so pleasant, telling her again and again that she was pretty but at the same time controlling and coercing her to keep moving towards the vacant block. He didn't explain to Linda why he was walking her across the road, but it soon became apparent to her what he intended to do.

Linda said that at the time, there was no reason for her to fight him. He wasn't horrible or rough as he walked alongside her, which left her feeling confused and conflicted. What made her even more uneasy was the fact that the area was deserted. So many thoughts raced through her mind. She didn't want to make this man angry, but she was also thinking that if her father found out she had gone with this man, she would get in trouble and perhaps even earn a few whacks with the leather belt for good measure.

When they reached the other side of the street, the man took her onto the vacant block, back behind some large, high dirt mounds that the local children used as a bike ramp. It was early evening, though, so no-one else was there. He led her behind the highest dirt mound and out of sight from both Streeters Road and Mooringe Avenue. There, he started to touch her. His mannerisms rapidly changed as he ushered her to the ground— not in a rough way, but helping her to sit down with a little bit of force. She described it as being similar to how you would push a dog's bottom down to get them to sit.

Linda was terrified and wondering how she was going to get herself out of that terrible situation. The man was very much in control. She was a little naïve but understood what was going on. Linda would look back and say she certainly lacked street smarts by today's standards. He continued to speak to her the whole time, controlling Linda with his words and tone. He told Linda that all she had to do was to sit there on the ground, that she was a pretty girl, that he had been watching her in the mornings going to school.

Soon, he became a little more forceful and started sexually touching her. His talking had become more subdued. As he was touching her, he said things like, 'This is all right, this is just showing you that I think that you are a pretty girl and I like you,' and, 'I am just showing you that I like you.'

Linda was a virgin and utterly inexperienced in any sexual way. She was a young, naïve teenager enjoying school and time with her friends. What this man was saying became worse, and the things that he was doing to her became terrible. Throughout this time, he was becoming sexually aroused, and then he raped her. As he was raping her vaginally, he used foul language. He could not finish the attack by just raping her vaginally, so he turned her over and raped her anally. He was then able to climax. Linda was unaware of just how long the whole attack took, but afterwards she recalls him becoming wholly wrapped up in himself, aggressive and closed off, as if she were to blame, saying things like, 'Now see what you made me do,' and, 'You got my pants dirty. You got dirt on my shirt.'

The place where the rape had occurred was very dusty, and all the man seemed to care about was his appearance. He ignored the fact that Linda was crying and that her school uniform was filthy. He didn't show any concern for her and the fact that her knees were scraped and bloodied, she had gravel rash, and she was bleeding from the rape. He was only concerned that his clothes had got dirty, and he blamed her for that, saying to Linda in a terse voice, 'See what you have done!' as he brushed the dust off his trousers.

On reflection, going through Linda's mind at this time was the silliest thing: as the man was trying to remove her underwear, she felt embarrassed about him seeing her white cottontails. As a grown woman, she felt that this was stupid of her, given what was happening, but in her confused young teenage state, that was how she felt. She also didn't think that the man was wearing underwear. Linda could not understand why he was so obsessed with his appearance and dirtying his clothes. Once done, he turned and walked away. She couldn't remember in which direction. Linda remained there for a while grazed, bruised, dazed, and distraught trying to make sense of what just occurred. With the benefit of hindsight in processing her rape, Linda concluded that it was all about him—his nice clothing and the soiling of his attire; nothing else mattered but him.

In the aftermath, Linda recalled getting home just before seven o'clock. What was usually a two-minute walk felt like two hours. The entire rape started between 6 and 6.30 pm, and by the time he had finished with her, she had settled down enough to make her way home.

As Linda walked through the door, her main concern was still about getting home before her dad did. Being raised in a European culture before emigrating to Australia, the father was the master of the house. Her mother did not question her dishevelled state; she merely told her to clean up before her father returned home. Linda did not say anything to her mother about what had happened but felt that her mother knew something wasn't right. Her mother appeared more preoccupied with getting dinner on the table to coincide with her husband arriving home—a sign of the times.

Linda felt that if she said anything to her father, he would either dismiss her story or belt her and tell her that she shouldn't have been there, that it was her fault for leading the man on. Linda then bottled this emotion up and said nothing to anyone. There was no form of safety or sanctuary in her home. She could not tell anyone because she was too scared. Also, who would believe her? She was trapped. She imagined the police visiting her residence to be greeted by her father. Of course, he would be nice while they were present, but as soon as they left he would bring out the leather belt, blaming Linda for what happened and also for the shame of the police arriving at their door. What would the neighbours say? Her stomach knotted in fear. Reporting the assault to the police at the time was not an option.

Only after a couple of years had passed did Linda see this man again on the same street corner. She had ignored him and walked in the other direction. At the age of seventeen, Linda could not live with the knowledge that she was living across the road from this predator and decided to leave home. She moved as far away as possible, but no matter where she moved, the memory of her rape remained imprisoned within her. This horrific event has affected every relationship she has had, and there seems to be nothing she could do about it. After Linda left her home, she lost control. She was drinking to excess, rebelling, and generally being troublesome. The couple she boarded with were kind to her and cared for her and were concerned about her behaviour, so they spoke with her about it.

For once, Linda decided to open up, not totally but enough to let them know about the rape. With her friends' support, she organised for a police officer to visit the house and speak with her about the assault. Upon the police officer attending and chatting with Linda, she was advised that the likelihood of bringing this man to justice was minimal due to the passage of time and lack of corroborative and forensic evidence. He also informed her that she would need to be medically examined and of the effects this may have on her.

The officer said he was willing to take her statement if she wished to make one, but after consideration, she decided to let it go. The deck was stacked against her. The predator would be believed over her. The officer is not to blame; this was the early 1980s. Pointing the finger at the clergy, the school teacher, the business leader, the politician, or the swimming coach was unheard of. Anyone who did was disbelieved and ridiculed. Over recent years, attitudes and processes have changed, which has encouraged once-reluctant sexual-abuse victims to tell their stories. Now they know that help is there.

In Linda's case, she was watching the news on television with her housemate when a story came on regarding the Beaumont children. They showed a picture of the Castalloy factory and Harry Phipps. She immediately stood up, with her stomach churning, her heart pounding and her head spinning. Linda pointed at the television exclaiming, 'That's him! That's the man that used to stand on the corner.'

Then she heard that they were digging up the area, so she rang her mother and asked her what was going on at Castalloy. She said, 'They think the Beaumont kids are there.' Linda finally told her mother about the rape, and that this man on the television was the man who had attacked her that day she had arrived home dusty and dirty. Her mother replied that Linda was lucky to be alive. In one terrible sense, Linda's mother was right, but in another sense, Linda felt that her mother didn't seem to care.

Linda later told Bill that she didn't know who this man was back then and had not asked him his name, nor did she know that he worked at the Castalloy factory. However, she instantly recognised him when his photograph was shown on the nightly news. Linda was in no doubt that the man who raped her was Harry Phipps.

Linda had moved on with her life as best she could, never speaking about what had happened—but she was now willing to do so. If Harry Phipps was involved in the disappearance of the Beaumont children, Linda realised that what had happened to her that day had likely happened to others. She hoped that by speaking out she might give others who had been abused by Phipps, or his associates, the courage and strength to do the same. She is confident that she would not have been his only victim. If this is so—and the authors believe it is—speaking up would help finally solve this mystery and also give everyone, particularly the parents of the children and other potential victims of Phipps, some closure.

We and experts who were present at the interview applaud Linda for coming to them and telling her story. She has named Phipps as her abuser in order to give herself some closure and obtain a release from the physical and mental pain that she has endured throughout her life since this rape.

Coming out with her story has indeed opened up old psycho-logical wounds, and at times she has fallen back into depression. However, close family members who had not been aware of what Linda had gone through now are. They have shown her love, compassion, and support. How many more are there who need the same understanding, love, and support for having to endure something that was not and never could be their fault, and are continuing to suffer in silence because of their treatment at the hands of a monster?

We hope that Linda will now feel some sense of relief and closure in finally getting to tell her story. It is also hoped that her courage in coming forward will provide guidance and encouragement for others to do the same and to report their abuse for some good to come out of this heartbreaking story.

Chapter 17:
Victims of Sexual Abuse

The impact of my dad's offending has had far-reaching effects and the ramifications have destroyed my life. He has sent a wrecking ball through my hopes and dreams.[57]

—Jeni Haynes

For decades, sexual abuse perpetrated against children went unchecked. The perpetrator went about their business unhampered, supremely confident their predatory paedophilic ways would remain hidden and disguised by the façade of a suit and tie, religious robes, or behind an entertainer's song-and-dance routine, all the while robbing the child of their potential and bright future.

We have learned over the last fourteen years that the debilitating effect child sexual abuse has on the victim is devastating. Most suffer irreparable mental and physical damage from these horrific acts of exploitation and remain in tortured silence for the rest of their lives. Many fall into alcohol and substance abuse as a coping mechanism; some turn to crime to feed their habits. All suffer from years of depression and chronic anxiety that manifests itself in lifelong low self-esteem. Victims become withdrawn and experience feelings of worthlessness.

They enter into relationships that soon become dysfunctional; marriages end up irreparable and broken. The survivors exhibit self-destructive behaviours and unexplained acts of anger and rage. Many suffer from suicidal tendencies and inflict self-harm. They experience unsettled sleep patterns and constant restlessness. Many are hypervigilant to the slightest touch. All are tormented by nightmares of the abuse. Holding down a job becomes difficult. As they grow older, mental health and physical issues become more pronounced. Their reliance on prescription medicines and regular visits to their GP and psychologist increase.

Child sexual abuse has a permanent effect, setting off a chain of events that lasts the duration of the victim's life. This horrific abuse not only cripples the survivor but can also split families and pit one sibling or relative against the other—a tragedy in the making. This has been the experience of Haydn Phipps, Linda, and another survivor of Phipps whom Bill is working with.

Most survivors of sexual abuse never tell anyone, fearful of the possibility of retaliation and further abuse once the perpetrator finds out. They have an overriding fear they will not be believed. As adults, many feel shame and embarrassment. Many could not face the humiliation that might be encountered if others found out. Instead, they leave things be—let sleeping dogs lie.

Others take solace in speaking privately to their medical practitioner, as Haydn did. Stuart obtained his medical reports after Haydn passed away several years ago. In places, Haydn speaks openly to his doctor regarding his abuse. The doctor states in writing, 'Haydn says he has continual disturbing dreams about his father abusing him in sexual and other ways.' Reporting a conversation between him and Haydn, he wrote, 'Haydn experienced sexual abuse during his childhood that has significantly impacted his health as an adult. This had led to anxiety attacks, depression, panic attacks, alcoholism, and chronic lower back pain.' It should also be noted the same doctor stated Haydn showed no significant cognitive or impaired judgement.

Some victims remain silent due to family loyalty. Simply put, one should not upset the apple cart. Others have a misplaced sense of self-blame for the abuse. The survivor believes that in some way they may have caused the violation. A comprehensive psychiatric study of the abused by Shirley Jülich was published in the *Journal of Child Sexual Abuse* in 2005 found that it is not unusual for the child to develop feelings for the paedophile,[58] which was not unlike Haydn, who held on to a lifelong desire for his father's approval and acceptance. When working at the Castalloy factory, he appeared torn between rage and the need for his father's approval.

The sexually abused will make concessions to decipher the good and bad behaviour of the perpetrator, trying to justify the predator's deviant behaviour out of sympathy, asking themselves whether they might have provoked it. Feeling they are in part responsible, they show concern for the paedophile's welfare. The survivor then becomes emotionally attached to their abuser. Haydn Phipps' attachment to his father is a classic example: there he was, giving an emotive eulogy at his father's funeral. Yet some of those attending knew of his hatred for his father. When meeting with Bill Hayes and relating his story, Haydn said on several occasions that it wasn't fair on his father for him to tell Bill the things that he was telling him 'as Harry is not here to defend himself'.

Haydn Phipps was terrified of Harry's regular night-time visitations, but he could not escape his horrific ordeal. His father threatened Haydn's physical and psychological survival if he ever spoke out. With nowhere to go and no-one to speak to, he was held as an unwilling compliant plaything by his captor. This deliberate isolation from others leads the survivor back to the abuser. They then seek nurturing and protection. Survivors can take this road while others, even at an early age, take their own lives. In the 1960s, 70s, and 80s, there were few escapes.

Haydn took the road that led back to Isola after his first marriage break-up. He had nowhere to go and was low on cash. Also, he was aware that if he got Harry offside, he could do him damage financially and socially. So, Haydn moved back into Isola with his young son, Nicholas. However, both were still very aware of Harry Phipps' sexual satin fetishes and no-go Saturdays.

Shirley Jülich's report on Stockholm syndrome can assist all of us in understanding why some victims become compliant and in part why they blame themselves for the predator's behaviour. Although this syndrome is usually linked with a kidnap or hostage situation, this also relates to some victims of child sexual abuse.[58]

Several people have pointed the finger at Haydn, suggesting he should have spoken out sooner. However, according to Darkness to Light child sexual abuse statistics, only thirty-eight percent of child victims disclose the fact they were abused.[21] The overriding fear is not being believed and the anxiety of losing the offender. The culprit may be important to the child or the child's family—the loving father or big brother or sister, the kind uncle or aunt, the local clergyman or clergywoman, or the friendly neighbour. They also do not tell anyone due to an offender's threat to hurt or kill them or someone they love, or the common fear that no-one will believe them and that they (the child) will get in trouble. Of course, this is always done by stealth. Abusers are the masters of manipulation.

The offender is most often an adult. Perhaps surprisingly, juveniles are offenders in up to 40% of cases. Offenders, be they adult or juvenile, can quickly and effectively shame and embarrass their victim, whether the victim is a child or an adult, castigating them for their disparaging and hurtful accusations. Hence the victims' desire to protect the offender and, in turn, defend themselves from any further public scrutiny.

Others do not wish to relive their darkest moments—moments that have all but destroyed their life. Hence a few pay an enormous price for perpetrators' sexual depravity. Adults who have a history of child sexual abuse are more than twice as likely to report a suicide attempt. What's also frightening is that the abuser is usually someone known to the victim—a parent or sibling, an uncle, teacher, scoutmaster, swim coach, or the local priest. How does a child victim try to comprehend that this sometimes loved, trusted, likeable, helpful individual is evil? In 2014, the Australian Institute of Family Studies found that ninety-five percent of sexual assaults are committed by someone known to the victim and often occur in the victim's or predator's home.

If the child or teenager speaks out, they are more likely to tell a close friend due to their profound distrust of authority figures. These friend-to-friend discussions do not always result in reports to the police. In the 1960s and 1970s, sexual abuse of minors and paedophilia was not a subject raised publicly, and the reporting would have been close to zero percent.

Institutions also failed to protect the child, most notably religious orders. They turned a blind eye to this inexcusable behaviour, moving the predator priest from diocese to diocese—not only poisoning the local pond but now the lakes and rivers. The clergy, corporate and media companies, and sometimes the extended families were more concerned with protecting their reputations than the victim.

Neither Haydn Phipps nor Linda stood a chance. The scale of sexual abuse in the 1950s, 1960s, 1970s and beyond was unimaginable. There are so many unseen and unheard victims, so many bystanders who allowed this abuse to continue and who regret not coming forward for fear of the impact on their family's reputation. These days have long gone. If you do not stand up for something, you will fall for anything.

As Freyana Irani wrote in an article in *The Australian* article titled 'No excuse for staying silent' on 15 December 2017, 'To change the future, we must do all that we can in the present to eradicate the failed responses of the past.'[59]

Child sexual abuse reports should be made to the state's child protection unit or directly to the police. Times have very much changed. You will be listened to and believed.

Chapter 18:
The Factory Dig

*My God, no man who was making this up would dare
be so tormented and worried as wanting the facts to
be corrected.*

—Brady Halls (email to authors on 28 April 2020)

On 5 September 2013, Alan Whiticker received an email from a David H, who had purchased a copy of *The Satin Man* and was disturbed to find out the Satin Man was indeed Harry Phipps. His email suggested he had 'some information' he thought Whiticker, Stuart Mullins, and Bill Hayes 'may be quite interested in'. In this email, David had a very interesting story to tell. He had been ringing the South Australia Police 'Crime Stoppers' line and leaving messages but had not received any response up to that time; later, he did get a response.

David and his brother Rob, born in June 1950 and November 1948 respectively, lived in North Plympton during the late 1950s, 1960s, and 1970s. During their teenage years, David and Rob worked at different odd jobs, from selling *Football Budgets* (a local sporting magazine sold at Australian Rules football games) to working as pin boys at the Glenelg Bowling Alley (where Haydn Phipps had also worked in a casual, after-school position, though they were not known to each other). They also picked up quite a bit of labouring work from a local builder. In addition to that, they did an activity through the Boy Scouts known as 'Bob a Job' work. David recalled a particular job that he and Rob had done at the Castalloy factory. As David recalled it, his father did some contractor work at Castalloy in the mid-1960s as a plumber, then had later gone on to work at a local council as a building inspector.

Initially, David found it difficult to pin down the year they undertook this job at Castalloy. Both David and Rob remember riding their bikes to get there, and that they would have been aged fifteen and seventeen.

Neither of the boys could remember much of the man who employed them for this job in terms of a description, but they did remember they had to dig a hole in the sandy area at the back of the Castalloy factory. It was a hot weekend, and the site was deserted. The hole was about their height or more in depth, a metre or so wide, and about two metres long, and the boys were supplied with shovels by the man who let them onto the site through a large, locked gate. It was definitely in sand, and it took them two full days to complete because the sides kept falling in. After the first day, the man came and looked into the hole and told them that it needed to be much deeper and to come back the next day; David clearly recalled that the man made it clear they had to have the hole dug out and finished over a weekend while the factory was closed.

Several times during the two days that they worked, the man drove a car into the area; he was the only occupant. He would remain in his car on the site and stare at them. He never spoke to the boys—he would watch for a while and then drive off.

Though physical details of the man aren't clear for David or Rob now, they recalled that the car he drove was green or similar in colour and was large with big rear fins and chrome—the car stood out because it wasn't the type often seen in Adelaide at that time. Phipps drove a Pontiac Parisienne at that time, a large US car with fins and lots of chrome and was dark green in colour.

They also knew approximately where they had dug the hole and could mark the area on a photograph if necessary. The other thing David remembered was that compared with other jobs that he and Rob had undertaken, they were very well paid. They were used to receiving a few shillings but, in this case, it was pounds (he couldn't recall the exact amount), a very large sum of money at that time. When the work was complete, the man told the boys to 'fuck off you little cunts and never come back'.

At that time and at their age, 'stranger danger' was unknown; however, they both remembered how 'eerie' it felt when this man watched them. The unusual circumstances around digging this strange hole and this person watching them were what have stayed with both men throughout their lives. They would remark to each other over the years at barbecues, 'Remember that weird job we did at Castalloy?' and, 'The time when we dug the grave at Castalloy?'—at no time realising that what they joked about might well have been the truth. David didn't recall ever having a serious conversation over it with his brother or anyone else. They had never connected any dots.

Based on this email, Bill met separately with David and Rob to discuss this information and to try to get an approximate idea of where, and precisely when, the hole was dug.

He found David and Rob to be academically well-qualified men of a solid background. They were both literate in their description of the events and were able to recall some of the issues with clarity.

On reflection, Rob remembered that he dug the hole the week before he started university, that being the first week in February 1966. You will recall that the Beaumont children disappeared on Wednesday 26 January 1966. From this, the brothers were able to ascertain that the hole was dug on the weekend of the 29th and 30th January 1966.

At that time, if a public holiday in South Australia fell on a weekday other than a Monday, then the following Monday would become the actual day off for workers rather than disturbing the middle of the working week. This meant that Monday, 31 January 1966 was the recognised day off from the previous week's Australia Day holiday.

It is also the case that Castalloy had closed all but essential operations for its annual shutdown throughout January 1966.

On 19 September 2013, David was contacted by a detective from SAPOL's Major Crime Investigation Branch who was following up on a report that David had made to Crime Stoppers prior to contacting Alan Whiticker.

David met the detective at Castalloy, where they walked onto the factory site trying to ascertain the location where David and his brother had dug the hole back in 1966. For David, the clue was the first gate into Castalloy at the rear of the factory in Kinkaid Avenue when travelling in a westerly direction from Streeters Road. The detective led David there from the front of the factory through the grounds and buildings, areas David was not familiar with, eventually ending in the area where he was advised by the detective that the first gate was situated.

As they made their way through the site, the detective questioned David, who felt that the detective was trying to confuse him, and at the site told David that his mind was made up that the children were not located in the sandpit. In fairness to the detective, it is Bill's opinion that the detective could merely have been testing the accuracy of David's memories of an event from so long ago.

In any event, David did his best to indicate the approximate area where he and his brother had dug the 'grave'. His brother, Rob, was also later interviewed by the same detective in October 2013.

Police enquiries ensued and, on 28 November 2013, police attended the Castalloy site and used ground-penetrating radar to survey and dig out the site. This development immediately received media attention and became front-page news, prompting talkback-radio conversations and current-affairs television programs. We were regularly interviewed by journalists over the days leading up to and after the dig, with any new leads or news regarding uncovering the mystery of the disappearance of Jane, Arnna, and Grant Beaumont attracting immediate media interest both locally and overseas. This extensive attention led Haydn to contact his cousin on the 24 November 2013 in an agitated state and say, 'They are digging in the wrong place.' The cousin then contacted Stuart with this information.

Nothing was found at that dig. Despite the disappointment felt by many, Mullins and Hayes continued their enquires.

In mid-2017, we were contacted by Michael Tamasi, then the general manager of Castalloy. At this point, the Castalloy business was owned by a US organisation and the land it sat on was owned by the South Australian Government. Up to then, and not surprisingly given the damage that can be done to businesses whose premises have been used for criminal activities, the owners of Castalloy, apparently on the instructions of SAPOL, had politely refused to allow us onto the site to make enquiries. However, it seems that by this time, Castalloy's US owners had decided to close the factory and move the operation offshore. Hence, their earlier position softened and Michael was able to speak with us and provide an aerial photograph of the Castalloy site taken in the mid-1960s. It was this photograph that allowed us to clearly see where the first search had gone wrong. From this aerial shot, we could see the gate where David and Rob said they had entered the site and dug the hole in 1966. The gate that David had been taken to by the detective was in fact a different business to Castalloy back in 1966 and therefore could not have been where they had dug the hole back then. We could now see the actual first gate to Castalloy as it was in 1966.

Given what we now know, this was an honest enough mistake considering the way David and Rob were brought to the area where this gate was by the detective. Who, again, may not have known what we had since discovered.

The aerial photograph showed the back gate in 1966 to be about fifty metres west from where David and Rob were taken and initially thought that it was, under the guidance of the detective. Tyre tracks leading from that gate into the sandy/grassy area at the back of Castalloy were visible. We knew the approximate distance from the gate where the boys had dug the hole so, using a car seen in the photograph as a guide (they were able to 'guesstimate' its approximate length), they measured the distance from the gate, along the wheel tracks, to a point where they felt the hole would be located. They were later found to have measured accurately as they were within half a metre of where the hole was later found to be.

Armed with this information, we continued our investigation with assistance from various people including Tony Zappia, Federal MP for Makin; South Australian Legislative Council member Frank Pangallo, who at the time was a reporter with Channel 7's local *Today Tonight* program; and Graham Archer, director of news and public affairs for *Today Tonight*.

After we had reached a stalemate with SAPOL, Tony Zappia spoke with the state premier at that time, the Honourable Jay Weatherill MP, and the then police minister and now State

Premier, the Honourable Peter Malinaskus MP. The minister considered the information on the case interesting enough to ask the police where they were with their enquiry.

From that point on, things began to accelerate. Thanks to the original exposure given by Channel 9's Brady Halls and then Channel 7s Frank Pangallo, a decision was made by Channel 7 in Sydney to make a documentary into our investigation.

The Channel 7 production team arrived in Adelaide under the guidance of Gareth Harvey, an outstanding producer with vast experience both in Australia and overseas, until he later moved to Channel 9. His replacement was Mark Llewellyn, again a very experienced and insightful producer who understood what was needed to get this story to the Australian public.

The production team also involved former NSW Police detective, investigator, and author Duncan McNab, who has assisted Channel 7 with various true-crime documentaries and who took to the task of finding the truth with great gusto.

Dr Xanthé Mallett also shared her great experience and expertise. Her depth of knowledge and insights into the workings of the criminal mind and the behaviours exhibited by paedophilic predators, sociopaths, and child molesters were invaluable to the authors.

The frontman for all of this was journalist Michael Usher, an entirely affable, thoughtful, and sensitive human being. Throughout the process, he conducted interviews with Linda, whose story we saw in Chapter 16, as well as various other witnesses, with total empathy and great consideration for the difficulties that speaking out would cause them. Michael is an all-around good guy and was the right man to present this story to the public.

The Channel 7 team, with Bill Hayes, engaged the skills of Dr Ian Moffatt, a senior research fellow in Archaeological Science from Flinders University in South Australia. He is a multi-disciplinary researcher, lecturer, and consultant in archaeological and earth science with particular expertise in geophysics, geochemistry, sedimentology, geoarchaeology, and spatial science and an altogether brilliant individual. Our very own Indiana Jones, Ian, was to conduct a geophysical survey of the area where the investigative team now believed the two boys had dug a 'grave-sized' hole back on 29–30 January 1966. This would essentially create a map of the sub-surface's archaeological features, which could detect not only natural structures but also anything that might have been buried amid the natural surroundings. Unlike other archaeological methods, a geophysical survey is neither invasive nor destructive, which allows the site to be preserved rather than excavated.

Ian and his team carried out the survey over four days in forty-plus-degree Celsius temperatures without shade. It is hard physical work, but Ian and his team never wavered in their commitment to the dig, knowing as they did what might eventuate from it. We give the team our heartfelt thanks for their enormous efforts. After several days of analysis, Ian presented the results of the survey. A number of things were revealed. Firstly, the 'primary' hole that the teenage boys had dug was clearly seen, even after fifty-two years. You could see that, after so many years, what had been the surface back then was covered in almost a metre of soil and sand mix. What was very disturbing was that a second hole could also be clearly seen. This hole was approximately the same dimensions as the first 'primary' hole dug in 1966 and was dug down to the same depth as the primary hole. It was set at right angles to the eastern side of the primary hole and formed something akin to the letter 'L', the base of the L being the new hole. This hole had obviously been dug at some time subsequent to the primary hole being dug.

There were no anomalies to be seen in that secondary hole, which prompted the question, why was it dug? This question was posed by a teenage David as he and his brother dug the primary hole all those years ago. As David asked of us, 'If it was dug to put rubbish in, why not get us to put the rubbish in and then refill the hole?'

But there was no rubbish where the boys had dug, nothing lying around that looked like it was going to be dumped; when they had finished digging, there was just a huge hole. Presumably, the man in the car would have needed to put whatever it was that he wanted to dispose of into the hole and then refill it, a very major job to do unless he had assistance.

Ian's geophysical survey showed an anomaly in the primary hole. It was not possible to be certain from the images just what the anomaly was or might be—this would only be shown by a dig—but the very fact that the primary hole had been found and that it contained an anomaly was a significant step forward.

However, the secondary hole was a matter of some concern, because it raised five serious questions:

1. Why was it dug?
2. When was it dug?
3. Who dug it?
4. What was put into the hole?
5. Who had filled it in?

There are a number of possible answers to these questions, and they became a matter of serious concern to us. We ask the following questions by way of trying to answer our concerns as listed above.

1. Was it a sheer coincidence that a second hole was dug over and down to the level of the primary hole?

2. Was there anything put into that second hole—for example, a genuine dump of rubbish? (The survey suggested this was unlikely, as no anomalies could be seen in the second hole.)

3. What was the purpose of digging the secondary hole if there was nothing put into it?

4. Was something put into that hole that was later removed or exhumed?

5. Was the hole dug to allow access to the first hole?

The first question could not be answered, and the second and third questions could only be answered by a dig of the site. As for the answer to the fourth and fifth questions, nothing was off the table.

It also occurred to Bill that there could be another reason that could offer an explanation to question five. He had seen rescues of children who had fallen into and become stuck in sinkholes, wells, and the like. In this type of event, the recovery of the victim is conducted not by digging down into the hole that they fell into but by digging a parallel hole down to the depth where the victim is stuck and then digging in at a right angle and pulling the victim into the rescue hole before taking them out through that means. This is a very successful way to conduct this type of recovery. Could it be that the person/s who dug the secondary hole were attempting to recover something from the primary hole?

As pure hypotheticals, we considered the following hypothetical scenarios.

There have been no known sightings of the Beaumont children since the day they vanished in 1966; therefore, it is reasonable to presume they were murdered by their abductor/s, who would have needed to dispose of them quickly. They (the murderer/s) would need to avoid, and where possible remove, any risk of detection.

The period after which the children disappeared was exceptionally hot. In that environment, human flesh begins to rot and smell within a very short period of time. If the worst possible scenario had occurred and the children were murdered soon after they were abducted, their bodies would need to be put somewhere in case someone came knocking and asking questions, perhaps even conducting a search for the children, or, if the smell drew attention, leading to the police being called.

Harry Phipps was a man of high intellect. He was also very resourceful and would have assessed the risk of being caught and would do what he needed to do to mitigate that risk. Hypothetically, the answer here might be to have a temporary place to put the bodies—and where better than in the ground where he had total control, such as Castalloy, buried deep down with a good covering of soil, where no smell could permeate? Having had the hole dug and placed the bodies—wrapped in the surfboard bags that Castalloy manufactured and that he kept his dresses in—into the hole, he would ask himself what the risk was that the two teenage boys would put two and two together and speak to the police. It was a possibility that he couldn't risk becoming a reality. Therefore, the hole that the young men had dug could only ever be a temporary resting place until such time as Harry could devise a permanent place to dispose of the bodies.

In the interim, he might place a dead animal or animal parts in the hole, say halfway to the bottom of where the children rested, so that, if the police did come and speak to him about the hole, he could say that it was a site to bury a dead animal. Police might then dig down, and partway down the primary hole they would find the remains of a dead animal, which would confirm what they had been told and the search would end there, leaving the real purpose for digging the hole a further metre below the level that they had dug to when finding the animal parts.

In time, Harry would be able to find and prepare a more permanent place or method to dispose of the bodies. Then the bodies could be exhumed and taken to a new place for burial or some other means of disposal.

Could that explain the secondary hole? It is hypothetical but worth considering and it might explain something that, to date, we have been unable to explain.

After their meeting to receive the results of the survey, Dr Ian Moffatt and Dr Xanthé Mallett met with the officer in charge of the Major Crime Investigation Branch, Detective Superintendent Des Bray, and his operations officer, Detective Chief Inspector Greg Hutchins, both experienced detectives and good, pragmatic police officers. Ian presented the evidence of the two holes that he had uncovered, supported by Xanthé in her role as a criminologist and forensic anthropologist.

It is worth stating at this point that before meeting with Ian and Xanthé, both men would have checked out and accepted their credentials before accepting their relative expertise and speaking with them. In the end, Harry Phipps was elevated to being a person of interest in the Beaumont case and it was agreed that a dig of the site would occur.

After further investigation by police, SAPOL announced that they would undertake a second dig at the Castalloy site. That dig occurred on a very hot summer morning on 2 February 2018, fifty-two years and one week after the Beaumont children were last seen. We arrived to what can only be described as a media frenzy. This level of attention really highlighted the effect that this story has had on the Australian psyche for the past five decades.

The street around the area where the dig would take place was teeming with all kinds of media and journalists from numerous newspapers, TV, and radio. They had gotten there early, but it was obvious that the TV stations had worked overnight to get prime positions to enable them to use cherry-pickers to look into the site and view the dig. Many were up on ladders at the Castalloy back fence; some were standing on a nearby roof. Combine that with the number of police and public milling about in a very small area, and the atmosphere was that of a football crowd or a pop concert. There was an air of excitement, an electric buzz in the air adding to the overall feeling of something special happening.

Channel 7, with whom we had been working, had a prime position in a small park immediately across from where the dig would take place. The police on the other side of the fence were well prepared with a large digger in situ, a shelter for shade, and a group of police and civilian experts to examine any remains that might be found. Police also had their senior media officer, Chief Inspector Col Cornish, present, who had worked hard throughout the day by organising up-to-date information from the dig to be disseminated to the waiting hordes, mostly through press conferences with Detective Chief Inspector Hutchins and at the final hole-side conference led by Detective Superintendent Bray. All were conducted with great clarity, professionalism, and openness.

The dig progressed over nine long and very hot hours. Overall, the police did a very detailed and exceptional job setting up and running the dig, and for that, they are to be admired and congratulated. Mostly it was humdrum sifting of soil taken from the excavation with not much for those watching to see. Then a flurry of activity would occur when something of note was found and, after an examination was made, it was back to digging and sifting.

The secondary hole was dug first, and as we and our team had feared, it contained nothing, not even a screw. This again raised the question: Why dig it to put nothing into it? The primary hole yielded the remnants of animal bones at a depth of about one metre, once again raising the question: Why dig it to a depth of two metres to place a few animal bones at a one-metre depth? It just didn't make sense. The big question for us was why did we find a 'scattering' of animal bones? If you were to bury a dead animal, wouldn't you bury the full carcass? What was found was a scattering of bones, not a full carcass. They could have just as easily been placed in a bin. Odd, to say the very least. It has a definite smell of being there as a distraction or decoy

We had conducted numerous interviews throughout the day with all manner of media. One of the media crews that carried out an interview with Hayes told him that through a third party they had been advised by a member of Harry Phipps' family that the search would find nothing but animal bones. This was before the dig began that day. This, too, prompts a question: How would this family member know what was in that hole? These bones were believed to be a few horse, cow, and sheep bones, but not full skeletons. Given that this hole was dug in 1966, who was around at that time from the Phipps family that would have known and remembered that there were only animal bones in the hole? A fairly minor detail to have recalled from those long-ago days, one could reasonably assume. Phipps lived in an urban environment—where did the horse, cow, and sheep bones come from? They were certainly not from his backyard.

In the end, no trace of human bones was found. Perhaps that would not be surprising, given the secondary hole that Ian's survey had uncovered. One major question to ask is was the hole or the holes a 'blind'? Put there as far from the real site as they could be to take police away from the actual site. As mentioned previously, Haydn told Bill and others 'they are in the pit'. The pit was behind the cottages on the far side of the site from where we dug. As Dr Xanthé Mallett had said, this hole was as far in a straight line as they could have dug from the pit that Haydn had spoken of.

We were invited onto the site for a final media call next to the excavation, where both were surprised by the size and depth of the hole. SAPOL had done an amazingly thorough job of the excavation. That only made the fact that Harry Phipps would have had to refill the hole by shovel once he was finished doing whatever it was that he had used the hole for even more perplexing.

The dig did leave more questions than it answered. At the time of writing, we were not aware of SAPOL's position going forward with the enquiry. Bill has been reliably advised that on the day of the dig, a large number number of calls—around seventy—were received by Crime Stoppers regarding the Beaumont crime and Harry Phipps. For Bill, if only five percent are deemed to be credible to some degree, in detective terms, that is a very good day indeed.

As for us, we will continue to investigate; indeed, our determination to find out what happened to the children has only increased. Sadly, Nancy Beaumont has now passed away, never knowing what happened to her children. Jim Beaumont, now well into his nineties, is in care and he, too, might never know the truth. The disappearance of Jane, Arnna, and Grant Beaumont remains one of Australia's enduring mysteries. The truth of what happened to them is a truth that is needed for all of us to have as human beings.

Chapter 19

Haydn's Cousin

*In a room where people unanimously maintain a
conspiracy of silence, one word of truth sounds like a
pistol shot.*[60]

—Czesław Miłosz

In 2017, Haydn Phipps' closest cousin and friend, Peter,
emailed a South Australian detective overseeing the Beaumont
children's cold case with knowledge and information he had
gathered over the decades since the crime. He did not receive
a reply. He followed up with another two pieces of correspondence and finally received a response from a detective thanking
him for the contact and indicating that someone would get back
to him. They never did. This was even after Mullins directly
emailed one of the more junior detectives associated with this
cold case in 2016, alerting him to this attempted contact by the
cousin.

His reply to Stuart:

Thank you for your email. Due to the number of Crime
Stoppers calls we receive relating to the Beaumonts, the
reports are allocated to a number of different investigators.
I can't speak for Peter's information, but we do try to phone

the caller back where we can about their information in a timely manner. If you can send me Peter's phone number, I will call him in relation to his information.

Mullins did pass on the phone number; however, Peter to this day has received no contact from any detectives. However, a detective did contact and meet Peter's younger sister a few years ago for an interview. Peter's opinion was that his sister did not know Haydn or the family as well as he did back in the 1960s. Being younger and a girl, Peter stated she never hung around the Phipps boys or the house the way Peter did, and she mostly visited when their parents visited. Peter is of the belief that the investigation may have been slanted to suit a particular narrative and desired outcome. He believed he could have added much more to Haydn's story about Harry Phipps and his obsession with making and wearing satin garments, about the rules of the Phipps house and about Haydn's attempts in later years to speak of the abuse he suffered at the hands of his father. Peter was the man Haydn confided in, but he was never interviewed by the Major Crime Investigation Branch.

According to Peter, as a young teenager, he and Haydn, with two other friends, would hang out around Glenelg and go on regular car trips down the coast on weekends. They all knew Haydn Phipps was a troubled boy from an early age. At times, he displayed erratic behaviour, taking unnecessary risks as if he had a death wish. Harry gave both the boys ample money to spend and cars when they were old enough to drive. There was certainly no want for material items, so Peter could not understand why Haydn would hate his father with such passion. Peter believed that both Haydn and his younger brother had personal problems over the years and also problems with Harry—Haydn with drugs and alcohol and the younger brother facing his own demons. He described Olga and Harry's marriage as dysfunctional. Harry appeared distant, detached, and unaffectionate. Olga, he stated, took good care of the boys. She was kind and considerate to them and was quietly spoken in what appeared to be a superficial marriage.

Peter, as with many others, was aware of Harry's expertise as a tailor and the fact that when around satin, he could not control his actions. As an example, at a Castalloy Christmas party, Peter saw Harry make a beeline for a woman wearing satin. It was clear that he needed to touch and feel this material. His fetish was well known in family circles and also among acquaintances. A strict dress code—do not wear satin—was in place when anyone visited Isola. Peter also knew well of Harry's no-go Saturdays when no-one was allowed anywhere near the house. As Peter remembers it, both Haydn and Wayne were paid to keep away.

Peter has maintained irregular contact with Haydn's son, who, according to Peter, also experienced first-hand this satin fetish and the no-go Saturdays. This narrative reinforces what Haydn said all along. Peter goes on to say that Harry Phipps had two personas: his public face and a very different one he showed in private.

Haydn was many things and could annoy people with his antics. He was unreliable at times and could exaggerate a bit. He was certainly no angel, but the apple never falls far from the tree. Person to person, however, Haydn showed his caring side and appeared to be desperately seeking affection. That being the case, he gravitated toward Peter's first wife, with whom he could talk about many things. Haydn spoke of his abuse to Peter many times over the years, and his story never changed. Peter has no doubt whatsoever that Haydn was telling the truth in this and in his account of Australia Day 1966. He never wavered in his recollection of seeing the Beaumont children in his yard that day.

Around 2008, an agitated Haydn called Peter after a senior detective from SAPOL Major Crime Investigation Branch contacted him by phone and asked him about his alleged sexual abuse at the hands of his father. Haydn, Peter said, was a broken man, and this detective clearly did not handle the approach well. According to Haydn when he was asked if he was abused, he denied it but had then called Peter, outraged, saying, 'Who in the fuck does this person think they are asking me such a question over the phone? I have said all that I had to say in my interview with Bill Hayes.' It is challenging for survivors to relive such traumatic events, and on many occasions, once they do relive it, they slip back into a depressive state.

In his clearer moments as he matured, Haydn confided further to Peter in the 2000s, firstly about horrific events he endured at the hands of his father, and later of seeing the Beaumont children in his backyard that fateful day and the 'sandpit'. This was during the publication of *The Satin Man: Uncovering the Mystery of the Missing Beaumont Children*, the first time anyone had written publicly about Harry Phipps' alleged involvement and the possibility of the children being buried in a sandpit at the Castalloy factory. Even though Peter believed Haydn was sexually abused, he thought it a stretch to consider Harry Phipps had something to do with the Beaumont children's disappearance.

However, after Stuart Mullins contacted and interviewed him and presented Peter with a wealth of damning corroborated information, Peter needed no further convincing.

Peter called Stuart Mullins several years ago after he bumped into an old friend from the 1960s, Norm Lockwood, who has since passed away. They had coffee and reminisced, and at one point, Norman asked, 'How is Haydn and that poofter [*a denigrating term used to describe homosexual men in Australia and some other parts of the world*] dad of his?' Peter asked why he asked. Norm went on to say how when he and his now wife were young bartenders at a private men's club in Adelaide back in the early 1970s, Harry would be there dressed up in women's clothing with other like-minded men. (We in no way condone or support Norm's comment regarding Harry, or indeed anyone, being a 'poofter' due to cross-dressing preferences.) He knew that the person was Harry Phipps because he had seen him several times when visiting Haydn in their younger years. Peter was shocked and asked Norm if he knew about what had occurred recently, as was shown repeatedly in the news and on current-affairs programs, and in discussions on talkback radio regarding Phipps and the Beaumont children. Norm was not aware, which only added to Peter's belief that Haydn was utterly truthful.

Adding further fuel to this story was the frantic phone call Haydn made to Peter during the first Castalloy factory excavation, in which Haydn told Peter that police were digging in the 'fucking wrong spot', which had many, not just Peter and the authors, asking the same question: what did Haydn know that he was not telling? Peter's younger sister is adamant that Haydn and Angela were untruthful, but Peter strongly disagrees with his sister's assertions.

Over the years, Peter and Haydn kept in close contact. They would regularly talk via phone, and Peter was one of the very few people Haydn trusted and confided in. It was Peter who organised for Haydn to meet with Mostyn Matters, the last of the Glenelg detectives still alive, in Cairns in Far North Queensland. During this meeting, Haydn took an immediate shine to Mos and they spent time alone together. It was here, again, that Haydn confided with Mostyn that he saw the Beaumont children in his backyard on 26 January 1966. Mostyn does not doubt Haydn's version, though he has noted, as have other people, that Haydn clammed up about what happened next but added that 'they are in the sandpit'.

Peter has had intermittent contact with some of his relatives over the past decade. These events have, of course, had a negative effect on all and caused divisions among them. Peter is unsure why some family members would deny Harry's satin fetishes or rule out of hand the idea that Haydn was sexually abused—to Peter, this shows that he was. What has been noticeable to Peter and others is that since SAPOL named Harry Phipps as a person of interest relating to the Beaumont disappearance, several vocal detractors have become very quiet.

Chapter 20:
The Younger Brother

Three things that cannot be hidden: the sun, the moon and the truth.

—Buddha

Journalist Nigel Hunt from *The Advertiser* interviewed Wayne Phipps and his wife, Eileen, for a general-interest piece on 18 February 2018. The headline read, 'The Beaumont children mystery: Harry Phipps' angry son says his father did not kill the Beaumont children'.[61]

The crux of the story was that Wayne accused his brother, Haydn Phipps, of being mentally ill and deranged and refutes his claims that their father, Harry Phipps, had any involvement in the disappearance of the Beaumont children. Wayne also denies Haydn's alleged sexual abuse occurred at the hands of his father. This article and all the allegations were made public after Haydn and Angela died, so we must work with what we know or can reasonably suppose to be true when examining the veracity of the claims.

Wayne and Eileen claim that Haydn and Angela had an axe to grind. Why? Because they were after revenge and money, having been left out of Harry Phipps' will. This, however, is not correct; indeed, Haydn was a beneficiary of his father's will. Transcripts of Harry's will and birth, death, and marriage certificates were obtained by the authors in 2012 through the former Adelaide research company Proformat Ancestral and local history researchers. These show that Wayne Phipps' claim is inaccurate.

Haydn was not left out of the will, as it says:

I give my sons Haydn Henry Phipps and Wayne Frederick Phipps as tenants in common and equal shares my house and land at Sussex Street Glenelg including all furniture, fittings and fixtures in it excluding all ornaments, decorations and collectables free of all State and Federal death, estate or succession duties. Also, to apply or to distribute the balance of the assets of the trust: as to one-quarter of it to each of my sons Haydn Henry Phipps and Wayne Frederick Phipps.

This does not relate to the main house, Isola, where Elizabeth resided. This is the residence next door to Isola, which Harry also owned. As with Angela, she had separated from Haydn years earlier and had little contact with the Phipps family. When speaking to us, Angela stated she has no expectation or any reason to think of being included in Harry's will.

Wayne Phipps told the journalist in the same *Advertiser* interview, 'My father never touched my friends or me, and never Haydn or his friends. If Hadyn had been abused, he would have told me, he would have told his mother—he was a blab-bermouth.'[61]

The organisation RAINN—the Rape Abuse and Incest National Network—in the article 'Sexual Assault of Men and Boys', says:

It can be hard to tell someone that you have experienced sexual assault or abuse. You may fear that you will face judgment or not be believed. Some men who have survived sexual assault as adults feel shame or self-doubt, believing that they should have been "strong enough" to fight off the perpetrator.[62]

The hard fact is that, unless there are credible adult witnesses who are willing to speak out or give video evidence, the prosecution is skating uphill on thin ice. The brave few who do speak out are further victimised. They end up suffering in silence and living a continuous nightmare.

Wayne and Eileen's thinking that they would have known if Haydn was abused and Harry was a paedophile is not unusual. But as we have seen, paedophiles work by stealth, in the shadows. They are incredibly brazen, and at times this behaviour beggars belief. Most of the adult population believe they can pick a paedophile; you cannot. Family members, relatives, and friends are rarely aware that any violation is taking place.

Paedophiles are meticulous, ensuring they are never suspected. They work to undermine the child's reputation, so if the child does speak up their story will not be believed. Predators like Harry Phipps are usually the average, likeable, engaging individual. Many are charismatic and charming and can come from any background in society. If the child abuser is the amiable parent, sibling, uncle, or grandfather, or someone else in the family they care about, the child may worry about getting that person in trouble by creating fault lines in the family unit. Hence, the predator continues to have free access. Some minors keep quiet because they feel that the sexual abuse is in part their fault. They are also fearful of retribution. So, Wayne and Eileen Phipps are certainly not alone in their thinking.

From the beginning of *The Advertiser* interview, Wayne and Eileen Phipps attempt to tear down Haydn's and Angela's accounts. However, much of what they say in this interview appears to lack accuracy. Haydn and Angela's account, however, has been corroborated by several individuals, including Haydn's closest cousin, Peter, past friends and neighbours, previous senior Castalloy managers and workers, relatives and acquaintances who knew Harry, and those, such as Archbishop John Hepworth, who knew of Harry Phipps and his movements within Adelaide's paedophilic circles in the 1960s.

Wayne went on to say that Haydn was 'mentally unhinged and needed help',[61] but he offers no evidence of his brother's mental state. Stuart Mullins is in possession of Haydn's full medical report at the time of his death—obtained by Haydn's son, from Uniting Care North Queensland, who passed it on to Mullins—which shows Haydn was psychologically damaged and sought help but was not deranged. In this report, Haydn speaks to his doctor regarding sexual abuse on numerous occasions. It is also clear that Haydn was being treated for conditions associated with abuse. His doctors' reports state that this sexual abuse had a significant impact on him as an adult.

Wayne Phipps also accuses us of basing our information on one mistruth after another, which is hurting the memory of Harry and Olga Phipps. More damning than any reputational damage, however, is the professional opinion of the many experts who regard Harry Phipps as the lead suspect in this case of the missing Beaumont children based on the information supplied to them collected from independent sources and by us through our own research.

In the same article, Wayne Phipps disputes Haydn's account of that fateful day on 26 January 1966—specifically Haydn's statement to Bill Hayes that he worked a shift at the Glenelg Ten Pin Bowling Alley before returning home for lunch around noon and saw the Beaumont children wander into his backyard as he sat in the 'cubby house' having a smoke. Wayne dismisses this, stating that Haydn never worked at the Glenelg Bowling Alley, that there was never a 'cubby house', and that Haydn 'hated cigarettes and never smoked as a teenager'.[61] These are, Wayne Phipps says in the article, examples of delusional statements.

However, when Stuart Mullins met with some of Haydn's former friends from the 1960s, one said they worked together at the bowling alley as pin boys in the early to mid-1960s, and they did have sort of a 'cubby house'—a few large planks of wood for cover from the elements attached to the fence. We would agree this 'cubby house' term used by Haydn would elicit an image of something a bit more grandiose than a few planks of wood cobbled together.

Likewise, a former friend told Mullins that he and Haydn did smoke a little in the 1960s. He used the term 'durries', another name for cigarettes at the time. Haydn said, 'Sometimes we wrapped some dead weeds in "roly papers".'

Wayne and Eileen also state in the same article that Haydn mentioned a tree house in the same book and chapter. However, there is no mention of a tree house in this book.

Indeed, according to two of Haydn's friends in the 1960s, the Phipps brothers had separate friendship groups, and Wayne did not hang around with Haydn and his friends because he was too young for them. In January 1966, the authors believe Wayne was ten at the time and turning eleven much later in the year.

This comment was backed up by Haydn's closest cousin, Peter, who is the same age as Haydn. He reiterated to Mullins that Wayne had his own circle of younger friends and did not hang around with Haydn.

Wayne said he shared a bedroom with Haydn until he got married at age twenty-one, and that he would have known if any sexual abuse occurred. However, the abuse happened in the early hours of the morning when the young brother was sound asleep.

The exploitation of Haydn stopped in approximately 1964. As described by Angela Phipps, this continued to occur up to three times a week for approximately eight years, from approximately 1956 to 1964. Wayne would only have been a newborn when the abuse of Haydn began and ten years old when it stopped because Haydn was fourteen years old and physically mature enough to defend himself.

From a newborn to age ten, the brother, we believe, was too young to be aware of anything unusual. The authors ask: How many children have been sexually abused right under the nose of adults who were never aware of what was going on until the child spoke up years later? Case in point: Australian and UK entertainer Rolf Harris, where none of the alleged sexual assaults happened in private, but in public settings. The youngest girl was eight. He was so brazen in what he did, and yet all was done by stealth in plain sight.

This type of abuse is difficult to fathom, and to many people, not just Wayne and Eileen Phipps, all this is incomprehensible and very difficult to reconcile.

Predators are very rarely caught. If they can easily fool adults, manipulating children or teenagers would be elementary. Again, Wayne's and Eileen's thinking is the norm, not the exception. At times, we are all left embittered by the sheer audacity of the paedophile. How did they get away with the sexual abuse for so long right under our collective noses?

A question has been asked by many: why would the Phipps brothers share a bedroom when their residence was large? According to relatives and neighbours, Isola has three large bedrooms. Could it be safety in numbers? Could it be that Harry and Olga Phipps had separate bedrooms? According to neighbours, friends, and business associates, this was the sleeping arrangement. They already knew the marital relationship was frosty, distant, dysfunctional, and lacking in love. In our opinion, siblings sleeping in the same bedrooms today may not be the norm, but it was in the 1960s. Or, was the other the room where Harry would fall asleep wearing his satin clothing? When he did, Haydn knew what was in store for him. In the same interview, when speaking to Nigel Hunt, Wayne Phipps says, 'Some people took advantage of him and my dead father for their own personal gain or revenge.'[61]

Yes, one person did: his father, Harry.

Wayne goes on to say Haydn's allegations are uncorroborated and casts serious doubts on their validity.[61] True, there are one or two statements Haydn made to us that are uncorroborated and lack validity. However, the majority of what Haydn and Angela have said has been corroborated by numerous credible sources. Wayne would know this. The fact that SAPOL's Major Crime Investigation Branch has raised Harry Phipps as a person of interest in the Beaumont case demonstrates that experienced investigators accept the overwhelming nature of the corroborated circumstantial evidence against Harry Phipps.

Wayne also casts doubt on his brother's sexual abuse based on the fact that Haydn moved back into Harry's residence with his son after his first divorce. Haydn's son, Nicholas Phipps, has read Wayne's newspaper account and, when speaking with Mullins, dismissed much of what he said to the reporter, saying Wayne appears to be hiding information about his father's satin fetish and the family dynamics. Yes, he did reside at the house, because they had nowhere else to go, but Nicholas stated that although Harry at times showered him and Haydn with money, Harry was evil and a deviant.

In a further conversation with Stuart, Nicholas, who was then in his forties, spoke about Harry's obsession with satin and the myriad of brightly coloured satin dresses he saw in the house. In a private room, he also saw other sexual paraphernalia such as codpieces and a phantom costume, all very similar to his father's recollections. Haydn's son stated he did not wish to swim in the backyard pool at the same time as Harry, as he tended to come too close. He moved out of the house when he was eighteen.

Stuart also found the idea that Haydn chose to move back into Harry's house challenging. To the rational mind, it doesn't make sense. But as Stuart spoke to more survivors, it became clear that this type of conduct is quite common. As mentioned in Chapter 17, this is behaviour is termed Stockholm syndrome.

This was very true for Haydn Phipps. Also, when Haydn was interviewed by Bill, he said he had moved back in as he was then older and stronger and could protect himself and his son.

However, for Wayne and Eileen, they are right to question this behaviour and his decision to move back into the residence where Harry resided and the sexual abuse occurred.

Wayne Phipps claims that Haydn's son—Harry's grandson—had made no allegations about Harry. This is not so. He has on numerous occasions and continues to do so. To put this into perspective, when Stuart first sent the book *Searching for the Beaumont Children* to Haydn's son in 2007, all Stuart wrote in a note placed inside the front cover of the book was, 'There is someone I would like to talk to you about. That you might know, in regards to this book.' When they met, Haydn's son stated, 'I know who this is to do with—my father and Harry.' How did he know?

Nicholas went on to say his father, Haydn, confided in him several times that he was sexually abused by Harry and also Harry had something to do with the disappearance of the Beaumont children, ending with 'They are in the sandpit'.

Although Haydn's son has stated to Stuart that he was never abused by Harry, he did say that his grandfather was deviant and a paedophile and has no reason not to believe his father. It is important to note that Nicholas has undergone a polygraph (lie detector) test with arguably Australia's number one polygraph expert, Steve Van Aperen, which is noted in Chapter 13. The result? Nicholas was being truthful regarding his accounts.

Wayne and Eileen go on to talk with the journalist accusing Haydn and Angela of making up fictitious stories after Harry died in 2004 when he could not defend himself. Again, this statement is inaccurate. Angela raised her concerns openly, not because Harry passed away. She raised them after reading Alan Whiticker's *Searching for the Beaumont Children* book, which was published in 2006.

Angela's justifiable concern was that if Haydn was sexually abused, as she believed he was, we might have not only an undetected alleged paedophile living near Colley Reserve in 1966, but one who matched the description and age range of the man seen playing with the Beaumont children that fateful day and was known to hand out one-pound notes. Then there is Haydn's statement that Harry had something to do with the Beaumont abduction. She had legitimate concerns, and her curiosity compelled her to ask a very reasonable question: could Harry Phipps be involved?

Angela also discussed the alleged sexual deviancy and abuse on numerous occasions with other relatives and Harry's second wife, Elizabeth Phipps, who asked the question, 'Is it true the boys were abused?' Note the use of the plural 'boys'. Angela also spoke with her sister, an officer in Victoria Police at the time.

Haydn Phipps raised his concerns when Harry was alive; however, he was quickly shot down in flames. Harry Phipps was wealthy, connected, and influential. He wielded a considerable amount of power and influence and was capable of having his son committed or locked up if he wished. Haydn *was* in a no-win situation here. Who would have believed him?

According to an online article, 'Child Sexual Abuse Statistics: The Issue of Child Sexual Abuse':

> Even with declining rates of sexual abuse, the public is not fully aware of the magnitude of the problem. The primary reason is that only about 38% of child victims disclose the fact that they have been sexually abused. Some never disclose.[63]

We are not surprised by this statistic. Having spoken to several victims of child sexual abuse over the last fourteen years, an overriding theme was who would believe them? They risked being shunned by family and friends if they did speak out. Also, many did not wish to relive the nightmare of what happened to them by telling the police usually several times of their ordeal.

According to the Darkness to Light web site's child sexual abuse statistics, even with declining rates of sexual abuse, the public is not fully aware of the magnitude of the problem. The primary reason is that only about 38% of child victims disclose the fact that they have been sexually abused. Some never disclose. Why so few? And why such consistency in the percentage over the years? Things appear not to have changed. Could it be because of the fear of not being believed and the inevitable negative repercussions that follow?

It is also worth noting that Wayne and Eileen Phipps chose to speak publicly only after Haydn and Angela died.

Wayne and Eileen also said to the journalist Nigel Hunt that they believe the material for *The Satin Man: Uncovering the Mystery of the Missing Beaumont Children* was provided solely by Angela as revenge against a man she saw as owing her financial support.[61] This claim is, quite simply, false. The information Mullins, Hayes, and Whiticker collected over the years came from multiple credible sources, which, when collated, became the 7 News documentary *The Beaumont Children: What Really Happened.*[52]

Journalist Nigel Hunt, in the article 'Beaumont children mystery: Harry Phipps' angry son says his father did not kill the children', states that SAPOL Major Crime Investigation Branch detectives became aware of the allegations in 2007 and found no evidence to corroborate Haydn's claims or any other evidence to link Harry to the Beaumont abduction.[61] Stuart Mullins and Bill Hayes have always believed that the police investigation back then into Harry Phipps was poorly executed, with glaring investigative shortcomings. For example, detectives never met or formally interviewed Haydn or Angela Phipps, or many other individuals who had damning information regarding Harry Phipps, yet they did meet with Wayne and Eileen and one or two of their supporters.

In our opinion, as well as that of several well-respected investigative journalists such as Duncan McNab, Brady Halls, and Graham Archer; former detective Mostyn Matters; former Head of Major Crime Ken Thorsen; and polygraph expert Steve Van Aperen, to name a few, Haydn and Angela should have been the first people to be formally interviewed. If done with an open mind and a desire to find the truth, these interviews would, in the authors' opinion, have established their credibility and honesty.

In the same article, Wayne Phipps states to journalist Nigel Hunt, 'Those who remember facts are either dead or too old to want this rubbish in their lives.'[61] This is not correct; they are not all dead, and they do not think this is rubbish. The journalist laments, 'It is a crying shame that each of the three key players in the latest chapter of the Beaumont children's disappearance is no longer alive.' In our opinion, this journalist had followed the case for more than a decade, but over those many years chose not to interview Haydn, Angela, and many others who could corroborate our information. Why?

The journalist also states in the same article, 'Certainly, if Harry Phipps were around today, the allegations linking him to their abduction would not have entered the public domain. If they had, those who made them would have found themselves in the Supreme Court on the wrong end of a defamation lawsuit.'[61]

This comment emanating from a well-educated professional is quite disconcerting, perplexing, and surprising. In this day and age, in our opinion, this information would have definitely entered the public domain. Harry Phipps' background would have been carefully scrutinised. Nowadays, the abused have a voice and are listened to and believed. Once others sexually abused by Harry Phipps believe they have a voice, they might also feel confident to step forward.

The journalist goes on to say, 'If Harry Phipps were around today, the allegations linking him to their abduction would not have entered the public domain. Also, he would also have a chance to either confirm or reject Haydn's allegation that he sexually abused him.'

Of course, Phipps would deny the claim. He would, however, have to explain the corroborated circumstantial evidence stacked against him and confront his accusers. In an email sent to Mullins in February 2018, Duncan McNab said:

> Many contested criminal cases are driven entirely by circum-
> stantial evidence of varying impact—geography, logistics,
> ownership of time, and so on. Harry's house location is
> compelling, but only after you have worked out the logistics
> of the Beaumont case. The police need reasonable cause
> to arrest someone, and this requires compelling evidence,
> including on many occasions circumstantial evidence. This
> might be two or three or a pile of circumstances, with Harry
> Phipps we have a pile.

In early 2018, Stuart Mullins was contacted by the same journalist regarding Wayne's account and was asked if he had any comment. Stuart raised the issue of the alleged rape of a teenage schoolgirl at the hands of Harry Phipps in the 1970s, to which the journalist stated, 'This cannot be corroborated.' In Mullins' opinion, there appeared to be little interest, concern, or empathy for this victim's plight and no mention of Haydn nor the abuse that he allegedly suffered. When Mullins raised some other interesting information regarding Wayne Phipps' past history, it did not appear to pique the journalist's interest.

Overall, the story told by Wayne and Eileen Phipps does not appear to be accurate. They may be, understandably, diverting attention from themselves. To be honest, who wouldn't do that in such a case? But Harry Phipps' deviant dark side is no longer hidden behind his past standing in the community; the overwhelming circumstantial evidence is here for all to see. The information we presented to SAPOL's Major Crime Inves-tigation Branch has been corroborated by multiple sources. However, the columnist appears to dismiss their information and the elevation of Harry Phipps to being a person of interest by SAPOL, instead preferring to talk about another Beaumont media frenzy and the hunt for a scoop every time new information regarding the case is put forward. We would respectfully like to remind this journalist he is part of the media and therefore part of his so-called media frenzy.

Steven Van Aperen stated, when speaking with the authors in 2018, 'When an individual attempts to divert attention away from themselves, they are hiding important information.' In an exclusive interview between journalist Nigel Hunt in the *Sunday Mail* South Australia on 18 February 2018 and Wayne and Eileen Phipps, it was not so much what they were saying—than what they were not saying. Haydn Phipps, on the other hand, has offered a lengthy, detailed account of his experience. We should ask the following:

- Was Haydn lying about Harry making and wearing satin garments?
- Was Haydn lying about his father exhibiting sexual deviancy?
- Was Haydn lying about his sexual abuse at the hands of his father?
- Was Haydn lying about his father regularly swimming at Glenelg and frequenting Colley Reserve?
- Was Haydn lying about his father's physical description in the mid-1960s?
- Was Haydn lying about working at the Glenelg Bowling Alley?
- Was Haydn lying about Harry handing out one-pound notes?
- Was Haydn lying about the family being highly dysfunctional?

- Was Haydn lying about seeing the Beaumont children at his house the day they disappeared?
- Was Haydn lying about seeing the children's brightly coloured beach towels and Jane carrying a shoulder-type carry bag and all having the same type of haircut?
- Was Haydn lying about the children being buried in the sandpit?

Stuart Mullins and Bill Hayes understand why family members react in different ways when a sibling or relative accuses an adult they all know of sexual abuse. Many will deny and cover up to protect the integrity of their loved ones and family name, which is entirely understandable. Or, in some cases, they will cover up for another sexual-abuse victim closer to home, not wanting their own sexual abuse to reach the light of day. There is also the stigma and perceived scandal of being linked to a paedophile, which can have an unfortunate and regrettable adverse effect on their children or grandchildren. However, Nancy and Jim Beaumont lived a nightmare for more than five decades. Indeed, Nancy went to her grave never knowing what had happened to her children—and we must never lose sight of that fact. We must do what is right and necessary to bring the truth to light.

Enter Harry Phipps

Top left: The sketch of the man seen playing with the Beaumont children.

Top right: Harry Phipps in the mid-to-late 1950s.
As he aged, his hair had turned to light brown.

By the early 1970s, his hair had turned grey

Bottom left: Harry Phipps in the early 1950s

Bottom right: Harry Phipps attending the end-of-year
Castalloy Christmas party, 1973.

Haydn Phipps accused his father of horrific sexual abuse when he was a child. Haydn also said that he saw the Beaumont children in his backyard that fateful day in 1966.

Haydn's account has been deemed truthful by polygraph experts.

Adelaide Advertiser January 2018

Harry Phipps named 'person of interest' in missing Beaumont children case

MAJOR Crime detectives have named a deceased man as a person of interest in one of South Australia's most notorious cold cases as they prepare to dig at a new site.

"THE DEVIL DOESN'T COME DRESSED IN A RED CAPE AND POINTY HORNS. HE COMES AS EVERYTHING YOU'VE EVER WISHED FOR"

A/General Manager
Palen Creek Correctional Centre
Ph. 07
Fax 07

Department of
Corrective Services

Palen Creek Correctional Centre

17 January 2006

Reference: Angela Fyfe

To whom it may concern,

Angela is employed as a Clinical Registered Nurse at Palen Creek Correctional Centre Medical Centre. Angela has been employed in this position since 2000.

During her employment at Palen Creek Correctional Centre, Angela demonstrated to me that she is a totally honest and reliable person who displays a genuine empathy for clients in her care. This behaviour is reflective of her active sense of community, in so far as, Angela has keenly sought and undertaken volunteer work for worthwhile community projects.

Angela adapted to the challenging environment of a Correctional Centre very quickly and is able to prioritise her work to meet ever-changing outcomes. Angela's clinical assessments and skills are unquestionable and administratively she produces work to an above average standard. Angela performs extremely well under pressure as has been demonstrated on numerous occasions, given the volatile nature of her work environment.

Angela is a valued team member, always willing to "work in" and is held in high regard by her peers and management.

I have no hesitation in endorsing Angela as a committed and valued employee and wish her continuing success.

Yours Faithfully

A world class corrective
services system

Mt Lindsay Highway   Palen Creek 4287
PMB 1 Rathdowney
Queensland 4287 Australia

A written reference obtained by the authors. That shows Angela as being honest, reliable, and trustworthy.

Angela believes her husband was sexually abused by his father, Harry, over many years. She gives valid reasons for making this judgement.

Top image: Some bolts of satin taken out of Harry's residence after he was placed into aged care. These were put to good use in a Christmas nativity play. His many other satin dresses, kaftans, and pyjamas were taken to the rubbish tip.

Bottom left: Remnants of Harry's satin cloth.

Bottom right: The last of Harry's satin pyjamas.

The Castalloy factory cottages. The smaller one to the right is where a young Christine was allegedly sexually abused by Harry Phipps and his associates.

At the direction of Harry Phipps, David and Robin dig a grave-sized hole at the back of the factory.
Saturday the 29th and Sunday the 30th of January 1966.
Three days after the children go missing.
Once completed, Harry pays them in pound notes and tells them to 'fuck off you little cunts and never come back'.
Images courtesy of Channel Seven Australia

240

This A4 note was placed on the main gate of the Castalloy factory, January 2016. The 50th anniversary of the disappearance of the Beaumont children.

Chapter 21:
The Adelaide Oval Abduction

I love you every day. And now I will miss you
every day.[64]

—Mitch Albom

Joanne Ratcliffe, aged eleven, and Kirste Jane Gordon, aged four, were abducted from the Adelaide Oval on 25 August 1973, and like the three Beaumont children, they were never seen again, as if they had vanished off the face of the earth.

In January 1968, John McGeorge, Australia's leading forensic criminal psychiatrist at the time, spoke with *Advertiser* journalist Ken Harrison. John was asked about his thoughts regarding the Beaumont children's abduction. His response to this journalist was chilling: 'The abductor of Jane, Arnna, and Grant would possibly strike again in three to four years.'[65] This prediction was startling to Bill Hayes and Stuart Mullins when they first read it.

This foretelling of another heinous abduction by John McGeorge was not far off the mark. In 1973, two girls were taken whilst attending an Australian (Aussie) Rules Football match with their family, Joanne with her parents and brother David, and Kirste with her grandmother. The South Australian public was yet again stunned and bewildered, and not surprisingly the abduction was compared with the Beaumont case seven years earlier.

Les and Kath Ratcliffe with their children, Joanne and David, then thirteen, enjoyed attending Aussie Rules matches to support their favourite team, the Norwood Red Legs. They were playing the North Adelaide Roosters, another popular team, so a large crowd was assured.

Halfway through the reserves match prior to the main event, Kath Ratcliffe spotted her friend, Mrs Rita Huckel, a fellow Norwood supporter. Rita was walking up the stairs of the grandstand with her granddaughter Kirste. Rita was looking after Kirste while Kirste's parents, Greg and Christine Gordon, spent the weekend visiting friends in Renmark, a Riverland town 254 kilometres north-east of Adelaide on the banks of the Murray River.

Kirste, being four, was a shy little girl, and the large crowd with their cheering and booing made her anxious. Joanne could spot this, so she invited Kirste to squeeze in next to her and hold hands. Kirste had made a friend in Joanne as they laughed and giggled together.

During the reserves match, they went to the downstairs kiosk together to get straws for their drinks. Shortly after, nature called and both headed to the toilets at the back of the grandstand and returned ten minutes later. Well into the main game, Kirste again needed to go, and Joanne obliged. When they had not returned after ten minutes, Les and Kath Ratcliffe went looking for them—but no trace of them was found. A parent's worst nightmare was unfolding.

Frantic with worry, Les and Kath alerted the secretary of the Adelaide Oval in his office to make an announcement that their two young girls were missing. They were informed, however, that an announcement could not be made during play because it would not be heard over the crowd. According to a reporter (name obscured) for *The News*, the secretary of the Adelaide Oval, on Monday 27 August 1973, stated, 'We cannot make a public appeal for every child who goes missing at a sporting event.'[66] This might be unheard of today, but in the 1960s this was a sign of the times. Much the same as the initial thought by detectives at the Glenelg police station the day the Beaumont children went missing, they thought that the kids would turn up soon.

The parents reluctantly returned to their seats to see if the children had come back. They had not. An announcement was finally made five minutes after the game. By that time, it was too little too late. A sense of despair and dread had overtaken the Ratcliffes and Rita Huckel.

As the hours passed, it was apparent this was an abduction. Mr and Mrs Gordon were notified while in the Riverland that the children were missing and immediately returned to Adelaide. What followed was a thorough police investigation. A description of the children was immediately released: Kirste was a cute four-year-old with blue eyes, faint freckles on fair English-rose skin, and curly honey-blonde hair. She was wearing a white pleated skirt with a purple jumper and brown lace-up shoes with white tights. Joanne had blue eyes and dark brown hair worn in two pigtails tied with rubber bands. She was wearing a white blouse and white cardigan, black jeans, white track shoes with blue stripes, and a white, mustard, and black tank top.

How this abduction unfolded was explained by several eye-witnesses, from whom the following was pieced together.

On their way to the toilets, Kirste and Joanne tried to entice some kittens from underneath a car parked near the large equipment shed, which was close to the men's restroom behind the grandstand. Joanne loved cats and dogs, so playing with and hopefully holding some kittens would have been exciting.

An eyewitness, sixty-one year old Ken Wohling, who was an assistant curator of the oval, was in the gardener's shed at the back of the Creswell stand where he was close enough to hear the girls say, 'Here, puss puss.' Wohling noticed a middle-aged man standing close to him, watching the children for about five minutes before he approached them. The middle-aged man struck up a conversation and then helped both girls attract the kittens. Within a short time, Joanne and Kirste were seen following this man toward the southern exit gate, until the older girl apparently became concerned as the man took Kirste under his arm. Joanne, clearly sensing this man meant no good, began to hit him with flailing arms as he took Kirste outside the grounds.[66]

Another eyewitness, thirteen-year-old Anthony Kilmartin, a vendor selling sweets and ice creams, said the man angrily spoke to the older girl as she was fiercely protesting: '"Go away, you little bitch," or something like that.'[67]

Anthony went on to say Joanne followed the man outside the grounds trying to protect a distressed Kirste. However, she was no match for this cunning and much stronger male and ended up being grabbed by him, too. Anthony did not raise the alarm because he thought this man was the girls' angry father.[67] This all unfolded just after 3.45 pm. The police were alerted at 5.12 pm—ample time for the predator to disappear. The suspect was described as a middle-aged man wearing a brown, broad-rimmed Akubra hat and brown trousers with a grey checked coat. Height approximated was five feet and ten to eleven inches, but he was slightly stooped.

To us, this abduction, unlike the Beaumont children's disappearance, was more opportunistic than a premeditated attack, although this possibility cannot be excluded. However, it would appear the abductor was at the football grounds for one reason, and it was not the game.

Detectives were confronted with little substantial information that would lead them in a positive direction. Joanne Ratcliffe's father was mystified when interviewed by police, because his daughter had been to the oval dozens of times and he did not believe that she would have left the oval voluntarily. She knew how to use a telephone and call an emergency number and was well aware not to talk to strangers. However, being a mature, responsible girl, protecting Kirste would have been her priority.

As Nicola Gage, a journalist from *ABC News*, in her article on Sunday 30 July 2017 during Missing Persons Week, states, 'Despite the time that has passed, Mrs Gordon said the heartbreak still felt as raw as the day it happened. 'It was the longest day I think I've ever lived in my life,' she said. 'When someone's missing, you have this ongoing rollercoaster of hope and hopelessness.'[68]

Christine Gordon went on to say, 'I suppose deep down there is an anger there that doesn't go away because this person did not have the right to interfere with those girls.'

Here we have two comparable abductions of young children only seven years apart, both groups taken from a distracted crowd in broad daylight where the perpetrator's anonymity is assured, with a similar physical description and modus operandi. The similarities between this crime and the abduction of Jane, Arnna, and Grant Beaumont are striking and did not go unnoticed by detectives, the media, and the general population. Stuart Mullins and Bill Hayes agree that if one solves the Beaumont case, it could well allow some inevitable similarities to the Adelaide Oval abductions to be made.

When police requested a watercolour impression of the suspect from an art teacher from the South Australian School of Arts, one could notice the strong similarities to the sketch produced seven years earlier of the man seen with the Beaumont children the day they disappeared. Detectives did not want this to become another Beaumont case. However, Superintendent Noel Lenton, the senior detective on the case, privately believed this was so.

In both abductions, the perpetrator used bait and a promise. In 1966, the set-up was stolen money, and the bait was the one-pound note. At the Adelaide Oval, it was kittens. The man kindly helped Kirste and Joanne coax the kittens out from under the parked car. Being unsuccessful, he may have used the ploy 'I have kittens in my car', or 'I spotted some around the entrance of the southern gate', and so the children happily followed him, to a point, much like the Beaumont children in 1966, where the children followed the lure of the pound. As Dr Xanthé Mallett states in her book *Cold Case Investigations*, 'When children are taken by a stranger, the most common tactic is to lure the child into a car with the promise of money, sweets, or to see some puppies or kittens, anything that might appeal to a young child.'[3]

In both abductions, a man appeared to size up the situation by watching from a short distance—lying on his beach towel at Colley Reserve and staring at Jane, Arnna, and Grant, and standing and watching Joanne and Kirste attempt to catch a kitten.

What alarmed Bill Hayes and Stuart Mullins was Anthony Kilmartin's statement to the police regarding his recollection of what the man said to Joanne. While she fiercely struggled to free Kirste from his clutches, the man angrily said, '"Go away, you little bitch," or something like that.[67]

It was the 'something like that' that pricked up the ears of Mullins. He had been contacted several years earlier by a gentleman claiming to have been a good friend of Anthony Kilmartin in the early 1970s. He stated Anthony had told him the man exclaimed to Joanne, 'Fuck off, you little bitch.' Also, this friend said he was left with an impression from Anthony that the last word was a little more colourful than 'bitch'. This type of language would make sense as this man was under pressure to disappear quickly. In our opinion, having Joanne fiercely punching him would draw unwanted attention. In anger, this little girl was causing trouble, and he was more likely to say 'fuck off' than 'go away'.

Anthony's alleged friend may be right; however, neither Mullins nor Hayes can corroborate what he was saying—only the original transcript of Kilmartin's interview with Major Crime could. Our opinion has always been Anthony would not have likely said the word 'fuck' to the press because, unlike today, this type of vocabulary was deemed inappropriate. So, he said 'or something like that'. If the police statement confirms he did use the word 'fuck', then a major red flag might be raised, because it might show a link between the perpetrator of the Adelaide Oval abduction and Harry Phipps. However, the reality is that this type of language could extend to almost anyone given the common usage of the word by certain types of people. At best there is a tenuous link to the known behaviours of Phipps and the man at the oval. Although there is some likeness to the photofit of the man at the oval, his personal description does not fit that of Phipps.

And lastly, there is the modus operandi of watching and waiting. This is common predatory paedophile behaviour. Before the man attempted his move on Joanne and Kirste, he spent time watching them, waiting for an opportunity to strike. At Colley Reserve, the man seen with Jane, Arnna, and Grant Beaumont lay on his towel staring as the children ran up from the water's edge and played under the sprinklers. In the 1970s, the rapist stood outside the Castalloy factory and watched his thirteen-year-old victim as she walked to school and from her girlfriend's place in the afternoons for several weeks, waiting for the ideal time to strike.

In the animal kingdom, lions hunt their prey in a defined area, their killing fields. What we have gleaned over years of research is that most serial killers are the same. The serial sexual predator will usually stalk its prey in a defined area, an area they are comfortable with, a city they know. In many cases, they already have planned where they will dispose of the body. Somewhere close, in a location they are familiar with. It's fair to assume the person responsible for these two crimes is an Adelaide local.

We know that there have been suspects nominated over the years, including, as we have said, Harry Phipps. There are more suspects, and it is not the authors' intention to go into those suspects in any detail in this book. Suffice it to say that the work goes on to find out just who the abductor or abductors are in this case as it does with the Beaumonts. The authors firmly believe that despite the passage of time, these cases can and will be solved. Someone out there has knowledge that will be key to solving this crime. It is time that they told the police just what they know to allow the family of Joanne and Kirste and the public of South Australia to have closure.

In closing this chapter, we must recognise the extreme bravery shown by Joanne Ratcliffe on this day. We feel certain that Kirste Gordon was the primary target of this abductor, as she was taken roughly under the arm of the offender away from the oval. According to witnesses, they were closely followed all the way to the River Torrens near the university footbridge by Joanne. Joanne was seen attacking this man, screaming, kicking, and punching him, and demanding that he let Kirste go, just as she had been seen to do at the Oval. In doing this and refusing to leave Kirste to her fate, Joanne had sacrificed herself for her little friend. There is no doubt that she could quite easily have escaped had she wished to. Remember that Joanne was only eleven years old, a small, slight little girl attacking a much larger and stronger man. We do recognise that perhaps, given that the focus of the investigation was elsewhere, Joanne has not been recognised for her actions and bravery, to say nothing of her self-sacrifice in giving her life to try to save Kirste on that day. It is time to correct that oversight, and we suggest that Joanne Ratcliffe should be recognised now with a posthumous award. It is not too late, and it is very much deserved.

Chapter 22:
Child Abduction and Murder

The hardest thing I've ever had to hear was that my child died. The hardest thing I will ever have to do is to live every day since that moment.

—A grieving mother

Few crime topics elicit as much fear, anxiety, and concern as child abduction and murder. Why do we have such a robust response from the general public? Emotionally, we feel personally connected. Losing a child, having them taken by a stranger, would devastate any parent, any family. The very idea rips at the heart and soul of not only parents but also the broader community. Hence this type of abduction can quickly morph into public hysteria, even though these types of crimes are rare.

Empirical research on this type of murderer is surprisingly scarce despite the interest in this topic. Most studies have looked at sexual murderers of adult women, which are more prevalent, neglecting to look at those who murder children. Why? The statistics regarding a child being abducted and murdered are extremely low due to their worldwide rarity. When reviewing Australia's child abductions and facts, Jeremy D Morley International Family Law states that there are approximately 170 reported cases of child abduction both into and out of Australia per year, out of a population of 25.5 million, which is mostly to do with a breakdown of the parents' relationship.[69]

When Helen Pitt, a journalist for the *Sydney Morning Herald*, wrote an article on 7 July 2019 regarding Australian child abduction and murder, the article suggests that occurrences were exceptionally rare. Since the Beaumont children were abducted and likely murdered in 1966, there have only been fourteen other cases in fifty-six years, with only very few of those unsolved.[70]

We have added a further two that had been missed in Helen's detailed research to bring it to fourteen: the case involving Arthur Stanley Brown abducting and murdering two girls in North Queensland in August 1970, and the abduction of Joanne Ratcliffe and Kirste Gordon from the Adelaide Oval in 1973.

According to Thor Benson, writer for *The Atlantic* and contributor to *The Daily Beast,* 'There is a one in 300,000 chance of a child being abducted off the street, playgroup or the beach. Even when a child is abducted, it's usually by someone known to the family; such as a relative or a friend.'[71]

In fact, a child may have more chance of being hit by lightning than being abducted by a stranger and a much smaller chance of being sexually assaulted and murdered by them. According to Elizabeth Nolan Brown, award-winning writer and senior editor at *Reason* magazine, 'A casual observer could be forgiven for thinking we're in the midst of a child-abduction epidemic. US kids are no more likely to be abducted today than they were decades ago, and much more likely to be returned safely when they are.'[72]

We believe the same goes for Australian children. Hence, a child being abducted and murdered is extremely rare. The abduction of multiple children is incomprehensible. This is what makes the taking of Jane, Arnna, and Grant Beaumont in 1966 and Kirste Gordon and Joanne Ratcliffe in 1973 so abnormal.

Being so incredibly uncommon due to their infrequency, these similar crimes taking place so close together in a city like Adelaide might lead one to the assumption that the same individual was involved. Why? Only a small number of paedophiles become murderers; therefore, the likelihood of Adelaide accommodating two within a short period is low.

Two others have been identified; the first was the kidnapping, sexual assault, and murder of sisters Sheila (aged twelve) and Katherine Lyon (aged ten), but this occurred in the United States. Here we have two siblings taken in broad daylight on a trip to a shopping mall in the suburb of Wheaton, Maryland, in March 1975, which resulted in one of the most extensive police investigations in the Washington area. The girls disappeared without a trace, and for thirty-eight years, this crime remained unsolved until Lloyd Welch was finally convicted of the abduction, sexual assault, and murder of the two girls.

The other case is closer to home. On 26 August 1970, Arthur Stanley Brown, aged fifty-eight at the time, allegedly raped and murdered Judith (aged seven) and Susan (aged five) Mackay and then left them for dead in a dry riverbed twenty-five kilometres south-west of Townsville in Queensland.

When a paedophile crosses the line and abducts and murders a child, the statistics are disturbing and profound and uncover a grim outcome. The most common methods of death in child homicides are strangulation/suffocation and stabbing. According to Ada Charalambous' thesis, *Behavioural Characteristics and Attributes of Child Sexual Homicide*, these were preferred due to the 'presumed vulnerability and engaging of control over the victims'.[73]

Kathleen Heide from the Department of Criminology at the University of South Florida suggests that sexual murderers of children tend to form a relatively homogeneous group, matching several characteristics of the sadistic offender.[74]

O'Meara, Davies, and Hammond in 2011 defined a sadistic personality as:

> A person who humiliates others, shows a longstanding pattern of cruel or demeaning behaviour to others, or intentionally inflicts physical, sexual or psychological pain or suffering on others in order to assert power and dominance or for pleasure.[75]

This is why few Australian crime topics evoke as much dread and distress as the cases of the Beaumonts and the Adelaide Oval abduction. As Jane's best friend Jenny told Stuart Mullins, she has shed tears over the decades thinking of the fate that befell her best friend Jane and her siblings and of how they might have suffered.

According to attorney Bob Ferguson at the Washington State Attorney-General's Office, the primary motive for the perpetrator of child abduction and murder in the cases studied is sexual assault. The stats are chilling: seventy-six percent of children are killed within three hours of being taken; 88.5 percent within twenty-four hours; ninety-nine percent within seven days; and 100 percent within one hundred days.[76]

Eric Beauregard, who holds a PhD in Criminology from Simon Fraser University, reported in a paper co-authored by Maryann Stone, Jean Proulx, and Patrick Michaud:

> It appears that sexual murderers of children are more often victims of sexual abuse during childhood and present

more often deviant sexual fantasies as compared to sexual murderers of women [...] sexual murderers of children more often use pornography prior to the crime, have contact with the victim prior to the crime, and commit a crime more often characterised by premeditation, strangulation, [and] the hiding of the body.[77]

Though there has been no proof that the Beaumont children or Kirste Gordon and Joanne Ratcliffe were murdered, the sad fact is that we all know this to be a high probability. The statistics garnered from an extensive report compiled by Dr Keppel, chief criminal investigator; Dr Weis, Professor of Sociology; and KA Hanfland, Violent Crime Investigations Supervisor with Homicide Investigation at the Washington State Attorney-General's office show that 'the typical child victim of an abduction–murder is a white female who is about 11 years old.'[78]

Joanne Ratcliffe was eleven; Jane Beaumont was nine.

She is from a middle class or 'blue-collar' family who lives in an urban or suburban neighbourhood, in a family residence. Her relationship with her family is stable, and the child is described as a 'normal kid'. In short, she is your average preteen girl.[78]

The same worldwide study showed that eighty-seven percent of murderers are male. The killing of children during an abduction, however, is almost a totally male domain of behaviour—an astounding 98.5 percent.[78] Going by these statistics, what is so heart-rending is the knowledge that as soon as this individual made contact with the children, they were never going home. Many paedophiles who murder display a distinct pattern, a similar modus operandi. So, if you think the Adelaide Oval and Beaumont children's abductions are connected, you might very well be right. Or could the Adelaide Oval abductions have been a 'copycat crime' done by another person to emulate the Beaumont abductions?

According to Kenneth A Hanfland and the team at the Washington State Attorney-General's office, two-thirds—sixty-seven percent—of the assailants had previously committed crimes against children with a similar modus operandi (MO).

The report goes on to state that: 'The similarities in MOs produced other surprises: They were most alike, by a large margin, in the 'commission of the offence,' […] using deception to gain control over an eventual molestation victim and later the murder victim.'[78]

This appears to have been the case in both the Beaumont and the Ratcliffe/Gordon abductions. The deception at Colley Reserve was the stolen-money scenario and, at the Adelaide oval, the possible suggestion of more kittens to play with. In both cases, the abductor deceived the children in order to lure them away.

Did this individual have premeditated murder planned after the sexual abuse, or did he not think that far ahead? Was he too overwhelmed by unbridled sexual lust, desire, and fantasy to think what he would do with his victims afterwards?

When Duncan McNab spoke to us in late 2017, he stated:

Like all crimes, some are planned, some are simply an opportunity presented. Like William Tyrrell (a three-year-old Australian boy who disappeared from his foster grand-mother's front yard in Kendal, New South Wales, in 2014). Whereas, Renee Aitken (aged five when she disappeared from a bedroom she shared with her brother Brad, aged eight on 16 February 1984 in the small country town of Narooma, New South Wales) was obviously planned. Yet the Adelaide Oval abduction is likely to have been opportunistic—and to us, exactly like the Beaumont's abduction. A confluence of opportunity, ego, arrogance, ability but not necessarily his habitual MO.

When we are dealing with the abduction of multiple children, a few variables come into play. Where a single child is abducted and sexually abused, there is a small chance of the child being found alive. For the child to speak about their ordeal would be extremely difficult, especially if what they have experienced is of a sexually sadistic nature. If the abuser is a stranger, the chance of identifying him would be small. Once the decision is made to abduct multiple children, the abductor would know the chance of them identifying him is more significant. Plus, as the children grow into adults, they may wish to speak out collectively. The risk of exposure for the paedophile is now many times greater.

Over the years, as the authors have investigated the Beaumonts' abduction, the one thing that has been asked of them many times is, how do you control multiple children in situations like these? At some point, the veneer of the charming, engaging, helpful, nice man would change. We had a glimpse of this at the Adelaide Oval when Joanne protested as the man attempted to lead the children out of the oval gates with Kirste under his arm. At some point in the abduction of children, the demeanour of the individual changes to verbal and physical aggression, which would be used to control the children. Any child in these circumstances would be cowered into submission and silence. To a sadistic paedophile, this cowering would be perversely pleasurable.

In general, the abduction, sexual abuse, and murder of children is rare; however, violent child sexual abuse is not. According to the National Sexual Violence Resource Centre, one in four girls and one in six boys (or about one in ten children) will be sexually abused before their eighteenth birthday.[79]

Gender is also a significant factor in sexual abuse. Females are five times more likely to be abused than males. This being the case, the reader may well know someone who has been abused.

The same study showed that ninety-six percent of people who sexually abuse children are male,[79] and seventy-six percent are married men.[80]

According to Darkness to Light, nearly seventy percent of child sex offenders have between one and nine victims and twenty percent have ten to forty victims.[63]

Many people have asked Bill Hayes and Stuart Mullins if they think Harry Phipps had other victims. Based on his characteristics and behavioural patterns, and the knowledge that the majority of paedophiles do not stop offending until they are caught, they believe that he did. The odds that Phipps struck again are high. He would have been unstoppable until caught. But Harry Phipps went to his grave without ever being held to account.

No parent ever wants to contemplate the thought of their child never returning home. But for Nancy and Jim Beaumont, Christine and Greg Gordon, and Kathleen and Les Ratcliffe, this became their lifelong reality. The authors feel that Jim Beaumont spoke for all parents involved when he said, 'If I could give my life right now for my kids to be returned safe and sound, I would.'[81]

Chapter 23:
The Evil Choir

*You're not a victim for sharing your story. You are a
survivor setting the world on fire with your truth. And
you never know who needs your light, your warmth,
and raging courage.*

—Alex Elle

In February 2019, Stuart Mullins met with sportsman-
turned-journalist Graham Cornes as a guest on Cornes' radio chat
show on local Adelaide radio station Five AA: 'Conversations with
Cornesy'. Graham is well known for delivering a series of behind-
the-scenes, insightful, enjoyable, and telling interviews with sports-
people, authors, businesspeople, musicians, and politicians.

The purpose of the interview was to discuss *The Satin Man*,
which Mullins co-authored with Alan Whiticker. This book
discussed the case of the missing Beaumont children and the
alleged involvement of Harry Phipps, though Phipps was not
named in that book.

Within hours of the radio interview, Mullins was contacted
by producer Leith Forrest, who reported that the Five AA
switchboard had been inundated with calls and information
about the case. Such events are not unusual when the Beaumont
case is discussed.

Most of the callers were well-meaning people who had a point to make, armed with theories or he-said-she-said whispers. One caller in particular, a mature male, captured Forrest's attention, and he immediately contacted Mullins, who in turn got in touch with Bill.

A sense of foreboding immediately struck them. What was once relegated to the realms of gossip about a mysterious Adelaide paedophile society surrounded by decades of conspiracy theories, hearsay, and rumour could well hold some truth.

The information that Leith Forrest passed on to us came from a well-respected, intelligent, articulate, experienced professional who had at the time chosen to remain anonymous. Hayes later ascertained this gentleman was a well-respected former private college principal; however, they agreed not to disclose his name. The authors will refer to him as Robert (not his real name).

Following an in-depth conversation, Hayes concluded that he was telling the truth as he believed it to be. Robert reported to Hayes that he had spoken to and met with a lady 'Christine and her brother Ted' (not their real names) on several occasions. Robert and the siblings discussed disturbing events they had experienced when Christine was a small child. Her brother Ted, also a child at the time, could corroborate what his sister had said to a point. At no time were names or circumstances of these conversations shared with others. Still, Hayes believes these conversations were recent and that Robert may have been acting in a counselling capacity to the lady and her brother Ted. The information they wanted to speak to Rob about involved Harry Phipps and a group of men who regularly met at a cottage on the Castalloy site at North Plympton.

We knew that Castalloy had two cottages. One cottage was used in the early-to-mid-1960s to make and shape custom

Castalloy-manufactured South Coaster surfboards and craft tailor-made canvas bags. This sideline business was managed by Dave (not his real name), whom the company employed. The boards, with the bags, were sold to department store Harris Scarfe®. In the end, the business was not profitable, and Harry Phipps closed it down. Dave went on to open his own surf shop in Adelaide. Recently, Stuart asked Dave whether he had any idea about the use of the second Castalloy cottage, as he had worked right next door. He did not, further adding that Phipps would have hidden his 'goings-on'.

The other cottage became known by some Castalloy factory workers as 'Harry's Cottage'. Harry Phipps was the only person with keys to this second cottage, and no-one else from the factory was allowed into it. This information was confirmed by several former Castalloy employees who worked in the factory at the time.

Robert told Bill Hayes that Phipps had decorated one of the rooms and fitted it out with the very best of toys, which would have been like a bee to a flower for small children. According to Rob's information, the play items were there to keep children occupied and happy for reasons that will soon become apparent.

Robert also told Hayes that this cottage not only housed Harry Phipps' fetish accessories, but it was where he gathered around him some 'birds of a feather'—a number of paedophilic men. These men—husbands and fathers—would bring their own small children to arranged meetings at 'Harry's Cottage'. They would put their children, male and female, into the 'toy room' to play with the toys. One could only hazard a guess as to what the paedophile fathers and Harry did while in another part of the cottage, the unsuspecting children played with the toys.

Eventually, the group would select a child for abuse. That child would be taken from the toy room and subjected to such depravity that is beyond understanding to anything less than the most twisted and black imagination.

In this case, as reported to Robert, the then-little girl Christine was the target of this group, in which her father and Harry were active. Her brother, Ted, who has confirmed his sister's story, was also brought along, not for abuse but to allow the father to take his daughter out without raising the suspicions of their mother.

According to Robert, this memory is very clear in Ted's and Christine's minds, and it appears that they were taken to Harry's Cottage on several occasions. Not surprisingly, Christine and Ted are both very damaged and hurt by the abuse and the tortured memories they carry from this episode of their young lives, a time they should have been safe and cared for by the very person who was, in fact, their abuser. After they spoke to Robert, Bill felt that Christine may have been receiving ongoing counselling from Robert.

Stuart Mullins and Bill Hayes fully respect the witnesses' decision to retain their anonymity. However, the authors continue to hope that the publication of this book will encourage them to reconsider their position and to further seek professional help. Those police officers who deal with the victims of such crimes are compassionate and well-trained officers who have undergone a rigid selection process and training to work in this role. Likewise, Commissioner Bronwyn Killmier, the present South Australian Commissioner for Victims Rights, and her staff will always ensure that victims of crime are given all necessary assistance to help them recover from their experiences. They do not need to go on living in hell as they have done for decades.

We feel that they must ask the question, could the Beaumont children have been brought to 'Harry's Cottage' for one of these meetings after they were abducted on 26 January 1966? Might they have been handed over to sick, deviant paedophiles who, like Harry, sexually abused children? If that were the case, what reaction would Jane have had if she or one of her siblings were selected for abuse? Knowing what we know about Jane, though only a child herself, we would conclude she would have exhibited a very serious reaction.

For this organised group of paedophiles, a non-compliant victim would have been a major dilemma. Perhaps their own children were so used to being abused by their fathers that the 'meetings' at Harry's Cottage seemed normal to them. Following this hypothesis, could these men allow this non-compliant child—Jane Beaumont—to leave? Of course they couldn't. To do so would mean the end of their illegal and reprehensible activities and a lengthy jail term, to say nothing of what would happen to them in prison. The majority of what were known in those days as 'decent, honest criminals' would not tolerate child molesters or 'rock spiders', as they are colloquially known. A paedophile's time in prison would likely be cut short. Therefore, the paedophile group's options were limited. The risk would need to be eliminated: the children would have to be disposed of.

Could this group tie in with meetings with the like-minded men at the Castalloy canteen or the private Adelaide gentlemen's club, as mentioned in previous chapters? Does it tie in with Haydn Phipps saying to Bill Hayes, 'Are you going to put these bastards in jail, Bill?' This question was raised by Haydn several years before the authors were advised of these paedophile fathers meeting at Castalloy. The use of the plural 'bastards' is chilling—was he referring to this group of paedophiles?

What is also chilling is the sign placed on the Castalloy fence on the 2018 anniversary of the abduction of the children that pointed to 'Harry Phipps and all his evil associates' being involved and said that 'the little boy is not buried here with his sisters', as shown in the image section.

If the sign on the gate is accurate, might Grant Beaumont have suffered a different fate than that of his sisters? Once again, hypothetically, if four-year-old Grant Beaumont did not die with his sisters Jane and Anna, he would likely retain little memory of his parents as time passed. Might he have been less likely than his older siblings to raise a fuss had he been kept by this group of paedophiles? It is too horrible to imagine what might have happened.

Stuart Mullins and Bill Hayes have been inside 'Harry's Cottage' on several occasions. It is an old, detached building now on the Castalloy site, but originally would have likely been a home prior to the site being built.

It is a typical building from the early twentieth century, with a rendered exterior and tin roof, and it is facing the main road. There is a front entrance through a single door. However, it appears that over the decades the back entrance facing the Castalloy sandpit was the main thoroughfare into the cottage. There are rectangular-shaped side windows on both sides of the cottage, which allow some light into the interior. The overall outside appearance gives the impression that the cottage was a well-built structure; however, with the march of time, it has fallen into disrepair, as the interior wooden floors have now mostly disintegrated, and the rooms are drab and dingy. Entry to the cottage is through the back door, then through a laundry, and into a small hallway. From there, to the left is where the kitchen would have been and to the right is a large room that at one time would likely have been the rear bedroom. The front part might have been a living room, possibly separated by a partition wall but certainly during its life as Harry's Cottage that room was one large room, as evidenced by some concrete work apparently laid to hold Harry's sewing machines where he made his fetish clothing. At the bottom of the hallway is a door leading into the living room and another door into what was likely to have been a front bedroom in the original home.

Every room in the cottage was in disrepair apart from one that appeared to be in better condition. This front room with the windows painted over faced the busy street. The walls were lined with varnished wood panelling, which became popular in the 1960s and 1970s. There were tacks still embedded on some parts of the walls that indicated paintings were hanging there at one time.

When we visited the site, it was a business day with traffic, both light and heavy vehicles, moving up and down the street. From within the cottage, very little could be heard due to the soundproof quality of the thick walls, the sturdy door, and blocked-out windows. In short, it was the ideal location to remain unseen and unheard inside.

What we found unusual inside this cottage is another room adjacent to the wood-panelled room. There were two very distinct concrete steel-reinforced blocks placed into the floor and poured in a way that the ends fit into the floor joists, thus securing them. Each block is around 1.1 metres long by 800 centimetres wide by 500 centimetres deep. The finish on the top is smooth and even. The authors estimate that each block would weigh something in the region of 1.5 tonnes. A great deal of concrete, indeed. The question is, why? Harry Phipps was known to sew dresses, so could these very large concrete blocks have been made to sit a sewing machine on? Industrial sewing machines can be quite solid and heavy, but would a 1.5-tonne concrete steel-reinforced block be required to hold one? Could this indicate a possible burial site? In all fairness, we cannot answer these questions and have no real idea what these blocks were used for. Only Harry Phipps could do so, but unfortunately, it is too late for that. Or is there someone out there who does know what went on in that cottage? Who is remaining silent? The authors are confident that there is.

From the description given by Haydn Phipps to Bill Hayes, from the back door of the cottages to the edge of the sandpit would have been no more than seven to ten metres. There had been a deep hole there, into which sand from the factory castings would be thrown and then covered by a grader that sat there for the purpose of covering and levelling. Harry Phipps was familiar with driving this grader.

In Haydn and Bill Hayes's recorded interview, listened to by Australian polygraph expert Steve Van Aperen and Mandy, a statement analysis expert in Europe, Haydn speaks about the cottage on Mooringe Avenue. This spot is important to him. He talks about the dump/sandpit. But later, he changes; his language around that spot goes from speaking of four acres of sand and a drop-off to a more expressive term—'shithole'—and then he calls it a 'shit pit'. This implies that his feelings toward this place have changed in a negative way. In Mandy's words, 'It can be connected to the [Beaumont] children.' This statement-analysis expert goes on to state that Haydn saw something that he was scared to talk about, and he blamed himself for not coming forward to report it.

We now ask, what happened in these cottages and the sandpit that scared Haydn into silence? Could what he said all along be true? Were Jane, Arnna, and Grant Beaumont abused and used as paedophile playthings in Harry's cottage—as Christine had been—to be discarded into the sandpit out the back and then bulldozed over? Did Adelaide have a privileged group of undetected paedophiles hidden under the disguise of respectable, well-presented Adelaide businessmen, politicians, members of the cloth, and judiciary? Were these perpetrators so bold, brazen, and supremely confident that they could hide in clear sight right under the collective noses of the Adelaide community? Dismissed by some as folklore, myth, and fiction, does this idea have some validity? It now appears to be so.

Chapter 24:
The Mullighan Inquiry

I believe good governments have nothing to hide.
We want to ensure we maintain confidence in our
public institutions.

—Jay Weatherill, former premier of South Australia

In 2004, the Children in State Care Commission of Inquiry, or the 'Mullighan Inquiry', was enacted by the parliament of South Australia to investigate allegations of abuse of children in state care. Commencing hearings in December of that year and meant to take only six months, this quickly ballooned into a three-year inquiry into the abuse of children in the care of the South Australian Government at a cost of 13.5 million dollars. The sheer number of individuals who were allegedly sexually abused as minors in state care and in general mostly from the 1940s to the 1970s was mind-boggling.

The Labor State Premier at the time was Mike Rann. He, like many, could not have foreseen that this investigation would uncover the extent of child exploitation, which was nothing short of appalling and shook the establishment to its core. The commissioner, the Right Honourable EP Mullighan, QC, personally interviewed 792 people who were victims of child sexual abuse, of which 242 had been children in state care at the time of their alleged abuse. Of the people who were victims, Mullighan had referred 170 people with information about 434 alleged paedophiles to the police. An edited version of the report has been prepared by Dr Robert N Moles of Networked Knowledge and states of the people who were victims, Mullighan had referred 170 people with information about 434 alleged paedophiles to the police. On 1 April 2008, Colin James of The Advertiser reported, Mullighan said he had been totally unprepared for the 'foul undercurrent of society' which had perpetrated child sex abuse against wards of the State between the 1940s and 1980s.

For many years, victims of sexual abuse in South Australia never had a platform to say what had happened to them. In speaking to the Mullighan Inquiry, an elderly woman, who had been in state care as a child, said early in her evidence, 'Who is ever there for frightened little girls in cupboards? Now you are there because you give me a voice and I wanted to say that.' Many of the sexually abused gave various reasons to the inquiry for not disclosing their ordeal, the main ones being the fear of not being believed or having to tell several members of a family and some friends in the hope that they would be believed. Many times, they were not, their accounts about the sexual abuse from 'Uncle Berty' or the ward officer being dismissed as sheer folly. One lady told the commission, 'You get told so many times not to say anything and someone suddenly says, "I want to hear what you have to say."' Another witness said:

> I never forgot nothing because I knew one day, through all I went through, that one day I would get a voice out there, out in the world. Because virtually, when I got brought up in the homes and taken away at six, it was virtually, I didn't know, the world was shut out to me.

One elderly woman gave evidence in the presence of one of her six children. That night, the children discussed at length what had happened to their mother, and a daughter later told Mullighan, 'We had always felt sorry for our mother; now we feel proud of her.' Some witnesses expressed their reasons for giving evidence to the Inquiry. One man told the inquiry, 'I've had days where I just wanted to give it all away and I just hope that this talk will end it.' A young woman said she hoped that her evidence will help police apprehend current abusers 'before they do it to another person'. We should have been shocked by Commissioner Mullighan's statement, reported by Colin James, but were not: 'While the full extent of the sexual abuse of children in State care can never be known, it is possible that the people who gave evidence to the inquiry are the tip of the iceberg'. We agree, as after fourteen years of investigation into the Beaumont case, nothing surprises us anymore.

The public and Commissioner Mullighan himself were still not prepared for what was yet to come regarding the horror of the sexual abuse and exploitation of children in state care by those in positions of trust and responsibility. What we found equally frightening were comments from this inquiry where victims spoke about paedophile parties for sexual gratification, facilitated by the supply of drugs and alcohol. Haydn and Christine may well be telling the truth about others being involved, as discussed in previous chapters of this book with Haydn saying, 'Are you going to put these bastards in jail, Bill?', the A4-sized note hung on the main front gate of Castalloy in January 2018 mentioning Harry Phipps and his 'evil associates', the bartender couple serving Phipps and 'like-minded men' at a private gentlemen's club in South Terrance, and the gathering of like-minded men inside the Castalloy canteen on selected weekends. Please note that we understand and accept that cross-dressing does not make one a paedophile.

Before the inquiry, many in the South Australian public had little understanding of the extent of sexual abuse of minors in South Australia and that people who had been abused felt a fear of not being believed and suffered in silence. In addition, victims felt that they may have contributed or had been responsible in some way for the abuse, which contributed to their silence. Due to this, the hearings were incredibly beneficial to the people making these disclosures, many expressing the importance of having been believed by someone 'in authority'. Because of these, more alleged victims of sexual abuse began stepping forward, knowing that for the first time since the 1950s, 60s, or 70s, they would be listened to.

Mullighan submitted his final report to the Governor of South Australia on 31 March 2008. The *Fourth Annual Progress Report in response to the Children in State Care Commission of Inquiry Report,* in part, states that many of the alleged incidents occurred in the 1960s and 70s, a period that Phipps and his cohorts appear to have been active. To the South Australian public, these children were sexually exploited, abused, threatened, and left vulnerable. Dozens of victims spent several days giving evidence to the enquiry and reliving for the first time in public their horrific and nightmarish childhood sexual abuse experiences. As the amount of damning sexual abuse information was still coming in, police only arrested two suspects out of 434 alleged paedophiles. With this type of statistic and unexplained inaction, the reader, like ourselves, can understand why many sexual abuse victims are hesitant to step forward. They can understand why the South Australian public is extremely sceptical, with a strong belief that a high-level, well-connected paedophile ring did, in fact, exist in the 1950s, 60s, and 70s. With so few being arrested, one might be led to ask the question, was there undue pressure emanating from sections of the old guard in government, the public service, or the upper echelons of South Australian society to place a halt to all this? Was the Mullighan Commission getting too close to those in power, whether it be current or former government officials, government ministers, law enforcement, the judiciary, or others in the higher echelons of business and South Australian society? The reality most likely is that there was simply not enough evidence to lead to those named being charged.

Shortly after the inquiry was completed, the public was gobsmacked that the South Australian government placed an eighty-year suppression order on portions of the Mullighan Commission, especially those who were named by the victims. This may be unfathomable in today's society. In fairness to the government, there are a number of very good reasons why names were not released. It is extremely likely that the order was placed on the advice of the Crown law department to the government to do just that. It is a question of whether those named are still living and if they have been brought before a court, charged, and convicted of these crimes. In the main, they have been named by victims without any other evidence, real or circumstantial, being able to be held against them. It doesn't mean that the victims were not believed—they were. Rightly or wrongly, it all comes down to our system of justice that is there to protect all, even the guilty if no evidence is available to support charges. If those named are now deceased, then they could legally have been named, but an all-enclosing suppression order was the most logical way to deal with it. We feel confident that the public of South Australia can rest assured that the suppression order was made for good and lawful reasons and not to protect paedophiles.

We, the people of South Australia, should congratulate Commissioner Justice Mullighan on the outstanding way this commission was conducted and on the startling findings made. He has given a voice to those unheard for so long. It is now down to the government to take action to ensure that these findings never need to be made again.

Chapter 25

The Purse

Coincidences mean you're on the right path.[82]

—Simon Van Booy

In June of 2007, Stuart Mullins met Elizabeth Phipps, Harry's second wife. They married not long after Elizabeth answered an employment advertisement in the local paper for a maid/cook. Born Daisy Ward, she grew up in Scotland before she moved to England and became a qualified nurse. After gaining valuable experience as a nurse, she emigrated to South Australia, obtaining work at a school-uniform garment factory near Adelaide. The owners described Daisy as a bit of a card, outgoing and streetwise. She knew how to play the game/rort the system, displaying an indifference to the truth and morality when it came to money, which appeared to dictate her decision-making abilities.

Hence, Daisy's downfall during her life was money mixed with heavy gambling. She always had an excuse for not being at work, which was a cover for her addiction.

Daisy was the type of woman who came and went as she pleased. According to the manager, the standing joke at the factory was, 'Has Daisy found her sugar daddy yet?' She made no secret this was her mission. The factory staff would humorously call out across the shop floor, 'Daisy, have you got a rich boyfriend yet?'

When Daisy secured the position at Isola after answering a newspaper ad and meeting the resident Harry Phipps, Daisy made no secret of the fact that she had struck the jackpot to her fellow factory workers and the owners. She gave no notice and left that day to begin her new role.

Once married to Harry, approximately a year later, she changed her name to Elizabeth Phipps—a name better suited to her new economic level and standing in the community. Spotted many times driving around Glenelg in her new Mercedes, Daisy Ward had finally achieved the standard of living she had yearned for, and no-one was going to take this away from her.

At the time of the meeting, Stuart Mullins was compiling a detailed dossier of corroborated information regarding Harry Phipps, which he forwarded to a SAPOL Major Crime Investigation Branch detective working on the cold case. With an ever-increasing amount of compelling information, Mullins believed that Elizabeth Phipps would be the next ideal person to meet. He passed her contacts to this detective, who informed Stuart his claims would be investigated.

Stuart received an email in February 2007 from this detective advising that he had met Wayne Phipps (who lived next door to Isola) and made arrangements to speak with Elizabeth Phipps. However, after five months passed with no update, Mullins decided to meet Elizabeth. He sought an introduction from a former senior manager from the Castalloy factory, David (not his real name), who knew her quite well.

David was intrigued by what Mullins had uncovered so far regarding Harry, and nothing that he had heard had shocked or surprised him. David, as with other senior managers at Castalloy, had heard of the satin fetish and was also aware of the intense hatred Haydn exhibited for his father. This hate was palpable, and David could not put it down to a workplace issue. Something must have been happening at home. Another senior manager at the factory corroborated this comment. Both described Harry's first marriage as frosty and distant and confirmed that the physical description of Harry matched closely the man seen with the Beaumont children the day they disappeared, and they also also noted how close Harry lived to Colley Reserve.

By June 2007, on David's referral, Mullins contacted Elizabeth by phone and, on David's advice, explained that he was conducting research into Castalloy and Harry Phipps. Both David and Stuart agreed that initially mentioning the Beaumont children in the same breath as the name Harry Phipps would not be appropriate.

Meeting Elizabeth at the front door of Isola, he soon realised how large the house was. A polished tiled concrete floor ran the length of the verandah's house frontage. The immediate coolness was noticeable. Elizabeth, now in her sixties, was a small woman with a Scottish accent, well dressed and pleasant. She and Mullins initially sat in the kitchen. The design was straight out of the 1950s, today known as old-world nostalgic/retro.

Mullins felt an instant rapport with Elizabeth as she showed him photos. Some snaps were taken of Harry in the 1920s to the late 1950s, but not much after that. One showed Harry with his tennis buddies in the 1950s, another with male friends lying on the beach at Glenelg in the 1940s. There was one of a five-year-old Harry wearing what appeared to be a frilly silk dress sitting on a tricycle.

When Mullins felt the timing was right, he mentioned having met Haydn Phipps. Her immediate reply was, 'Oh

God! What has he been saying?' This provided a valid opening for Mullins, replying to Elizabeth that Haydn alleged he was sexually abused by Harry. Mullins also raised Haydn's comments about Harry's making and wearing satin garments coupled with a deviant sexual nature. Mullins also informed Elizabeth that Haydn mentioned Harry may have had something to do with the Beaumont children and their disappearance. Mullins then showed her the book *Searching for the Beaumont Children*. At this point, Elizabeth quickly snatched the photos off the kitchen table and left the book without touching it. She became decidedly agitated and quickly retorted, 'The Beaumont children? Next, you will say he is involved with the taking of Joanne Ratcliffe and Kirste Gordon.' Mullins was taken aback by the quick association and replied, 'You certainly know your history.'

Mullins was now on full alert and reassured Elizabeth that to properly assess Haydn's claims, he needed to follow through with these allegations to ascertain their credibility. With this comment, Elizabeth was more at ease, so they adjourned to the living room. Again, this room was a throwback to the 1950s, with everything in pristine condition.

Elizabeth offered a cup of tea, and once settled, Mullins asked, 'Has a detective from Major Crime contacted you to discuss these issues?' She assured him there had been no discussions and no contact with any detective. Mullins was now more determined than ever to pursue Harry Phipps and to find the truth about the Beaumont disappearance. Mullins also felt deceived by this detective as his words were not being met with action.

Mullins spoke about Haydn and Angela's allegations of sexual abuse over many years. He also spoke of Harry making an array of satin dresses and when wearing them becoming sexually aroused. He told Elizabeth other relatives had corroborated this deviant sexual behaviour and asked if she had asked Angela, 'Is it true the boys were abused?'

Elizabeth denied this and entered into a long diatribe regarding Haydn's alcohol abuse and erratic behaviour. She also accused Angela and Haydn of having an axe to grind and being after money and revenge. Needless to say, after Harry's death, Elizabeth received the car, one and a half million dollars, and the house. But the focus of this conversation was to ascertain a possible attempted deception on Elizabeth's part and whether she was aware of Harry's addiction to satin.

This does not, of course, make him a paedophile. However, coupled with his deviant sexual behaviour, it certainly rings alarm bells. It is, therefore, understandable that Elizabeth showed distress when questioned about her knowledge of this behaviour.

In 2010, Mullins had discussions with Gary and Mary, former owners of the school-uniform garment factory that employed Elizabeth, who claimed she had asked them to take out loads of satin fabric and garments—coloured dresses—from the house after Harry was placed into care, saying, 'You have no idea what I have got myself into.' Yet when meeting Mullins, she denied any knowledge of any of that.

From Mullins' source within the extended Phipps family/ friends sphere, he was sent email conversations in 2015 between individuals relating to Elizabeth. The correspondence indicated that several people were aware of her predicament, stating that she had bitten off more than she could chew. Several noted in one discussion that Elizabeth's judgement was clouded by the almighty dollar and the dread of losing all. This was followed by, 'Harry was a bad egg; guess she found out too late. *The Satin Man* book does not surprise but still a shock.'

Even though it was clear to Mullins that Elizabeth was withholding information, it should be noted that Haydn had been harassing her by leaving several immature, silly messages on her answering machine, the likes of, 'Not a bad way to get the money—marry the bastard,' and, 'I know what you did,' with a bit of silly giggling in between the statements.

'See what I have to put up with!' she exclaimed as Mullins listened. It was apparent Haydn was intoxicated and being a nuisance, mostly speaking in derogatory terms.

Mullins understood, as he was well aware that Haydn had his moments. As a rapport was developing, Elizabeth was happy to show him around the house. She mentioned the large attic and the cellar, which Angela had told him about. Elizabeth was now well into her sixties and walking up the steep stairs to the attic was a difficult task for her, whereas the cellar off the kitchen was down just a few steps.

The basement was cool, with rows of shelves on two sides and a small window at ground level facing the backyard. There were neatly organised books along one shelf with an antique-style vase and a lamp from the 1920s or 1930s on another. On the floor were two brown vinyl suitcases in immaculate condition, straight out of the 1950s. The lack of damp, dust, and sunlight combined with the coolness to create the feel of a time warp for these antique pieces. Mullins noted a spotless printing press that would look more in place in an antique store. He mentioned to Elizabeth that this item would be worth a bit of money at an auction house or an op shop, and she agreed.

What raised Mullins' curiosity was a small, older-style beige clip purse in pristine condition lying by itself on the third tier of the bookshelf. He was aware that Jane Beaumont had a clip purse with her that fateful day. This item had a silver goldish trim at the top and two baubles that wrapped around one another to click the purse closed—the type and style of purse Mullins remembered from his childhood. He felt a cold chill knowing that in crimes like this, many paedophiles collect 'souvenirs' from their victims and rarely discard them.

For Mullins, this was the one feature that was out of place, because Harry and Olga had two boys. Mullins didn't say anything to Elizabeth at the time but was thinking on his feet. Should he grab the purse while Elizabeth was not looking? Wishful thinking on his behalf—the cellar was small, and she was standing close and to his right side where the stairs led up to the kitchen. The scenarios running through his mind were many. If he snatched and ran, he might knock an elderly Elizabeth over, and things could go astray very quickly. He could inconspicuously take the purse, but would he mess with the DNA? In retrospect, Mullins thought he might have watched too many TV crime series. In the end, the cellar was too small for him not to be noticed taking an item.

As Mullins was leaving the house after a pleasant ninety minutes, he thanked Elizabeth for her valuable time and understanding and later sent a thank-you note with flowers. Within minutes of leaving Isola, he contacted Alan Whiticker to confirm whether Jane Beaumont did indeed have a clip purse the day she vanished. Whiticker replied that she did and, going by the original police report, it was white. However, the purse Mullins spotted was light brown or off-white at best. Even though there was a colour discrepancy, Mullins had to return. He and Whiticker both knew how crucial this purse could be.

Mullins contacted Elizabeth that afternoon asking to return the next day due to an item he spotted in the basement. A time was set up to meet the following day, but when he arrived at Isola, he was greeted not only by Elizabeth but also by her close friend. The atmosphere was noticeably frosty compared to the previous day. This friend, it should be noted, was one of the emailers mentioned previously.

Mullins asked if he could view the purse in the cellar, because Jane Beaumont had carried one similar. They reluctantly agreed. Both the basement and the mood were decidedly cold. Hence, Mullins got straight to the point. He asked about the purse, and they opened it in front of him. The interior was beige, but there was nothing inside, and they quickly closed it. 'What is it doing down here?' Mullins asked. 'Harry had two boys.' Elizabeth quickly said she had bought the purse from an op shop a week earlier. Mullins replied, 'Then why would the purse be down here if you just bought it?' After that remark, he was asked to leave.

Mullins alerted the Major Crime Investigation Branch detective that he had met Elizabeth and was aware that he had neither contacted nor met her, which contradicted his previous email saying that he would make contact. This spurred the detective into action and he visited Elizabeth soon after, only to be informed she had thrown the purse out.

In Mullins' opinion, this action of discarding the purse did not seem to faze the detective, who later told Mullins he was beating his head up against a brick wall. However, Mullins was convinced this officer had been duped by the streetwise Elizabeth Phipps who, in his opinion, was a calculating, cunning woman and appeared to have conned several other detectives over the years, all to protect her wealth. However, the more Mullins continued his hunt for the truth, the easier it became to untangle the deception.

The question about Elizabeth's story is worth considering. She, a very wealthy woman, would have us believe that out of the blue she had attended an op shop and purchased this little, old-fashioned purse. Instead of placing it in her handbag to use, she had instead put it on a shelf down in an unused basement. There it had remained until noticed by Mullins, who advised her that Jane Beaumont had owned a similar purse. She later gets a visit from a detective from SAPOL whom she advises that, for no apparent reason, she has thrown this little purse out.

After Mullins' second visit to Isola, Elizabeth contacted her solicitor who, in turn, sent a letter to Mullins stating that he was an unwanted presence. The letter also suggested that Mullins hadn't been interested in photos of Harry and had used this as an excuse to get the appointment with Elizabeth. It also stated that he had accused Harry Phipps of abducting the Beaumont children.

Mullins diplomatically replied, addressing each of the issues and, in many cases, discrepancies in her account, also asking the solicitor that, if he was an unwanted presence, how did that account for his one-and-a-half-hour visit/stay? After this, Stuart received no further correspondence from the solicitor. Another detective, who visited the residence not long after the purse incident, said to Stuart that Elizabeth had accused him of gaining entry by impersonating a police officer. This was easily debunked, and Stuart gave the detective the contact of the former Castalloy manager that had referred him to her.

The detective did not visit Elizabeth for six months. At this point, Mullins enlisted arguably South Australia's foremost private investigator, Bill Hayes. Soon after a meeting was arranged with Bill, Stuart, and a different detective who had been assigned to follow up on the information presented regarding Harry Phipps. Why a new detective? Having Bill's support did open a few more doors and alerted SAPOL that he and Stuart meant business.

The SAPOL detective and Hayes were interested in this purse, and after extensive research, the question of colour was still an issue. Mullins and a senior detective exchanged several emails in 2009 as this officer was very interested in the shape, size, and colour of the purse. They requested, if possible, an image of the item seen. Mullins could find many images of small white clip purses. However, he stated in these email exchanges the purse he saw was not white, saying the item in question was off-white at best or light brown. He sent an image of the size and shape but not the exact colour, which was proving difficult to find. In the original 1966 police report, the colour of Jane's purse was described by her mother Nancy as white. But in 2018, when Stuart Mullins met Jane Beaumont's best friend Jenny, she contradicted the original police report. Knowing Jane well in their formative years, Jenny described Jane's purse as being beige in colour, not, as always thought, white. This revelation sent shudders down our respective spines.

Chapter 26:
The Police Investigation

Police officers put the badge on every morning, not knowing for sure if they'll come home at night to take it off.[83]

—Tom Cotton

L aw enforcement around the world is a demanding and challenging job that regularly involves trying to carry out sometimes-onerous duties while under-resourced. Many detectives investigate numerous cases simultaneously, where a balancing act must be performed. Which one takes priority? Is one crime more important or more urgent than the other? What are the chances of the crime being solved in a reasonable amount of time? Do they have the necessary tools at their disposal? Are they working under strict budgetary guidelines?

We all should understand that these investigations are not carried out as they are in a fictional TV crime series—where the evidence conveniently falls into place and the crime is neatly solved within an hour's viewing time. These TV shows highlight detectives exhibiting acute insight, impressive intellect, and quick wit, with an intelligent answer to every question thrown at them. Internet speed is impressively fast, and the software utilised is remarkable. Every resource is at their disposal, and the cost factor is not an issue. Evidence pops up at the most convenient time, and a positive outcome is always assured.

However, in real life, the police are not paid actors, nor do they have a script at their disposal—also, a definite conclusion to a case is not always achieved. For the most part, law enforcement officers are professionals carrying out an, at times, thankless job under the most trying circumstances. Police departments are usually under-resourced and under-staffed, and their office surroundings are a throwback to the 1970s. As Ken Poirot, award-winning author, entrepreneur, and public speaker states, 'How disappointing when the fantasy is better than the reality.'

There are also high expectations from the public, political circles, and the media. There is the expectation that police need to be perfect at all times—no mistakes, no errors of judgement, and no indiscretion or human failings. Police services worldwide are used as bureaucratic basketballs to suit the purposes of political parties and what captures the vote. The pressures departments face to achieve immediate results to suit the politicians' narrative is constant. They are also continually jumping through layers of government red tape. Detectives must be extremely careful in choosing their words so that their comments are not taken out of context or distorted by the media. Misconstrued comments can give grieving family members and a concerned public false hope, which can invariably lead to even greater media fodder. They must always be cognisant of tempering expectations, as the public and the media at times get ahead of themselves in the search for answers or a front-page headline.

The police deal on a face-to-face, day-to-day basis with tragic circumstances involving parents, children, relatives, and friends and, on occasion, with fallen officers cut down in the line of duty. Comments must be tempered to minimise the negative impact on family, friends, and the public.

As a detective with South Australia Police for more than ten years, Bill experienced many and varied events within the force that he would not wish upon the public. He has seen how these situations have affected some of his closest colleagues over the years. With this in mind, the authors collectively say a massive thank you to all of our police officers and appreciate the work that they do.

Being mindful that police have a difficult job, a minority of abduction and murder investigations have been mishandled—where the investigation has been inadequate, incompetently conducted, shoddy, or indeed amateurish, and in the worse cases, deceitful, with detectives covering their trail—placing and tampering with evidence or allowing evidence to go missing. Leads have not been followed up and protocols not adhered to. Facts have been distorted to suit the narrative and discount the obvious. Lies have been perpetuated and attitudes unshakably stubborn in the face of the conspicuous, all culminating in writing questionable and slanted reports.

These detectives are eventually held to account, most often exposed and castigated by their own colleagues. However, they do stain an otherwise very professional organisation. A minority of police and detectives who fall into this bracket need to understand that it is not a badge and uniform that defines a person. Wearing this attire or holding a senior position in the ranks does not place anyone above scrutiny. It certainly does not entitle anyone to instant respect or standing in the community. Like all of us, you must earn it.

The most notable botched investigation in Australia in recent times was that of the disappearance of Daniel Morcombe, a thirteen-year-old boy abducted from a bus stop in broad daylight on the Sunshine Coast, Queensland in 2003. On 5 April 2019, the finding of the coronial inquest that was handed down by Terry Ryan, the Queensland State Coroner,[84] beggared belief, highlighting that officers could have done more in the early stages of the investigation into the disappearance of Daniel Morcombe to focus on Brett Peter Cowan. If it weren't for the persistence of Daniel's parents, Denise and Bruce Morecombe, over the years to bring their son's killer to justice, Brett Cowan would highly likely never have been charged. The parents' relentless drive, perseverance, and tenacity resulted in a government inquiry into the initial police investigation. This probe found the detectives' case examination wanting. Evidence was contaminated or misplaced, DNA samples taken from Cowan's car were not examined for eight years, even though they should have been given priority, and leads were not followed up. What was especially frightening in this case is that Cowan already had two previous convictions for sexually abusing children and he lived in the region where Daniel disappeared.

Initial findings found that the original detectives could have looked more closely at Cowan, 'particularly having regard to his admissions that placed him at the scene of Daniel's disappearance'.[84] There were also noticeable gaps in his alibi. To a new team of Queensland detectives placed on the case, this information rang alarm bells. After a prolonged undercover investigation, Brett Cowan was brought to justice and sentenced to life imprisonment thanks to the outstanding work of the second team of detectives given the task.

A South Australia Major Crime Investigation Branch investigation carried out between 2007 and 2017 into Harry Phipps and his alleged involvement in the disappearance of the Beaumont children appears to have some of these similarities. We believe the initial examination of the corroborated accounts presented in dossier form to the head of Major Crime and several senior detectives was mismanaged. A myriad of individuals noted in the book *The Satin Man* were never met and formally interviewed. The people who followed up with a phone call or letter to Major Crime received a standard departmental letter or nothing at all. Maybe, as the saying goes, 'Most people miss opportunities because it is dressed in overalls and looks like work'.

The cold-case enquiry into Phipps appeared to be based on subjectivity. The Beaumont case, more than any other, has been weighed down by conspiracy theories, false leads, misrepresentation, and plagued by media gossip, erroneous reports, and hearsay—was this a case of 'here we go again'?

South Australia's Crime Stoppers continues to receive calls on a regular basis five decades after the crime was committed. These calls need to be followed up, and this sometimes can wear a bit thin. We believe that what they presented to the police was compelling circumstantial evidence. However, from the outset, simple policing mistakes were made.

Mullins had asked Bill Hayes and several other current and former police and detectives whom they believed should have been met and formally interviewed first. Without exception, all agreed: the two primary individuals who spoke out regarding Harry Phipps. They are Haydn Phipps and his former wife, Angela Fyfe. Only then could a detective ascertain if they were truthful.

This was never done. According to Bill Hayes, this did not follow standard policing procedure and was a grave miscalculation. As both Haydn and Angela resided in Queensland, there may have been department budgetary constraints. Were they under-resourced or time-poor? In the authors' assessment, the cold-case investigators should have been judicious in their assessment and careful to not mix their personal opinions with their professional opinions to dictate their actions and therefore deviate from department protocol, as appears to have been the case here. With the corroborated information presented to the Major Crime Investigation Branch, did a detective cherry-pick witnesses and therefore only interview a few select family members who had refused to speak to Mullins or Hayes, resulting in them making a premature judgment call about Haydn and Angela's credibility?

If detectives had built a solid rapport with both Haydn and Angela, the initial outcome might have been different. However, the detective who previously told Stuart Mullins he was beating his head up against a brick wall also allegedly said to brothers David and Robin while overseeing the first factory dig at the Castalloy factory in 2015, 'My mind is made up on all this.'

Bill Hayes took the view that until otherwise disproved, Haydn Phipps was sexually abused and did see the Beaumont children in his backyard on the 26th of January 1966. Both of us were aware that victims of sexual abuse have a distrust of authoritative figures and that speaking out is incredibly difficult, so we treated Haydn carefully with in our dealings with him. Some detectives could have done the same. Haydn could have been lying, as the original cold-case detectives may have believed, but by not meeting and formally interviewing him, how could they possibly form a conclusion one way or the other?

However, a conclusion to this case may very well have already been left on an epitaph that was hung on the front fence of the Castalloy factory early on 26 January 2016 (the fiftieth anniversary of the abduction) by a yet-to-be-identified person:

JANE ARNNA AND GRANT

R.I.P

'TODAY IS THE 50th ANNIVERSARY OF THE MISSING
BEAUMONT CHILDREN * JANE ARNNA GRANT *
'Two little girls are buried here. The little boy is not buried
here with his sisters.
I hope and pray your little souls have passed over. You all
will never ever be forgotten. R.I.P
HARRY PHIPPS and all his EVIL ASSOCIATES were
involved in this. Well planned, well groomed. These grounds
will eventually be dug up by a wealthy businessman.'

C.S

This note was discovered by a senior employee, who took a photo before contacting the Major Crime Investigation Branch. They were immediately paid a visit by the same detective Mullins had had interesting dealings with.

This employee presented the note, asking if the officer would also like to have the security footage. However, this detective apparently declined the offer but took the note.

Before the second dig at the factory in 2018, the same senior employee met the new cold-case senior detectives and asked what they thought of the note found on the gate now in the Major Crime Investigation Branch's possession. Their response was a little surprising as these new detectives appeared to have no knowledge of the note. Once the phone image was viewed, their interest was raised. This occurrence was concerning to us. Their first thought regarding the note had been fingerprints. Perhaps the individual who created the note could be traced if fingerprints were evident or indeed if there was DNA evidence. The second was: if it was a case of simply not passing relevant information and evidence on to your superiors, it begs the question, why? And where is the original document now? An additional concern was why refuse to look at the security footage, if indeed any footage existed that might have identified the person who left the note? This would open up a new line of enquiry.

This is where we are obliged to ask whether this detective may have not shown this A4 note and kept or discarded it. Then did Elizabeth Phipps hand the beige clip purse seen in the basement by Mullins over to this detective? Notwithstanding that, this detective stated to Mullins that Elizabeth threw the purse away. This is speculation, of course, but worth asking.

The perceived lack of investigative will in regard to Harry Phipps was likely based on a senior officer's original report, which laid down preconceived ideas before the detectives began their investigation. Until otherwise warranted, senior officers would not question the initial investigation. It is accepted that there must be a high degree of trust in each detective's abilities and professionalism. Otherwise, micromanaging and scrutinis- ing every detective's investigative report would be time-con- suming and, of course, lead to a breakdown of confidence in their abilities to manage a case effectively. So, it appears the initial investigation into Harry Phipps was never questioned.

Mullins and Hayes carried out further investigative work, uncovering more compelling information linking Harry Phipps to his alleged involvement in the disappearance of the Beaumont children. They presented the information to Ken Thorsen, retired and former Head of Major Crime in the 1980s, who commented, after reading some of the information, 'If this information is corroborated, this material has red flags all over it. Let's shake the tree and see what falls out.'

They also presented copies of Haydn Phipps' recorded interview and statement-analysis report to the Major Crime Investigation Branch. Do they still have these items, or have they been lost or discarded? They were also sent to Brady Halls, a journalist for Channel 9's award-winning *A Current Affair* programme, and to Frank Pangallo, an award-winning journalist from Adelaide's *Today Tonight* and now a South Australian politician. These dedicated reporters, in turn, have since beaten the Harry Phipps drum loudly and clearly.

Mullins sent several registered-post letters to the then-South Australian Minister for Police Peter Malinauskas and the head of Major Crime detailing some shortfalls in the investigation. He was pleasantly surprised to receive positive replies to both by phone and by letter, which Hayes viewed as a constructive move. Bill has always pointed out the positive side of police work and the pressure officers are under and that it is imperative that they are guarded with information and that conclusions are not jumped to.

In the meantime, Hayes, still highly respected in the law-enforcement community, met the Head of the Major Crime Investigation Branch and other detectives. He also contacted his long-time friend and federal MP Tony Zappia. Tony was so concerned with the information Bill had provided to him that he, in turn, contacted the then-South Australian Premier Jay Wetherill, whom the authors believe may have made a few well-placed calls. As to what Bill discovered? There appeared to be 'some new movement at the station', with different detectives quietly going about their investigation into Harry Phipps out of sight of prying eyes. Bill stated that Major Crime would not say if they were further pursuing lines of enquiry into Phipps, to avoid unnecessary media attention. As Hayes said, it can be a juggling act, and SAPOL must be mindful of not giving false hope. With new eyes looking into cases, investigations can be re-evaluated and reinvigorated. Hence, there was a renewed interest in Harry Phipps. We also believed that Major Crime's new-found exuberance regarding investigating Phipps may have been due to this initial request that came from above.

Mistakes, however, were still being made. One of the most damaging, according to Haydn, was his treatment and the surprise, unwelcome phone call made by a Queensland Police detective where he had come at Haydn with no finesse at all, causing Haydn to hang up on him. There was then reportedly a follow-up call from a SA detective who, according to Haydn, had badgered him and spoken in an insistent, aggressive manner. Haydn claimed that he told this detective that everything that he had said to Bill Hayes was a lie. That seemed to satisfy them, and they terminated the call with Haydn. Haydn immediately rang his cousin and told him what happened and was extremely unhappy with their approach to him. Saying, 'Who in the fuck do they think they are? I have said all I want to say to Bill.'

Afterwards, Haydn did not wish to speak with anyone, Bill and Stuart included.

It took a least two years for Haydn to rebuild trust with them.

These detectives should have treated Haydn as a victim of child sexual abuse until convinced otherwise. Neither the Queensland detective who made the first call nor the SA detective who made the second call appeared to do that. In a later call between Mullins and the SA detective, they had stated, 'People with mental issues say these things.' Mullins' first response was, how could this detective make this type of judgement by only talking to Haydn over the phone? This detective did not appear to be qualified in the field of working with victims of child sexual abuse, nor did they appear to be a practising clinician, to the best of our knowledge. Therefore, what did they write in their reports?

If a detective is going to interview an alleged victim of child sexual abuse, they should be aware of pertinent information.

There is a multitude of information and professional narratives relating to statistics and summaries in this area. Some of these are quoted in *Darkness to Light: Child Sexual Abuse Statistics* and the National Center for Victims of Crime, to name a few.

According to these child sexual abuse statistics, eight percent of victims aged twelve to seventeen are male.[21] A child has to tell seven adults of suspected abuse before he or she is taken seriously. The male ego is conditioned by society with an aversion to weakness, and the crime of molestation incites a lifelong haemorrhage of self-esteem that can become fatal if not treated. Rates of suicide among male victims of childhood sexual abuse are fourteen times higher than the norm, and they are thirty-eight times more likely to die from a drug overdose.[85] Much of this section relates directly to Haydn's experience.

The hard fact is unless there are credible adult witnesses who are willing to testify or provide video evidence, the prosecution of a paedophile is like ice-skating uphill. As with Haydn and another of Harry Phipps' victims, the brave few who speak out find themselves further victimised by the persona of the paedophile or close family or friends flocking to their defence cultivated to disguise their true nature. This has been evident regarding the champions of Harry Phipps' character while Haydn's and Linda's lives spiralled downward.

Another, more senior, detective assigned to the Harry Phipps case informed Stuart Mullins that she had met Elizabeth Phipps, and Elizabeth had claimed that Mullins had gained entry to her home by impersonating a police officer. However, Mullins informed the detective over the phone he was introduced to Elizabeth by one of the former senior managers at Castalloy factory as carrying out research into Castalloy and Harry Phipps. The question is, what else has Elizabeth Phipps lied about? This attempted deception did not appear to faze the officer. To others, it raised red flags. Also, if you are going to lie, you better have a good memory.

As one detective is replaced by another, which is the usual rotation policy within SAPOL, the new replacement may have a different way of approaching a case. Over time, and with Bill and Stuart's persistence and determination, assisted by many exceptional professionals, the Major Crime Investigation Branch committed more time and effort to investigate Harry Phipps. Mullins was in email contact with a new detective on the case, and Bill worked with some detectives and the media who all met at the Castalloy factory in late 2017 to discuss the factory dig, as mentioned in Chapter 16.

As of early 2018, Harry Phipps was raised to be considered a person of interest by the South Australian Major Crime Investigation Branch, as we believe he should, along with the many professionals already mentioned in this book who consider Harry Phipps as the lead suspect. We were encouraged by Des Bray's comment to 5AA radio breakfast personality David Penberthy. Bray said he doesn't like the term 'cold case' because it suggests it's gathering dust in a drawer somewhere: 'These cases are not cold; they are active cases and there are guys who have devoted their careers to solving them.' However, out of the media spotlight, the department's words do not appear to be matched by their actions in regards to further looking into Harry Phipps. To us, there still seems to be a reluctance to thoroughly investigate this individual. At every turn, we feel as though they have been trying to feed a petulant child who does not wish to eat their greens even though these are good for them. A more recent case in point, and mentioned in this book previously, regards Linda (not her real name), who alleged Harry Phipps sexually abused her as a thirteen-year-old schoolgirl across the road from his Castalloy factory in North Plympton in 1979. Her account has been viewed by millions since she appeared in the documentary *The Beaumont Children: What Really Happened.* The experts present at the time, watching Linda being interviewed, had no hesitation in saying she was being truthful. Yet the Major Crime Investigation Branch has not appeared to make a concerted effort to speak to and hopefully meet her, why? It is fair to say here that when the police officer that took over the case heard about Linda, he asked to speak with her. Her decision, relayed a considerable time before this call to Bill and based on her initial dealings with police when reporting her rape, was that the police had their chance and blew it when she had made her initial report. She didn't wish to speak with them. However, should the point have been pressed by the investigators to try and get her to relent? Had this been put to Bill, then he would have spoken to Linda to see if she would change her mind and speak with the police. This is not a criticism of the police, just a question that needed to be asked. For what it is worth, it is Hayes's opinion that she probably would not relent from her original decision.

The authors also believe there still does not appear any genuine effort by detectives assigned to this cold case to effectively continue looking into Harry Phipps' background.

It is our belief that the answer to this case may well be buried at the Castalloy factory. As such, they believe that digging up the entire sandpit area is not only important, it is imperative.

If Haydn Phipps was truthful in his account, as the authors, along with Steve Van Aperen and other professionals, believe he is, then there is a need for the state government to loosen the purse strings. There is a need for several diligent detectives to be placed on this case who can re-examine the initial investigation and plan and coordinate a major excavation of the entire sandpit area at the Castalloy factory and Harry Phipps' real-estate assets. Only then can we be assured that a thorough investigation of Harry Phipps has been carried out and a comprehensive, meticulous search of the entire sandpit area conducted. Let's not die wondering.

Chapter 27:
Previous Suspects

Where there is smoke, there is fire.

—John Heywood's Proverbs (1546)

Since the disappearance of the Beaumont children in 1966, there has been a lot of speculation regarding who committed the crime. This abduction, more than any, has left the police, the public, and the press confounded. Any mention of a new lead creates a media free-for-all, which is to be expected for a case that has baffled and shocked us all for decades—not just in Australia but internationally—and left us trying to come to terms with the inexplicable and attempting to make sense of this brazen act.

Of course, the media has been littered with a litany of conspiracy theories, false leads, and dead ends. Over the decades, a multitude of names have been presented, most based on hearsay, and any new person of interest presented as a possible suspect leads to a flurry of media attention and speculation.

In the past five decades, only six individuals have been raised as persons of interest in this case. However, with most suspects, their age, physical description, and proximity to Glenelg at the time are questionable. We conclude that most of these individuals can be discounted due to these facts. Also, paedophiles hunt in a defined activity space and display distinct patterns regarding the type of prey they hunt. Knowing this, Dr Xanthé Mallett, Duncan McNab, and Graham Archer agree that out of the six persons of interest, Harry Phipps stands out head and shoulders above the others. The authors have set out below the additional five persons of interest presented over the decades.

Alan Anthony Munro was a successful businessman and millionaire who lived for many years in Siem Reap, Thailand, where he ran a well-known ladyboy bar and arranged financing for orphanages. Cambodian officials were investigating Munro regarding offences perpetrated by him relating to these institutions. He left Cambodia to return to Adelaide for tax reasons and was arrested at the airport on child sex charges.

In Australia, Munro, a former scout leader, had pleaded guilty to child sex offences as far back as 1962 in and around Adelaide, ten in all including buggery and indecent assault. However, regarding his alleged involvement in the abduction of Jane, Arnna, and Grant Beaumont in 1966, Munro was twenty years old. He did not fit the height or age, nor the description of the man seen at the Colley reserve with the Beaumont children that day. However, he cannot be ignored as being a possible associate and accomplice of Phipps in this case. Glenelg is an area that Munro was very familiar with, almost a local. Did he know Phipps as a fellow paedophile? In fact we firmly believe that he has been identified as having been in Glenelg that day by a reliable witness. His possible involvement as an accomplice does need further investigation to confirm or negate that possibility. Munro is still serving time and is due for release in December 2023.

Bevan Spencer von Einem was nineteen in January 1966. At age thirty-seven, he was sentenced to life in prison for murdering fifteen-year-old Richard Kelvin, the son of an Adelaide television newsreader, and he was suspected of killing five others.

Police initially looked at him for a possible connection to the Beaumont children's disappearance because several elements seemed to fit. He somewhat resembled the description and police sketch from 1966, was roughly six feet (182 centimetres) tall, which fitted the height range, and was known to frequent Glenelg beach to 'perv' on the change rooms. However, he was described as preoccupied with young men; sexually abusing young children was not his modus operandi. He was also noticeably much younger than the suspect seen with the children in 1966. Von Einem refused to cooperate with police inquiries. As reported in the *Adelaide Advertiser* on 15 September 2019 under the headline 'Debi Marshall: Interview with Bevan Spencer von Einem', she asked about a witness who told authorities that von Einem had admitted to being involved in the disappearance of the Beaumont children, to which he replied: 'He was a jail snitch. Everything he said about me, he did it for the money. I didn't do it.'[86]

Arthur Stanley Brown was fifty-three in January 1966 and lived in north Queensland.

He was charged in 1998 with the murder of the MacKay sisters—seven-year-old Judith and five-year-old Susan—in Townsville. They were abducted from a bus stop 200 metres from their home on their way to school on 26 August 1970; their bodies were found several days later in a dry creek bed twenty-five kilometres away.

Stories regarding Brown emerged in the late 1960s about him molesting young girls who were extended family members. Even though Brown bore a similarity to the man seen at the beach with the Beaumont children, there is no proof that he visited Adelaide in 1965 or 1966. Indeed, Brown's age, along with the sheer tyranny of distance—2,400 kilometres—and the fact that he was unfamiliar with the Glenelg and Adelaide areas, makes Brown an unlikely suspect.

His modus operandi when abducting children was different from that of the 1966 and 1973 abductions. One was a snatch-and-grab, with bodies dumped to be found, whereas the others required a degree of persuasiveness, and the bodies have never been found. Predators have their own defined activity space where they feel comfortable operating—Glenelg was not his.

James Ryan O'Neill is a convicted murderer and suspected serial killer; he was jailed for life in 1975 for the murder of a nine-year-old boy in Tasmania. Of the places O'Neill visited, children had gone missing in seven of them. Though he has only been charged with one offence, police detectives believe that O'Neill has likely committed many more of these types of crimes.

O'Neill was nineteen in 1966 and too young to be the man seen with the Beaumont children at Glenelg beach. O'Neill stated to police officers that he had never visited Adelaide. However, he frequently visited Coober Pedy, South Australia, for his work fossicking and selling opals. The roads travelled from Melbourne, where he lived, to Coober Pedy pass through Adelaide, but his age alone would discount him, nor did he fit the description of the suspect in the Beaumont case.

In the 2005 Australian documentary *The Fishermen: A Journey into the Mind of a Killer*, the South Australia Police were asked for their opinion. The officer in charge of major crime investigations, Detective Superintendent Peter Woite, confirmed that O'Neill had recently been interviewed. However, Woite said that 'no evidence was found to support this person's involvement in the disappearance of the Beaumont children'. O'Neil is serving a life sentence.

Derek Ernest Percy was a convicted child killer linked to the deaths of nine children aged three to fifteen in the 1960s. He died at St Vincent's Hospital in Melbourne in 2013 and has been linked to some of Australia's most notorious child killings. In 1966, Percy was seventeen years old and too young to have been the man seen with the Beaumont children.

With Percy, von Einem, Brown, O'Neill, and Munro, no-one fits the age range, and only two fit the facial description: Arthur Stanley Brown and Harry Phipps. Of the two, only Phipps was known to tip in and hand out pound notes.

Over the decades, the Beaumont case continues to elicit strong and, in some cases, very opinionated views of 'whodunnit'. Many people have their theories and they are sticking to them. Quite a few vehemently believe that Anthony Munro and his cohort Max McIntyre are involved and the bodies are buried in a now filled-in sinkhole on McIntyre's property on the Yorke Peninsula in South Australia.

Others believe that Arthur Stanley Brown is responsible, because he bears a resemblance to the man seen with the children that day at the beach. Then there is talk of the 'von Einem family murders', a series of homosexual killings in the 1970s and 1980s. One theory held was this was the work of an Adelaide predatory group of influential people and that von Einem was involved with others who took part in paedophilic activities. The allegations are based on information that was neither firsthand nor corroborated, but this talk about an elite, well-connected Adelaide paedophilic society remains strong. Adelaide had a hidden dark side, as noted in Sean Fewster's book *City of Evil: The Truth About Adelaide's Strange and Violent Underbelly*.

One Australian newspaper journalist, in a superb 2005 piece on the City of Churches, wrote, 'The shaken city, a town already burdened with a reputation for bizarre crimes and cover-ups, searched for literary analogies in Arthur Miller's *The Crucible* and Shakespeare's *King Lear*. "'Through tattered rags small vices do appear; Robes and furred gowns hide all.' Does that sound like Adelaide?" asks author Susan Mitchell, whose book *All Things Bright and Beautiful* is about the sins of this outwardly respectable city.'[87]

Through all the smoke, the fact remains that there are more pieces of corroborating circumstantial evidence linking Harry Phipps to the abduction of the Beaumont children than against the other five combined. He had the opportunity and familiarity with the surrounding area; this was his 'turf'. The way the children were enticed indicates to profilers and criminologists such as Kris Illingworth, Dr Xanthé Mallett, and Duncan McNab that this abduction was well planned. The predator enticed the children with his well-meaning and caring façade. By doing this, the paedophile would have the children out of sight reasonably quickly without drawing the attention of onlookers. An abduction of this nature requires a high degree of intelligence, cunning, and maturity. Of the six persons of interest, the one who was never caught has all these attributes. That person is Harry Phipps.

Chapter 28:
Last Man Standing

A day and meeting I will never forget for as long as I live.

—Mostyn Matters

This chapter is dedicated to Mostyn Matters, the last remaining detective on duty at the Glenelg police station on that fateful day, 26 January 1966, and the first to meet a distraught Nancy and Jim Beaumont. We also remember Mostyn's fellow detectives with whom he worked closely: Senior detective Ron 'Wings' Blight, and detectives Peter Vogel, Lloyd Brand, and Peter Tremalick.

Mostyn's early life was marred by tragedy when, as a three-year-old being held in his mother's arms in the front seat of the family car, he was involved in a horrific accident. His mother Beryl, father Frederick, and family friends, the Buchanans, with their thirteen-month-old child Patricia, were to spend a day out having a picnic at Strathalbyn, a picturesque country town sixty kilometres south-east of Adelaide.

Tragically, the vehicle his father was driving collided with the Victor Harbour Express train at a level crossing not far from their destination. The train had blindsided Frederick travelling at speed coming out of the cutting and around a bend.

In 1938, South Australia did not have level crossing boom gates or flashing lights to indicate that a train was approaching. The locomotive impacted the vehicle at the centre of the passenger side. According to the *Adelaide Mail* newspaper on 29 January 1938, the car was shunted 123 metres along the track before the train pulled up, the impact sending the vehicle and its occupants over the side of the Strathalbyn bridge plummeting nine metres into the river below.

Mostyn's mother Beryl, along with Mr and Mrs Buchanan, were killed. His father Frederick, young Mostyn, and baby Patricia survived. At the time, this was the most horrific car accident in South Australian history. Newspaper photos of the car would indicate that they were indeed lucky to have survived the mangled wreck.

This event changed their lives forever. Mostyn's father believed he was responsible and suffered what we term today post-traumatic stress disorder. Grief-stricken by the memory of losing people he loved dearly, Frederick immersed himself in his work. For a time, Mostyn became secondary and Frederick requested his in-laws take care of him for a while as he moved away, attempting to start a new life. However, the memory of this horrendous event followed him to his grave.

Over his formative years, Mostyn lived with his grandparents, Percy and Cristiana, before moving several times between relatives. He quickly became a resilient young lad adapting to his new transient surroundings. He is described by several who knew him as being independent and his own man. As Elizabeth Edwards, bestselling author, states, 'Resilience is accepting your new reality, even if it's less good than the one you had before.'[88]

After Frederick remarried in 1940 and found balance in his work and life, Mostyn moved back to live with his father and his new stepmother. Over the next few years, Mostyn was greeted by two stepbrothers with whom he is still very close today.

At Unley High School, Mostyn became known as Mos, and this name has stuck ever since. He excelled academically, but his heart was in sports, specifically cricket and Australian Rules football. Later he played first grade with the Brighton Cricket Club, which was one step away from the South Australian state side, and he played first grade for the Glenelg Tigers in the SANFL (South Australian National Football League) through the mid-1950s to early 1960s. Mos was a very handy player in both sports. Several men who played against Mostyn described him as a 'hard nut and not to be messed with'.

Straight out of school at the age of sixteen, he began work for Rapid Shoe Repairs in the Adelaide CBD, a shop his father owned. Shortly after that, he was offered a job at Arnold Shoe Repairs. He took this job mainly because they had a company motorcycle that was used to collect shoes that required repairs from stores and homes around Adelaide and surrounding suburbs. He remained there for a few years, and this experience of riding motorcycles would come in handy a few years later.

In 1956, at the age of twenty-one, Mostyn married Margaret Evans and bought a house at Dover Gardens, fourteen kilometres south-west of Adelaide and six kilometres from Glenelg. Dover Gardens was a new middle-class war service and housing trust suburb. They had two wonderful daughters and a home Mos still resides in today. He and Margaret amicably divorced several decades later.

The year 1956 also saw Mos join the South Australia Police, firstly as a uniformed police officer on the beat. After twelve months of pounding the pavement, he was promoted to constable and joined the motorcycle squad for three years. This is where he had the opportunity to ride his first Golden Triumph—by today's standards a much sought-after collector's item.

Mostyn always held aspirations of becoming a detective, and in 1961, he got his wish, transferring into the Vice Squad where he investigated gaming and licensing offences in addition to prostitution and brothels.

It was at this time Mos was introduced to alcohol. He recalls that, on one occasion, he was sent down to a hotel in Port Adelaide to investigate licensing issues and to gather evidence against a local bookmaker. Mos was happy drinking lemon squash until the bookmaker arrived, at which time he would begin to gather evidence. However, the publican had other ideas. He pointed out to Mos that he was standing out like a sore thumb at the bar drinking a fizzy drink. He needed something a little stronger to blend in. The following week, Mos turned up again with the intention to catch the bookmaker in the act and started drinking beer not long into the afternoon. By 5 pm, Mos was inebriated. In fact, he was so intoxicated the publican rang the police to come and get him.

Later the same year, Mos was transferred to the Adelaide CIB, and within twelve months he was again transferred, this time to the Glenelg police station where he initially held the rank of detective constable. It was this transfer that would change Mostyn's life forever.

By 1965, he was promoted to detective senior constable. The station was located at the end of Jetty Road, which was the final destination of the Adelaide to Glenelg tram. This tram would make its twelve-kilometre round trip from the CBD of Adelaide to the seaside suburb of Glenelg many times a day and still does. The station also backed onto the Colley Reserve, an open lawned area just fifty metres from the seashore. The building that housed the police station is still there but is now believed to be the Glenelg post office.

Glenelg was and still is an upper-market suburb and seaside town, popular with holidaymakers and local Adelaideans. Crime in the area consisted of what Mos would term several known pickpockets, small theft, lost property left at Colley Reserve, a house or shop break-in or an occasional assault, a report of a 'pervert' at the change rooms, or a lost child wandering the reserve during the busy summer months. The town was known to be a safe place.

At the Glenelg police station on 26 January 1966, the day left an indelible mark not just on the detectives at Glenelg, but on the psyche of the Australian public.

Mostyn was the first detective to meet a distraught Nancy and Jim Beaumont, who had arrived at the police station to report their children, Jane, Arnna, and Grant, missing. This first encounter is something that Mostyn will never forget. One of the reasons it still haunts him is that his first thought was that the parents were overreacting; he thought the children would soon turn up. Lost children always did in cases like these. There was always a simple explanation.

No-one could have imagined what followed. This initial meeting left Mostyn and the other Glenelg detectives mentally scarred for the rest of their lives. They were all family men with young children, and the thought of losing three children coupled with a deeply distressed Mr and Mr Beaumont shattered them all. Mostyn, along with Ron Blight and each of the other detectives, took this case personally, always feeling they could have done more. Mostyn still thinks this more than five decades later.

What unfolded in the days, weeks, months, and years later created collective anguish, and grief took its toll. Some say that Ron Blight died of a broken heart.

Sarah Ockler, author and writer in the United States, sums up this grief and heartbreak: 'Weeping is not the same thing as crying. It takes your whole body to weep, and when it's over, you feel like you don't have any bones left to hold you up.'[89]

Even as this tragic event changed them, it also bonded the team closer together. Each one looked out for the other and their families. They were all very close-knit and kept in contact over the ensuing decades. Even with all these trials and tribulations, Mostyn wrote in his journal: 'Stationed at the Glenelg CIB were the best years of my policing career.'

Mostyn became close friends with Tom Patterson, who was the Somerton and Somerton Park postman for decades. Everybody in the surrounding suburbs knew 'Tom the Postie', as did Jane, Arnna, and Grant Beaumont. Mos first met Tom when he was interviewed at the station several days after the abduction. Tom had seen the children when they had made their way over to Colley Reserve from the Mosely Street bus top. For decades until Tom's passing, Mos and Tom were lawn-bowl buddies and members of the Somerton Bowls Club, where Mostyn still plays.

By 1970, Mostyn had transferred to Darlington Police Station two kilometres from Stuart Mullins' old family residence at Seacombe Gardens. By 1974, Mostyn made detective sergeant first grade and was stationed at Police Headquarters in Adelaide CIB as part of a team of thirty-two detectives. By the time he left the service in 1989, Mos had been awarded the National Police Service Medal. To this day, Mostyn is still well known and referred to as the detective who first met a distressed Nancy and Jim Beaumont.

Every story has a silver lining, and Mostyn's has his. He had caught the eye of a pretty, younger lady, Diana, who was working at a large sports club where Mostyn was on the executive committee. Di and her friend decided to follow Mostyn a few afternoons by car. However, being a wily ex-detective, Mos cottoned on to these two from the get-go. He gave them a few days of playing cat-and-mouse, then pounced. As he approached her car in the club's car park, Diana was sitting in the driver's seat very conspicuously pretending to read the newspaper. He asked her why she had been following him, to which Diana replied, 'I find you a good looker and would like to go out with you.' The straightforwardness and bravado enamoured Mostyn; he was a no-bull former detective and enjoyed her direct approach. He couldn't say no. After they were together for several years, Mostyn proposed. Diana accepted, and they married at the Somerton Bowls Club in 2015.

Diana had experienced ongoing health problems and was mostly confined to a wheelchair, but she had promised Mos she would walk down the aisle with him on their special day. And true to her word, she did. To Mos, Diana was the love of his life. Vivacious, outgoing, and quite the conversationalist. She never had a bad word to say about anyone. She always saw the best in people. Sadly, Diana Matters passed away due to health complications in 2019.

Although Diana's death has left Mostyn at times feeling empty and alone, he knows he is well supported by his two lovely daughters. They are always there to help and visit Mos regularly. Also, Stuart and Bill keep in close contact. From time to time, Mostyn also receives a surprise call from South Australian MP Frank Pangallo. Mos plays lawn bowls at his favourite club surrounded by friends that he has known for decades, so assistance and companionship are not far away. He also potters around his sizeable backyard with its myriad fruit trees and spends time in his shed with an array of framed photos and scrapbooks of his decades in the police force and photos, awards, and trophies from his days playing cricket and Australian Rules football. Mos and his then-wife Margaret moved into their Adelaide suburb in the 1950s and, to him, this will always be home, where he has wonderful, happy memories. However, one can see Mostyn very much misses the love of his life, his lady Diana.

THE NEWS

LAST

Adelaide: Monday, August 27, 1973   7c'

WEATHER

ABDUCTED

GIRLS MAY BE STILL ALIVE

By Staff Reporters

"If the person who took the little girls has them hidden somewhere, please let them free unharmed."

This dramatic appeal was flashed from Police Headquarters today as police intensified their search for Joanne Ratcliffe, 11, and Kirste Gordon, 4.

Kirste Gordon and Joanne Ratcliffe went missing while attending an Australian Rules football match at the Adelaide Oval on 25 August 1973, where both walked between the grandstands to the toilets and were never seen again. Image courtesy of News Ltd.

The actual abduction took place behind the John Creswell stand next to the ladies toilets to the right. Image courtesy of News Ltd.

"Grief is love with
no place to go"
KAREN GIBBS

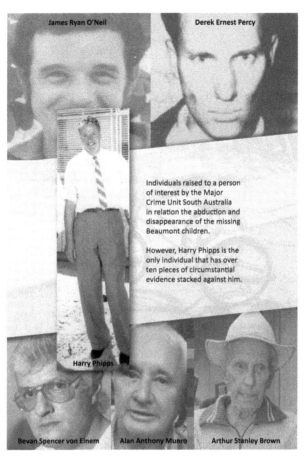

The last detective standing. Mostyn Matters with Bill and Stuart, 2022.

Nancy Helen Ellis Beaumont was born on the 5th of August 1927 and passed away on the 19th of September 2019 never knowing what happened to her children.

Now she is reunited with her ever smiling children Jim Beaumont is now in his mid to late 90s and resides in an aged residential community Adelaide.

We believe this is the last known photograph of Nancy, who was out in Glenelg with her carer. The photo was sent to Stuart by an unknown person. However, we thank them for this.

Epilogue:
Where to Next

Let us shake the tree and see what falls out.

—Ken Thorsen, former head of
South Australia Major Crime Unit

If detectives in 1966 had known a lot more than they did—that a local man fit the description of the individual seen playing with the Beaumont children that day at the beach, that this person was an alleged paedophile who exhibited deviant sexual behaviours, that this man was a regular swimmer at Glenelg beach and frequented Colley Reserve, that he was a wealthy, connected establishment man known to hand out pound notes, that he lived 190 metres in direct sight of Colley Reserve where the Beaumont children were last seen playing and 200 metres from Wenzel's Bakery, where Jane was last seen paying for lunch with a pound note before she and her siblings disappeared— whose residence might they have visited first?

The officers did not have this information in 1966, but SAPOL does now. All this is coupled with other corroborated circumstantial evidence that links Harry Phipps to the disappearance of the Beaumont children. We, along with many professionals in the fields of criminology, profilers, investigative journalists, former detectives, and several politicians, believe the case against Phipps should be cast wide open and Phipps exposed for who he really was.

Stuart Mullins and Bill Hayes are reminded of the naysayers over the years who have said that this type of case will never be solved. These individuals cannot give any valid reasons why, except if it hasn't been resolved now, this investigation will never be taken to its conclusion. Some sections of the media and public have suggested that the authors are after book sales, notoriety, or simply their day in the sun. Or that their research into Phipps has been loose with the truth, flawed, based on fiction, scandalous, and directed at destroying Harry Phipps' legacy. However, the facts speak louder and clearer than the barbed word. Or as Mullins states, 'The truth lingers to sort out the mess of the lies.'

Can this case be solved? Of course, it can. The pieces of the jigsaw have been placed together one by one over the past fourteen years to produce a clear picture of what may very well have happened that day and, more importantly, the individual likely involved: Harry Phipps.

When Mullins spoke to a detective from SAPOL in early 2018, he was not flippant in saying, 'Stuart, we need to dig them up.' Which, of course, may be true—but where to start?

The reaction of many regarding Harry Phipps is like a deer in the headlights. For others, the answer to this abduction and murder of three innocent children lies at the Castalloy factory and squarely at the feet of Harry Phipps. For years—as far back as the early 1990s—Haydn Phipps had been saying that the children were buried in the sandpit.

Phipps would have disposed of the bodies not too far from home, a location well known to him with easy access for him to control, and somewhere he could remain smug and confident enough that they would never be found. It was also a place he could take a perverse pride in the fact that only he knew where the bodies were and would get a sick pleasure from regularly viewing the burial site. The majority of sex offenders commit their crimes relatively close to their home base. Phipps was no different. Castalloy at North Plympton was one such location and Colley Reserve the other.

Harry Phipps owned several properties: a house across the road from his Castalloy factory on Kinkaid Avenue, one on Cygnet Street at Kingston Park near Seacliff, a few beachside suburbs south-east of Glenelg, and a property at Flagstaff Hill, fifteen kilometres south of Adelaide. He also owned a holiday house at Goolwa, a coastal town located near the mouth of the Murray River and three properties on Augusta and Sussex streets in Glenelg. In all locations, Harry had total control. These backyards, together with the sandpit area at the Castalloy area, should be thoroughly excavated.

It is the general consensus from the likes of Dr Xanthé Mallett, Terrance G Lichtenwald, Duncan McNab, and Graham Archer that Phipps is highly likely to be the individual who abducted the Beaumont children. If this is the case, there must be a firm commitment and backing from the South Australian Government to provide the Major Crime Investigation Branch with the necessary budget, time, and resources to fully reinvestigate Phipps and leave no stone unturned.

They should interview individuals, those who are still alive, who are so important to this case yet have never been spoken to by the police. Detectives should also re-interview Wayne Phipps and his wife to ascertain the full facts of their narrative as told to the *Adelaide Advertiser* journalist. Are they being truthful or withholding information that would be important in exposing Phipps as a paedophile? If they are, detectives must ask, why?

All Major Crime investigations need detectives with commitment and a good dose of curiosity who are up to date and informed regarding the characteristics of the sexually abused and the persona and predatory habits of a paedophile—those open to working with criminologists, profilers, and statement-analysis experts. This would be a positive start.

Of paramount importance is determining exactly where the Castalloy sandpit was located in the 1960s, followed by a return search of the Castalloy factory. As Mostyn Matters stated, 'Dig the whole fucking lot up.' All of Phipps' properties must be examined. If the remains of Jane, Arnna, and Grant Beaumont were found, the authors believe that other remnants of child victims might be, too. How much would this cost?

What price are we placing on the lives of these children? Is there a monetary value connected to each child, and once the budget is exhausted, do we move on? Or do we believe this case can be and will be solved?

Many respected professionals, such as investigative journalists, politicians, private investigators, criminologists, and former detectives believe that we may have the answer and now we need the patience, commitment, and determination to see this through. We can no longer hide behind some public sentiment that advocates not re-traumatising the parents and allowing the children to 'rest in peace'.

The children and Nancy are at peace. It is the public that is not. We are all obligated, for the sake of the children and parents, to bring Jane, Arnna, and Grant Beaumont home.

Postscript by Bill Hayes

The authors are aware that ongoing enquiries and allegations such as those made in this book can be difficult for the family and friends of both the Beaumont and Phipps extended families.

We respectfully request that those who read this book understand that this is an open wound that must be healed in the case of the Beaumont family. However, it is still difficult for them, given its ongoing nature; it is done in the hope of getting answers to this enduring mystery. Since commencing this investigation fourteen years ago, we have been conscious of the need to conduct our inquiries with that in mind. We hope that we have conducted the investigation in a manner that would have caused the least amount of upset to the family. Both Stuart and I also ask you, the reader, to respect the family's privacy.

Concerning the Phipps family, we also understand just how difficult it must be for them to read the allegations that have been made against their family member. We make no apologies for making these allegations as we are acting on tested information that we have received or that our investigation has uncovered. Nevertheless, we do understand the pain this must be bringing them. We urge the reader to accept that the extended Phipps family are totally innocent of any wrongdoings alleged against Harry Phipps. Please treat them with respect and consideration as they too are innocent victims in all of this.

Likewise, the current residents of Isola have nothing to do with this investigation and are simply trying to live their lives as a normal family. Please respect their right to privacy and to live in peace.

Bill Hayes and Stuart Mullins

Thanks To

It only takes one voice, at the right pitch,
to start an avalanche.

Diana Hardy

Many individuals need to be thanked for standing up and speaking out. Individuals who assisted us in any way possible over the past fourteen years to shed light in dark places. Some people placed their reputations on the line, while several relatives of the Phipps family who dared to speak up were told to recant their stories or to face the consequences. We want to say a collective thank you to them and the professionals listed below. Without your assistance, Harry Phipps may have never been elevated to a person of interest by the South Australia Police.

To Alan Whiticker, author of the 2006 publication *Searching for the Beaumont Children*. Without this well-researched book, the name Harry Phipps highly likely would never have made the light of day.

To Angela Fyfe (née Phipps), the lady who stood up and spoke out against a backdrop of naysayers and vilification: she spoke with clarity and honesty when others remained silent.

To Haydn Phipps, who suffered decades of mental and physical anguish caused by his father: the eldest son found the courage and conviction to speak his truth, knowing he would revive and relive his nightmare ordeal of sexual abuse.

The same goes for Linda, a lady who knew that discussing her sexual abuse at the hands of Harry Phipps would reignite the mental trauma suffered for decades. Despite this psychological and physical anguish, she stepped forward and spoke out. For this, the authors are eternally grateful.

Also, to 'Christine and Ted' for stepping forward with their incredible and startling account of the sexual abuse of children at the hands of Harry Phipps and his perverted group of associates.

To Mostyn Matters, the last of the detectives who was stationed at the Glenelg police station that fateful day in 1966. Mostyn's invaluable insights into this day and the weeks, months, and years afterwards clarified the unfolding drama, and the emotional pain suffered not only by Mr and Mrs Beaumont but the many individuals associated with this case.

To Jenny, Jane's best friend, for her heart-warming account of their time spent together.

To Peter, Haydn's closest cousin, for his honest account of his time spent with Haydn and the Phipps family.

To Tony Zappia, federal politician and Member for Makin, South Australia, who worked tirelessly behind the scenes, opening doors that were otherwise inaccessible. Most notably to Jay Wetherill, the then Premier of South Australia, and Peter Malinauskas, the then Police Minister.

Many thanks to state politician Frank Pangallo, who for many years was a well-respected, tenacious investigative journalist with Adelaide's top-rated *Today Tonight* current-affairs program. He worked tirelessly to expose Harry Phipps over many programs and still offers his assistance to us today.

To the entire award-winning Adelaide's Channel 7 *Today Tonight* team. Especially Graham Archer, an investigative reporter and producer who, along with the team, relentlessly pursued Harry Phipps.

To Brady Halls, investigative reporter for the top-rating Channel 9's *A Current Affair* program, who also exposed Harry Phipps as a deviant paedophile and the individual most likely to have abducted the Beaumont children. He continually offers his assistance in any way possible and advises behind the scenes.

To Duncan McNab, former detective, award-winning true-crime author, TV producer, and investigative journalist with Channel 7 who, together with Michael Usher, journalist and TV presenter, and the team, produced an extraordinary documentary, *The Beaumont Children: What Really Happened,* and continued to provide assistance/insight and sage advice.

To highly credentialed and knowledgeable Dr Xanthé Mallett, criminologist, forensic anthropologist, and television presenter, for her invaluable, insightful, comprehensive, and extensive examination of Harry Phipps' psychology and behavioural patterns.

To Dr Ian Moffat, senior lecturer in Archaeological Science at Flinders University, South Australia, for his and his team's assistance at the 2018 dig at the Castalloy site.

To Steven Van Aperen, Australia's top statement-analysis and lie-detection expert, who offered his expertise into the mind of Haydn Phipps.

To Mandy and Yvette from the Netherlands who provided us with their insightful and in-depth analysis of Bill's interview with Haydn as well as the letter sent by Angela to the SA Police.

To Ken Thorsen (now deceased), former head of the South Australia Police Major Crime Squad in the 1980s, for his insights into corroborated information presented by us.

To Kris Illingsworth, former detective, criminal investigative analyst, and criminologist, for her insight and analysis of how the abduction unfolded.

To Michael Tamassi who, when permitted, gave us unrestricted access to and valuable information about Castalloy.

To Terrance G Lichtenwald, PhD, for his insightful analysis of the behavioural and personality characteristics of Harry Phipps.

To Ocean Reeve Publishing for the enthusiastic support, faith, and professionalism they have shown all the way through this book publishing process.

A big thank you to Julia Garnaut and the team at the Holdfast Bay Historical Society for providing exceptional images of Glenelg beach and foreshore and Colley Reserve in the 1960s.

To Gus Marmitt, graphic artist at Gold Coast Graphic Designs for the front and back book covers and for designing Bill and Stuart's Beaumont Children Facebook® and Instagram® posts.

To Yakk, a social media strategy company on the Gold Coast, Queensland, Australia for guiding us and the story through the social medial maze.

And Jared at Camera House Robina, Queensland, Australia for the retouching of the Beaumont family's black-and-white photos to living colour.

To Nat and Matthew at Elite Media Melbourne for filming and editing Stuart's and Bill's numerous YouTube episodes regarding this abduction that are available for viewing now. We say a heartfelt collective thanks to the many others who stepped forward with information regarding Harry Phipps. Their insights and recollections in regards to the Phipps family are well documented in *The Satin Man: Uncovering the Mystery of the Missing Beaumont Children*. If they did not have the courage to come forward, then Harry Phipps would have slipped between the cracks. We have chosen not to name them here as this may expose them to unwanted phone calls, trolling, or the media presenting themselves at their front door. To the above collective of all people that stood up, we are immensely grateful.

To anyone who comes forward as a result of the publication of this book and provides even the smallest piece of relevant information, we thank you in advance; the truth is out there.

And last but not least we would like to say a big thank you to our wives, children, extended family, friends, and work associates, all of whom wholeheartedly supported our efforts over the last fourteen years to bring Harry Phipps to justice. To them, both are eternally grateful.

In closing: this book is not the end of this investigation. It is ongoing and will remain so until there is nothing more to be found. Ever the optimists, we are always hopeful that the investigations that we have done will continue to pay dividends. We firmly believe that the one important piece of information to bring this all together is just around the corner. Never give up hope; we won't. Finally, one wonders just how the police would have reacted had it been they that uncovered the evidence outlined in this book as opposed to us. We ask this because of what was said to us by police—'We won't be told by civilians how to solve crime.'

Really?

References

1   J McCollister, *Echoes from the Smithsonian: America's History Brought to Life*, Spotlight Press, Champaign, Dec 2004, p. 113.

2   A Whiticker and S Mullins, *The Satin Man: Uncovering the Mystery of the Missing Beaumont Children*, New Holland, Wahroonga, 20 May 2013.

3   X Mallett, *Cold Case Investigations*, Macmillan Australia, Sydney, 27 Aug 2019.

4   K Anderson et al, 'Missing: The Beaumont disclosures', *The News (Adelaide)*, News Limited, 21 Feb 1968.

5   CS Lewis, *The Lion, the Witch and the Wardrobe (The Chronicles of Narnia)*, HarperCollins, New York, 2 Jan 2008.

6   Juvenile Justice, 'Reason to Hope: On the Front Lines with John Walsh', *Juvenile Justice Journal*, vol. 5, no. 1, May 1998, https://ojjdp.ojp.gov/sites/g/files/xyckuh176/files/jjjournal/jjjournal1598/hope.html, accessed 6 May 2022.

7   The News (Adelaide), 'Calls Pour In', *The News*, 2 Feb 1966, p. 2.

8   The News (Adelaide), 'New Witness Found', *The News,* 2 Feb 1966.

9   F Pangallo, 'Beaumont detective', *Today Tonight,* Seven Network, 17 Jun 2015, https://www.todaytonightadelaide.com.au/beaumont-detective/, accessed May 2022.

10 The Advertiser Friday the 28th of January 1966 'No Clue in Massive Hunt: Father Fears Three Abducted'.

11 M Day, 'New Sex Attack Fears', *The News,* 28 Jan 1966.

12 The News (Adelaide), 'Chase after three children in car'; 'Hectic chase through the Eastern Suburbs', *The News (Adelaide)*, News Limited, 31 Jan 1966.

13 The Advertiser (Adelaide), 'A secret search for the bodies of the Beaumont Children is being made by Victorian Police on four small islands near Port Phillip Heads', *The Advertiser*, 11 Feb 1966.

14 Washington State Office of the Attorney General, '2006 Abduction Murder Study', 2006, https://www.atg.wa.gov/child-abduction-murder-research, accessed 6 May 2022.

15 A Whiticker, *Searching for the Beaumont Children: Australia's Most Famous Unsolved Mystery*, John Wiley & Sons Australia, Milton, 11 Jan 2006.

16 Sunday Mail (Adelaide), 'Sex Crime Now Feared', *Sunday Mail*, 31 Jan 1966, p. 3.

17 B Bosker, 'Ben Huh Stars As A Lolcat, Talks Twitter, Memes, And Going Viral', *Huffington Post*, 6 Dec 2017, https://www.huffpost.com/entry/ben-huh-stars-as-a-lolcat_n_756498, accessed 17 May 2022.

18 R Berryman, 'Missing: A mythical horse they once had', *The News*, 20 Feb 1968.

19 F Weedn, *Forever*, Cedco Publishing, San Rafael, 1999.

20 B Aurora, *Raw*, CreateSpace Independent Publishing Platform, 12 Feb 2014.

21 Darkness to Light, *Child Sexual Abuse Statistics*, n.d., Darkness to Light, North Charleston, 2022, https://www.d2l.org/wp-content/uploads/2017/01/all_statistics_20150619.pdf, accessed 9 May 2022.

22 M Everson and B Boat, 'False Allegations of Sexual Abuse by Children and Adolescents', *Journal of the American Academy of Child and Adolescent Psychiatry*, 1 Apr 1989, p. 231, https://www.researchgate.net/publication/20229836_False_Allegations_of_Sexual_Abuse_by_Children_and_Adolescents, accessed 9 May 2022.

23 BBC, 'Rolf Harris: Woman says assault claim 'not for cash'', *BBC News*, 22 May 2017, https://www.bbc.com/news/uk-39998240, accessed 9 May 2022.

24   Belfast Telegraph, 'Rolf Harris jailed for five years and nine months for indecent assault', *Belfast Telegraph*, 4 Jul 2014, https://www.belfasttelegraph.co.uk/news/uk/rolf-harris-jailed-for-five-years-and-nine-months-for-indecent-assault-30407049.html?msclkid=-8f5a6132cf4411ec98824d67afa4ad5e, accessed 9 May 2022.

25   S Cannane, 'Rolf Harris indecently assaulted blind, disabled woman in hospital, London court hears', *ABC News*, 17 Jan 2017, https://www.abc.net.au/news/2017-01-17/harris-indecent-ly-assaulted-blind-woman-at-hospital-court-hears/8186598?ms-clkid=e8917684cf4611ec906a3382cee6f96b, accessed 9 May 2022

26   F Pangallo, 'Beaumont update part 1', *Today Tonight (Adelaide)*, Seven Network, 25 Nov 2015.

27   S Fewster, 'Anglican Church of South Australia 'swept child sex abuse under carpet'', *The Advertiser*, 15 Dec 2010.

28   B Carey, 'Preying on Children: The Emerging Psychology of Pedophiles', *The New York Times Company*, 29 Sept 2019, https://www.nytimes.com/2019/09/29/us/pedophiles-online-sex-abuse.html?msclkid=b8fcf933cf4c11ecb3bd615b26dff30a, accessed 9 May 2022.

29   L Little, '60 MINUTES: Paedophiles 'born, not made', controversial study finds', *Nine News,* Nine Digital Pty Ltd, 3 Nov 2019, https://www.9news.com.au/national/60-minutes-paedophiles-genet-ic-study-doctor-james-cantor/42a85591-d1b8-4914-a766-10de5e-279b62?msclkid=7a6d4167cf4e11ecb2459518f158d2d2, viewed 9 May 2022.

30   M Szegedy-Maszak, 'Mysteries of the Mind: Is your unconscious making your everyday decisions?' [via Internet Archive], *Health & Medicine*, US News & World Report, 28 May 2005, https://web.archive.org/web/20050301001555/http://www.usnews.com/usnews/issue/050228/health/28think.htm, accessed 9 May 2022.

31   K Essex, *Dracula in Love*, Allen & Unwin, St Leonards, 2011.

32   The News (Adelaide), 'New Clue Revealed by Police', *The News,* 25 Jan 1967.

33   S Meyer, *The Host*, Sphere, London, 2009.

34 J Medeiros, 'How geographic profiling helps find serial criminals', *Wired*, 18 Nov 2014, https://www.wired.co.uk/article/mapping-murder, viewed 20 Jun 2022.

35 J Chopin et al, 'Sexual Homicide of Children: A New Classification', *International Journal of Offender Therapy and Compartive Criminology,* Sage Publications, 2 Mar 2019, https://journals.sagepub.com/doi/10.1177/0306624X19834419.

36 K Rossmo, 'Overview of Geographic Profiling', *Center for Geospatial Intelligence and Investigation,* Texas State University, n.d., viewed 20 Jun 2022, https://www.txstate.edu/gii/geographic-profiling/overview.html.

37 A Current Affair, 'Beaumont Children: Fresh Claims In 'Satin Man' Book, *Nine Network,* 2013, https://www.nfsa.gov.au/collection/curated/beaumont-children-fresh-claims-satin-man-book, viewed 20 Jun 2022.

38 M O'Leary, 'Modeling Criminal Distance Decay', *Cityscape*, vol. 13, no. 3, 2011, Hud User, https://www.huduser.gov/portal/periodicals/cityscpe/vol13num3/Cityscape_Nov2011_Modelling_Criminal.pdf, viewed 9 May 2022.

39 P Brantington and P Brantington, *Crime Pattern Theory*, Macmillan, New York, 1984.

40 J Herman, *Trauma and Recovery: The Aftermath of Violence - From Domestic Abuse to Political Terror*, Basic Books, New York, 2015.

41 Royal Commission into Institutional Responses to Child Sexual Abuse, *Final Report*, Commonwealth of Australia, 15 Dec 2017, https://www.childabuseroyalcommission.gov.au/final-report, accessed 10 May 2022.

42 M Rezendes, 'Church allowed abuse by priest for years' [via Internet Archive], Boston Glove Media Partners LLC, 6 Jan 2002, http://web.archive.org/web/20150213041036/https://www.bostonglobe.com/news/special-reports/2002/01/06/church-allowed-abuse-priest-for-years/cSHfGkTIrAT25qKGvBuDNM/story.html, accessed 10 May 2022.

43   C Radish, 'Alex Gibney Talks Catholic Church Sex Abuse Documentary MEA MAXIMA CULPA: SILENCE IN THE HOUSE OF GOD, His WikiLeaks Film, and More', Collider, 4 Feb 2013, https://collider.com/alex-gibney-mea-maxima-culpa-interview/, accessed 10 May 2022.

44   C Sutton, 'Broke, homeless, shunned: disgraced TV star Robert Hughes' miserable new life', *News.com.au*, 14 Feb 2020, https://www.news.com.au/national/crime/broke-homeless-shunned-dis-graced-tv-star-robert-hughes-miserable-new-life.

45   Herald Sun, 'Former Hey Dad star Sarah Monahan opens up about sexual abuse', *Herald Sun*, 14 Jun 2017.

46   J Herman, *Trauma and Recovery*, Basic Books, New York, 2015.

47   ABC News, 'Robert Hughes trial: Former Hey Dad! star found guilty of sexually abusing girls in 1980s', 7 Apr 2014, *ABC News, ABC*, https://www.abc.net.au/news/2014-04-07/robert-hughes-found-guilty/5372728, accessed 10 May 2022.

48   T Dimoff, '11 Known Facts About Sex Offenders [Updated]', SACS Consulting & Investigative Services Inc, 2 Jul 2020, https://sacsconsulting.com/2020/07/02/facts-about-sex-offenders/, accessed 20 Jun 2020.

49   M Davey, 'Paedophile priest Gerald Ridsdale sentenced to 11 more years in jail', *The Guardian*, 31 Aug 2017, https://www.theguardian.com/australia-news/2017/aug/31/paedophile-priest-gerald-rids-dale-sentenced-to-11-more-years-in-jail, accessed 20 Jun 2022.

50   7 News, 'Extra year in jail for ex-Bega Cheese boss', 7news.com.au, 11 May 2019, https://7news.com.au/news/crime/extra-year-in-jail-for-ex-bega-cheese-boss-c-106013, accessed 20 Jun 2022.

51   C Oksana, *Safe Passage to Healing: A Guide for Survivors of Ritual Abuse*, iUniverse, Bloomington, 2001.

52   7 News, 'The Beaumont Children: What Really Happened?', 5 Feb 2018, https://www.youtube.com/watch?v=GWN3cHKeuCw, accessed 20 Jun 2022.

53   K Anderson et al, 'The Beaumont Disclosures', *The News,* 21 Feb 1968.

54 S Kassam, http://suzykassem.com/.

55 A Solzhenitsyn, 'Nobel Lecture in Literature 1970', *Alexandr Solzhenitsyn—Biographical*, Nobel Prize Outreach AB, 2022, https://www.nobelprize.org/prizes/literature/1970/solzhenitsyn/biographical/, accessed 10 May 2022.

56 D Pelzer, *A Child Called 'It': One Child's Courage to Survive*, Seven Dials, Kent, 2019.

57 T Barlass, 'Woman with multiple personalities to read impact statement in different 'alters'', *Sydney Morning Herald*, 31 May 2019, https://www.smh.com.au/national/woman-with-multiple-personalities-to-read-impact-statement-in-different-alters-20190530-p51sqi.html, accessed 12 May 2022.

58 S Jülich PhD, 'Stockholm Syndrome and Child Sexual Abuse', *Journal of Child Sexual Abuse*, vol. 14, issue 3, 17 Oct 2008, https://www.tandfonline.com/doi/abs/10.1300/J070v14n03_06, accessed 10 May 2022.

59 The Australian Thursday February 2nd, 2023. 'Child sexual abuse royal commission: No excuse for staying silent', Freyana Irani.

60 C Milosz, 'Nobel Lecture in Literature 1980', *Czeslaw Milosz—Biographical*, Nobel Prize Outreach AB, 2022.

61 Buzz Admin, 'Beaumont children mystery: Harry Phipps' angry son says his father did not kill the children', *Unmasking the killer of the Beaumont children blog*, 28 Feb 2018, https://thebeaumontchildren.com.au/beaumont-children-mystery-harry-phipps-angry-son-says-father-not-kill-children/, accessed 12 May 2022.

62 Rape, Abuse & Incest National Network, 'Sexual Assault of Men and Boys', *RAINN*, RAINN, n.d., www.rainn.org/articles/sexual-assault-men-and-boys, accessed August 2022.

63 Darkness to Light, 'Child Sexual Abuse Statistics' [digital booklet], n.d., www.d2l.org/wp-content/uploads/2017/01/all_statistics_20150619.pdf, accessed August 2022.

64 M Albom, *For One More Day*, Hyperion, New York, 2008.

65 K Harrison, 'Beaumont Disclosures', *The Advertiser* (Adelaide), 21 Feb 1968.

66 The News (Adelaide), 'Abducted: Girls may still be alive', *The News,* 27 Aug 1973.

67 The News (Adelaide), 'Vendor Eyewitness', *The News,* 28 Aug 1973.

68 N Gage, 'Missing Persons Week: Kirste Gordon's parents recall day she disappeared from Adelaide Oval', 30 Jul 2017, *ABC News*, ABC, https://www.abc.net.au/news/2017-07-30/parents-re-flect-on-disappearance-of-daughter-kirste-gordon/8754968#:~:tex-t=Despite%20the%20time%20that%20has%20passed%2C%20 Mrs%20Gordon,of%20the%20longest%20four-hour%20 drives%20of%20her%20life, accessed 12 May 2022.

69 Law Office of Jeremy Morley, 'Australia and Child Abduction: Some Facts', Jeremy Morley, n.d., https://www.international-di-vorce.com/australia_child_abduction3.htm, accessed 21 Jun 2022.

70 H Pitt, 'Australian abduction cases and missing children', *Sydney Morning Herald* [via Internet Archive], 7 Jul 2019, http://web.archive.org/web/20211023023532/https://www.smh.com.au/national/australian-abduction-cases-and-missing-chil-dren-20190705-p524k6.html, accessed 21 Jun 2022.

71 T Benson, 'What You Really Should Know About Child Kidnapping', ATTN:, Inc, 2 Apr 2016, https://archive.attn.com/stories/6974/odds-of-child-getting-kidnapped, accessed 21 Jun 2022.

72 E Nolan Brown, 'Enough Stranger Danger! Children Rarely Abducted by Those They Don't Know', *Reason*, Reason Foundation, 31 Mar 2017, https://reason.com/2017/03/31/kidnap-ping-stats/, accessed 12 May 2022.

73 A Charalambous, 'Behavioural Characteristics and Attributes of Child Sexual Homicides', MSc thesis, University of Hud-dersfield, West Yorkshire, Aug 2014, https://www.researchgate.net/publication/266374595_Behavioural_Characteristics_and_Attributes_of_Child_Sexual_Homicides, accessed 21 Jun 2022.

74 K Heide et al, 'Sexually Motivated Child Abduction Murders: Synthesis of the Literature and Case Illustration', 8 Jan 2009, Taylor & Francis Online, https://www.tandfonline.com/doi/full/10.1080/15564880802561770, accessed 21 Jun 2022.

75   A O'Meara et al, 'The Psychometric Properties and Utility of the Short Sadistic Impulse Scale (SSIS)', Feb 2011, https://www.researchgate.net/publication/49834950_The_Psychometric_Properties_and_Utility_of_the_Short_Sadistic_Impulse_Scale_SSIS, accessed 21 Jun 2022.

76   R McKenna, 'Case Management for Missing Children Homicide Investigation', US Department of Justice Office of Juvenile Justice and Delinquency Prevention, May 2006, https://agportal-s3bucket.s3.amazonaws.com/uploadedfiles/Another/Supporting_Law_Enforcement/Homicide_Investigation_Tracking_System_(HITS)/Child_Abduction_Murder_Research/CMIIPDF.pdf, accessed 21 Jun 2022.

77   E Beauregard et al, 'Sexual Murderers of Children', *International Journal of Offender Therapy and Comparative Criminology*, May 2005, https://www.researchgate.net/journal/International-Journal-of-Offender-Therapy-and-Comparative-Criminology-1552-6933, accessed 21 Jun 2022.

78   K Hanfland et al, 'Investigative Case Management for Missing Children Homicide Investigation', US Department of Justice Office of Juvenile Justice and Delinquency Prevention, May 1997, https://www.ojp.gov/pdffiles1/Digitization/201253NCJRS.pdf, accessed 12 May 2022.

79   National Sexual Violence Resource Centre, 'Statistics In-Depth', NSVRC, n.d., https://www.nsvrc.org/statistics/statistics-depth, accessed 16 May 2022.

80   YWCA USA, *Child Sexual Abuse Facts* [digital booklet], YWCA USA, September 2017, www.ywca.org/wp-content/uploads/WWV-CSA-Fact-Sheet-Final.pdf, accessed August 2022.

81   The News (Adelaide), 'The lonely future', *The News*, 26 Feb 1968.

82   S Van Booy, *Love Begins in Winter: Five Stories*, HarperCollins, New York, 2009.

83   T Cotton, 'Senator Tom Cotton's Remarks on Crime and Justice in America', Hudson Institute Inc, 19 May 2016, https://www.hudson.org/research/12505-senator-tom-cotton-s-remarks-on-crime-and-justice-in-america, accessed 16 May 2022.

84 Queensland Courts, *Inquest into the disappearance and death of Daniel James Morcombe*, 5 Apr 2019, https://www.courts.qld.gov.au/__data/assets/pdf_file/0004/608476/cif-morcombe-d-20190405.pdf, accessed 16 May 2022.

85 P Mullen, et al, 'Suicide and fatal drug overdose in child sexual abuse victims: A historical cohort study', *The Medical Journal of Australia*, vol. 192, issue 4, February 2010, DOI:10.5694/j.1326-5377.2010.tb03475.x.

86 D Marshall, 'Debi Marshall: My meeting with softly spoken, charming murderer Bevan Spencer von Einem', *The Advertiser,* Nationwide News Pty Ltd, 14 Sept 2019, https://www.adelaidenow.com.au/truecrimeaustralia/debi-marshall-my-meet-ing-with-softly-spoken-charming-murderer-bevan-spencer-von-einem/news-story/fceb6f28d5dd402719da22c0501a4e10, accessed 16 May 2022.

87 'Fears, rumours lurk in heart of Adelaide', *The Age*, 16 Apr 2005, https://www.theage.com.au/national/fears-rumours-lurk-in-heart-of-adelaide-20050416-gdzzke.html, accessed 17 May 2022.

88 'Elizabeth Edwards On "Facing Life's Adversities"', *All Things Considered* [podcast], NPR, 7 May 2009, www.npr.org/2009/05/07/103895496/elizabeth-edwards-on-fac-ing-lifes-adversities, accessed August 2022.

89 S Ockler, *Twenty Boy Summer*, Little, Brown and Company, Boston, 2010.

Printed in the USA
CPSIA information can be obtained
at www.ICGtesting.com
LVHW010024150324
774551LV00033B/897